A QUIET VICTORY FOR LATINO RIGHTS

A Quiet Victory for Latino Rights

FDR and the Controversy over "Whiteness"

Patrick D. Lukens

The University of Arizona Press
Tucson

The University of Arizona Press
www.uapress.arizona.edu

 Published 2012
First paperback edition 2017

Printed in the United States of America
22 21 20 19 18 17 7 6 5 4 3 2

ISBN-13: 978-0-8165-2902-5 (cloth)
ISBN-13: 978-0-8165-3728-0 (paper)

Cover design by David Drummond
Cover photo: Immigration application of Timoteo Andrade, 1929

Publication of this book is made possible in part by the proceeds of a permanent endowment created with the assistance of a Challenge Grant from the National Endowment for the Humanities, a federal agency.

Library of Congress Cataloging-in-Publication Data
Lukens, Patrick D., 1966–
A quiet victory for Latino rights : FDR and the controversy over whiteness / Patrick D. Lukens.
p. cm.
Includes bibliographical references and index.
ISBN 978-0-8165-2902-5 (cloth : alk. paper) 1. Hispanic Americans—Civil rights—History—20th century. 2. Hispanic Americans—Legal status, laws, etc.—History—20th century. 3. Hispanic Americans—Race identity—History—20th century. 4. Roosevelt, Franklin D. (Franklin Delano), 1882–1945—Relations with Hispanic Americans. 5. Roosevelt, Franklin D. (Franklin Delano), 1882–1945—Political and social views. 6. United States—Politics and government—1929–1933. 7. United States—Politics and government—1933–1945. 8. United States—Social policy. 9. United States—Race relations—Political aspects—History—20th century. I. Title.
E184.S75L85 2012
323.1168'0730904—dc23
2011027211

♾ This paper meets the requirements of ANSI/NISO Z39.48-1992 (Permanence of Paper).

To my beautiful wife, Jerri, and my lovely daughter, Victoria.
Thank you for your love, your understanding, and your patience.

Soli Deo Gloria

Contents

Illustrations

Preface

DURING THE LATER YEARS OF MY UNDERGRADUATE EXPERIENCE AT New Mexico State University, I remember a history professor telling the class something like this: "As history majors, you are going to have to move beyond studying the history of 'dead white men.'" My first thought was that most everything I had learned about history in grade school and high school had been traditional political history. Most of what I learned in my survey courses was also largely traditional. It was not until my upper-division undergraduate years that I was really introduced to a broader array of historical fields. In my undergraduate senior writing seminar, our required sources were the slave narratives edited by George P. Rawick and gathered by the Federal Writers Project of the Works Progress Administration. The words I read and the paper that I wrote were eye openers to me.

An additional insight occurred when I took Professor Darlis Miller's New Mexico History course. In that class, she assigned a family history paper, and I started out quite happy that my mother's family claimed Josefina Jaramillo, Kit Carson's wife, as a relative. But after perusing a few books on Carson, I quickly realized that none of that mattered. Even if it were true, Josefina Jaramillo was merely a distant relative, and this was to be a paper about my immediate family. My final paper mentioned nothing at all about "Uncle Kit" or "Aunt Josefina." It was a history of Mom's lesser-known relatives, the Espinosa family, starting with her grandfather, Jose Rafael

Rosendo Espinosa. When Dr. Miller returned the graded paper, she had written, "You have the makings of a true historian." That was quite a compliment to a fledgling undergraduate history major.

As I began my graduate studies, also at New Mexico State University, I sort of fell into public history, thanks to the guidance of Professor Jeffrey P. Brown. Under the direction of Professor Louis R. "Ray" Sadler, I also pursued the history of Mexico and US-Mexican relations. I have lived within 100 miles of the border since the age of eleven and have always loved Mexico, its culture, and its people.

When I began applying to PhD programs, Jeff Brown helped guide me to Professor Noel Stowe's Public History Program at Arizona State University. At ASU, I discovered and trained in a subset of public history that has actually put a new face on traditional political history: public policy history. I also continued my studies in Mexican history and US-Mexican relations under the tutelage of Professor F. Arturo Rosales.

Early in my PhD program, Arturo threw a new twist at me. He advised me that since I was (half) Latino and working toward a PhD in Mexican history, I would be expected to know Chicano/a history as well. This, said Arturo, is an expectation not placed upon Anglos with a PhD in Mexican history. Looking around the profession, I concluded that whether or not it had to be true, it certainly appeared to be true from my perspective as a graduate student.

The result of my training as a historical public policy analyst and a Mexican historian who is versed in Chicano/a history is this book. I was introduced to Timoteo Andrade one day when Arturo handed me a slim file from Mexico's Secretaria de Relaciones Exteriores, their equivalent to the US State Department. Arturo had made some use of it, but he realized that it had much more potential. He had also moved beyond any topics to which it would be relevant, so he offered it to me as a foundation for a dissertation. What I saw piqued my interest from every perspective of my academic training. Clearly, it was a foreign policy issue. It was Chicano/a history that included elements of race and ethnicity relevant on both sides of the border. It dealt with immigration and naturalization. Domestic policy implications were written all over it. The culmination of my research is this book.

Completing this study also reminded me of my undergraduate professor who said, "you are going to have to move beyond studying the history of 'dead white men.'" Perhaps I misinterpreted what that professor meant, but I believe that I overinterpreted it. For a few years after hearing that comment, I thought that the history of dead white men was passé. But through my PhD program, and especially through the process of researching and writing my dissertation, the foundation of this book, I came to a conclusion: during the period that this work analyzes, white men (who are now dead) made the decisions. Some fought to deny nonwhites their civil rights, and others fought for them. While this book is on many levels a very traditional political history, it is a history of everybody's contribution. It is a history of the government of Mexico and Mexican American civil rights activists, and it is a history of the white men who opposed them and, of course, the white men who helped them.

I view Timoteo Andrade's case almost as a prism, through which several aspects of history can be separated out and examined independently. This book serves as both a magnifying lens and a reverse prism in which all of these streams of light are considered and then recombined into white light, or the whole story. It intertwines the story of nativists, debaters in Congress, civil rights activists, Mexican immigrants, the government of Mexico, and the FDR administration.

As a policy study, this book shows how the policy approaches of the decision makers worked for the benefit of a minority group. In deviating from the methods of policymaking that dated back at least to 1789, the State Department explored options that circumvented the federal judiciary and the Congress and put more power in the hands of the bureaucracy. Although in this case their intentions were enlightened, I have found that such policy approaches are not always the best. While the policy was initially successful, it had unintended consequences. Further, although it took three more years, the traditional process did indeed achieve positive results. Just as important, I have come to believe that one should always consider the potential that bureaucrats, lacking the checks and balances of the Congress and the judiciary, may wield such power without enlightened goals in mind, and possibly even to achieve malevolent ends.

As a study of race, ethnicity, and civil rights, I show in this book that FDR's State Department went to great lengths to do a remarkable thing for Latino/as, but not necessarily for the benefit of civil rights. While the State Department's agenda was foreign relations, fortunately for the nonwhites involved, the department developed a good rapport with the Mexican ambassador and listened to the input of Mexican American civil rights activists. And fortunately, the nonwhites left a detailed record of their role, so at least it cannot be said that only dead white men wrote the history.

To revisit my overinterpretation of "dead white men": I certainly agree that we need to broaden our view and both teach and research much more than just the traditional political history that those of us over forty years old were taught in grade school. However, as a result of my participation in the Policy History Program at ASU, and through the process of writing this book, I have also come to realize that we cannot neglect it. Without exploring the role of the decision makers, both those who stood for and those who stood against civil rights, we can never understand how we arrived where we are today.

I often ask my students, "In a society where only white men voted, how did women and minorities acquire the vote?" In some countries, people fight and die for that right. But a violent suffrage revolution did not occur in the United States. Here, white men fought against white men at the beginning of that process. After that, if there had not been white men throughout history who had been willing to vote to enfranchise women and minorities, to fight for rights, we would not be able to celebrate the fact that we no longer have only white men's portraits hanging in the hall of US presidents today.

Acknowledgments

A GREAT MANY PEOPLE CONTRIBUTED TO THIS WORK. FIRST, I WANT to thank Professors F. Arturo Rosales and the late Noel J. Stowe. This book would not exist had it not been for the support and encouragement of Arturo Rosales. First, he provided the foundation of this research when he gave me the *Andrade* file as a dissertation topic. Second, even several years after I completed my degree from Arizona State University, Arturo continued to send me information to feed the fire that drove me to work on this, despite my full-time teaching load at a nonresearch institution.

Although Noel Stowe's contribution ended when I completed at ASU, his influence on my development there shaped this book. He helped me to grow a strong sense of public and policy history, which helps to explain how this research ended up in the arena of policy analysis.

I also must thank Gregory Rodríguez, Irvine Senior Fellow at the New America Foundation, a nonpartisan public policy institute in Washington, DC, and a regular contributor to the *Los Angeles Times* opinion section. One of the "reminders" from Arturo Rosales that kept me working on this project was Rodríguez's book, *Mongrels, Bastards, Orphans, and Vagabonds: Mexican Immigration and the Future of Race in America* (2007). Arturo was the first to notice that several pages of his book summarized and cited my dissertation. About five minutes after I e-mailed Mr. Rodríguez to thank him for taking note of my work and utilizing so much of it, he telephoned me to talk about our respective works, and he also encouraged me to continue the process of publishing my findings.

Along the way, several scholars read drafts of this work and provided invaluable feedback. Professor Thomas Guglielmo of George Washington University was one of the earliest. Tom's feedback helped place this work within the greater context, but, more important, he opened my eyes to the Nationality Act of 1940, Section 303 of which was a direct result of the State Department's efforts to counter the *Andrade* ruling. Thanks, Tom. I would have missed that one without your feedback.

Needing a legal scholar's point of view, I asked Professors Guadalupe Luna of the Northern Illinois University College of Law and Richard Delgado of the Seattle University School of Law if they could read and comment on a later draft. I want to thank Professor Luna for her support overall, and for helping me fine-tune some of the legal aspects of this work, and for pointing me toward a few additional scholars whose work was quite useful. Although Professor Delgado declined due to time constraints, I would still like to thank him for his encouragement and willingness to consider my request.

Finally, I would like to thank the anonymous peer reviewers selected by the University of Arizona Press for their comments, criticisms, and advice, and especially for their support of this publication.

Research at the Franklin D. Roosevelt Presidential Library was made possible in part by financial support from the Graduate Research Support Program at Arizona State University.

A QUIET VICTORY FOR LATINO RIGHTS

1

Introduction

ON DECEMBER 11, 1935, IN BUFFALO, NEW YORK, FEDERAL JUDGE John Knight of New York's Western District denied the citizenship petition of three Mexican expatriates named Timoteo Andrade, Porfirio Bravo, and Francisco Velez. Although naturalization petitions are denied almost as a matter of daily routine, in the case of Timoteo Andrade, Judge Knight also wrote a detailed opinion explaining why he had denied the petition. Although all three had been denied, Knight probably focused on Andrade simply because he appeared first in the alphabet. Knight ruled that Andrade was "not a free white person" as defined by Section 359, Title 8, of the United States Code, which allowed that only "aliens being free white persons, [or African]" could be naturalized.[1] He further asserted that not only was Andrade ineligible under existing US naturalization laws, but that most Mexican nationals were also ineligible due to their race. Knight's judgment, therefore, provided the United States with a firm legal definition of the racial status of Mexican natives at a time when world intellectuals were still debating that very issue.

This ruling came at a time of transition in American history. In the previous decade, a conflict had emerged between "old America" and "new America." Among the controversial issues about which Americans quarreled during the 1920s were Prohibition, evangelical fundamentalism (e.g., the Scopes Monkey Trial), morality, and immigration. With respect to immigration and race, the US Congress passed the Johnson-Reed Immigration Act (the 1924 Immigration Act). This law "ranked [immigrants] in a hierarchy of desirability" and helped to construct "a white American race." By default, the act made non-European immigrants, including Mexicans, "unalterably foreign and unassimilable to the nation."[2]

That time of transition in the 1930s included the beginning of the Great Depression and the election of Franklin Delano Roosevelt to the US presidency. Roosevelt had launched his Good Neighbor Policy, and Knight's decision put Roosevelt's State Department in a predicament where it had to balance that policy with US immigration and naturalization laws as they existed in December 1935.

The 1930s also saw the early origins of the Mexican American civil rights movement, which would also be instrumental in fighting Knight's ruling. This movement, which historian Thomas Guglielmo has called a "Caucasian rights" movement, was in part a reaction to the 1924 Immigration Act. The racial constructs that emerged from the 1924 Act made "'Mexican' . . . a wholly negative racial category, which comprised both Mexican immigrants and Mexican Americans in the United States."[3] Much of the early Mexican American civil rights struggle was a fight to continue to be classified as white, which is how Mexican Americans had appeared in every US Census until 1930.

Knight's ruling on Timoteo Andrade was the culmination of efforts headed by Valentine Stuart (V. S.) McClatchy, the executive secretary of the California Joint Immigration Committee (CJIC). McClatchy's plan was that Andrade would appeal the ruling and that federal appeals courts and ultimately the US Supreme Court would uphold the decision. If that had happened, Knight's ruling would have changed history. First, it obviously would have made Mexican nationals ineligible for naturalization in the United States. But the main issue behind this effort was immigration. Under the rules of Section 13 of the 1924 Immigration Act (Asian Exclusion, which was also the result of McClatchy's efforts), if a foreign national was ineligible for naturalization, then he or she was also ineligible to immigrate into the United States. Therefore, Judge Knight's decision would have substantially curtailed, if not ended, legal Mexican immigration to the United States because of the large percentage of Indians and mixed-race individuals in Mexico.

In addition, the decision would have further diminished the status of Mexican Americans. Prior to the 1930 Census, Mexican Americans had been classified as white. In 1930, the Census Bureau used the classification Mexican, which helped to hasten the erosion of Mexican American civil rights. Like African Americans, Latinos/as faced segregation. However, *Plessy v. Ferguson* applied only to African Americans, and therefore segregation of Latinos/as was arguably not legal, because Latinos/as were generally considered to be white (at least until the 1930 Census). Civil rights activists fought segregation and, in a few instances (the most notable being the 1931 Lemon Grove, California, case), they had defeated school segregation in court.[4] But had Knight's ruling been upheld by the Supreme Court, it would have undermined further court cases similar to the Lemon Grove case because it may have applied *Plessy v. Ferguson* to Latinos/as, and it certainly would have placed them in a legal position similar to that of Asians—nonwhite and, in the eyes of many white Americans, non-American. Finally, Knight's decision would have applied California's Alien Land Law (which had been aimed at preventing Japanese from buying California farmland) to Latinos/as.

Objectives

McClatchy's efforts toward Mexican immigrants and Judge Knight's ruling on Andrade's naturalization petition have been little noticed by historians. The *Andrade* case is mentioned briefly by F. Arturo Rosales,[5] and two other authors write about Knight's ruling in slight detail. The first is a published work by Gregory Rodriguez and the second a PhD dissertation by Michael Calderón-Zaks. But both authors' discussion of *Andrade* is limited because they place the decision in a much larger context of Mexican and Mexican American history. Rodriguez's book ranges from 1519 to 2007, and Calderón-Zaks's dissertation from 1884 to 1940. Further, both authors' main source of information on the *Andrade* decision is an earlier draft of this book.[6]

A few other researchers have come close to uncovering the issue of *Andrade* and the State Department. Of those, historian Mae

Ngai probably came closest, although she followed the story only to a February 5, 1929, memorandum from Labor Secretary Davis to Representative Albert Johnson, chair of the House Immigration Committee. Ngai wrote of McClatchy's efforts: "In addition to their demands for a quota on Mexican immigration the CJIC also called for excluding Mexicans on the grounds of racial ineligibility to citizenship. But the Labor Department concluded there was no basis to pursue such a policy" due to a Supreme Court decision, *In Re Rodriguez* (81 Fed. 337, May 3, 1897).[7] But with Judge Knight's ruling against Andrade six years later, the CJIC came very close to succeeding in racial exclusion by overturning *Rodriguez*.[8]

One of the main reasons that the *Andrade* decision has been relegated to obscurity is that both the State Department and the government of Mexico sought to keep it obscure. Initially, word of Knight's decision traveled fast. The story hit the Associated Press (AP) news wire and appeared in the *New York Times* and Mexico City's *Excelsior*. The government of Mexico issued a press release that appeared in the *New York Times* as well as in Mexico City's *El Nacional*. But after discovering that they had a common agenda of making this situation disappear, both governments made every effort to end press coverage of *Andrade*, and it did indeed end quickly.

Despite its obscurity, the circumstances surrounding the ruling do in fact have vast historical significance. The potential of this ruling to change the face of immigration to the United States paralleled the significance of the 1924 Immigration Act itself. This act, of course, is arguably one of the most important events in US immigration history. In a theoretical legal sense, Knight's ruling should have applied the most restrictive measure of that act to Mexican immigrants. Why, then, if Judge Knight's ruling had such tremendous potential to influence the flow of immigration to the United States, has it not been the topic of historical scrutiny?

The answer to that question is simple. While earth-changing events become a well-known part of the historical record, some events that could reach that magnitude never realize their potential. Such events may fade into historical obscurity for several reasons; in this situation, it happened because Roosevelt's State Department developed and implemented an administrative policy that circumvented Knight's ruling without changing his interpretation of existing law. It is the efforts of the State Department, the government of Mexico, and the Mexican American civil rights movement, not the decision itself, that are the most historically significant aspects of this study. The ultimate implementation of an administrative policy that classified Mexican immigrants and Mexican Americans as white was, in fact, a solution that reflected a relatively new direction in policymaking, administrative law.

The State Department's efforts brought two results. First, in June 1937 the administration adopted a uniform policy of classifying persons of Mexican nationality or descent as white. More important, the US Census Bureau followed this policy in the 1940 Census of Population and Housing, which is the major source for US racial and other statistics of that era. This policy emerged as a result of the efforts of senior State Department officials, who developed it and pushed for its implementation on an administration-wide basis, in an effort to avert the possibility of a minor international incident. Second, Section 303 of the Nationality Act of 1940, which was chiefly written by many of the same individuals, completely removed the racial barrier to naturalization of Mexican, non-white Canadian, and Latin American expatriates.

The racial classification policy was driven by cooperation between the State Department, the government of Mexico, and the Mexican American civil rights movement. However, the earliest historiography of this topic gave most of the credit to the third group.[9] Only within recent years have scholars begun looking at the role of governments in initiating (rather than responding to demands for) racial policy. Again, in this particular case, this is because the State Department and the government of Mexico went to great lengths to make things happen, but also took measures to prevent publicity of those efforts.

Context Within Current Historiography

While the origins of the administration's racial classification policy and the 1940 Nationality Act are the focus of this work, the multifaceted nature of the issue lends itself to analyses of several aspects of US and Mexican history. For example, this study incorporates or examines several elements of policy history, New Deal history, Chicano/a history, critical race theory and its subbranch LatCrit theory, Latin American history, and US immigration history to explain many of the circumstances that both contributed to and emerged from the *Andrade* ruling.

Policy History

This book is primarily a policy history. It is about activists on both sides who fought to set an agenda, but the foundation of this work is the policymakers in all three branches of the U.S. government and the executive branch of the government of Mexico who wrestled with the issues. The driving force behind the implementation of the policy and the legislation was senior State Department officials who sought to prevent negative repercussions in US-Mexican relations. This work describes the processes that the State Department followed to achieve this goal. The State Department officials followed two very different and conflicting methods of policymaking. In the first method, referred to in this work as the traditional model (or the constitutional model), the legislature formulates policy, the executive implements policy, and the judiciary determines its constitutionality.[10] This method took substantial time to achieve policy ends, which pushed policymakers to develop the second mode. Referred to here as the technocratic model, the second model became the FDR administration's method to combat the Great Depression. In it, the executive formulates and implements policy, while the legislature only passes laws that allow for the general framework of the administrative policies. The time involved is much shorter. In this case, using the technocratic approach, the administration implemented a policy in 1937. Various officials in the State Department still insisted on following the traditional model, but they did not achieve legislation on this issue until 1940. Also, the role of the judiciary in the technocratic model of policymaking became a point of contention during FDR's first term in office, as the federal courts continually struck down New Deal measures as unconstitutional.

In their efforts to counteract Judge Knight's decision, State Department officials first pursued the traditional approach. But after achieving little initial success, they began searching for faster options. Following examples set by other departments in the Roosevelt administration, many of which were achieving success with policies that they had both written and implemented, State Department officials began to look for administrative solutions to their problem. Ultimately, they developed a policy that would counter Knight's decision. With the help of Mexican Ambassador Francisco Castillo Nájera, State Department officials worked to employ this policy administration-wide to provide a stronger hand against the possibility that the judiciary would attempt to counter the policy before the FDR administration could follow up with legislation.

New Deal History

In New Deal history, the conflict between the FDR administration and the judiciary is well known. This change in policymaking created a shift in the balance of powers between the presidency, the Congress, and the judiciary, which had a direct impact on the State Department's approach to the *Andrade* ruling. As Roosevelt went about building his "strong presidency," New Deal Democrats in Congress acquiesced because, as the New Deal architects argued, Congress could not act quickly enough to respond to the crises of the Great Depression. New Dealers believed that only through the centralization of policymaking and implementation in the executive branch could the federal government deal with the nation's problems.

However, between the elections of Abraham Lincoln and Franklin Roosevelt, Americans had elected only two Democrats to the presidency. This meant that the vast majority of federal judges were Republican appointees. This Republican-dominated judiciary was unwilling to give the president such unlimited power, unlike the New Deal Democrat Congress. After being reelected in 1936, however, Roosevelt forced a shift in the judiciary toward his way of thinking via political pressure and appointments of politically sympathetic Democrat judges and justices.

Viewed in this context, this narrative presents an interesting but little-known example of one New Deal–era issue where the executive branch prevailed over the judiciary. At the time that Knight handed down his decision, older Republicans still dominated the judiciary. This generation was responsible for interpreting the racial prerequisite for naturalization ("white persons") in such a way that all but those who were of entirely European blood were excluded.[11] But while State Department officials were in the process of finding a way to manipulate federal policies around the judiciary, the overall political position of the federal courts was shifting in the New Deal's favor. By the time the policy was formalized in the 1940 federal Census, the judiciary had largely acquiesced to the New Deal. Although the Andrade decision was not one of the issues that helped to cause that change, it certainly did benefit from Roosevelt's victory in the executive-judicial struggle of the mid-1930s.

Mexican American History and LatCrit Theory

Within the same general time frame as Judge Knight's ruling, and because of the political realities of the era, Mexican American civil rights activists had been pushing their own agenda of having themselves racially classified as white. One of those fundamental realities was that citizenship was "not solely a creature of the state, but [was] partially constituted by the citizenry [and] being 'American' meant being white."[12] One major factor in that "whiteness" was the "eugenicists' concern about the establishment of an unassimilable people" as citizens.[13] Therefore, asserting whiteness became a common approach to acquiring US citizenship in the early twentieth century.

Being a citizen or, for the immigrant, being eligible for citizenship went hand in hand with civil rights. While African Americans had the Fourteenth Amendment to make them citizens and at least theoretically protect their civil rights:

> Mexicans and Mexican Americans were engaged in a struggle for their rights and their humanity even before the establishment of the Fourteenth Amendment and before the concept

> of "equal protection" came into common discussion in American society. They were citizens earlier than African Americans and they were in a position to debate the issue of whether they were white or not. African Americans never had to debate the issue of whiteness, while Mexican Americans continue that debate even today.[14]

The primary issue at hand here is what scholars have termed the "black/white binary paradigm." Juan Perea defines this paradigm as "the conception that race in America consists, either exclusively or primarily, of only two constituent racial groups, the Black and the White."[15] Perea goes on to criticize this model because it "binds and organizes racial discourse, limiting both the scope and the range of legitimate viewpoints in that discourse."[16] The paradigm oversimplifies racial ideas in much the same way that a freshman-level survey history course takes a broad view of centuries of time. Further, Perea states, "Many scholars of race reproduce this paradigm when they write and act as though only the Black and the White races matter for purposes of discussing race and social policy with regard to race. The mere recognition that 'other people of color' exist, without careful attention to their voices, their histories, and their real presence, is merely a reassertion of the Black/White paradigm."[17] Finally, the worst impact on Latinos/as, according to Perea, is that the black/white binary "counts only Blacks as significantly disadvantaged by White racism [and] posits that non-White immigrant ethnics are essentially Whites-in-waiting who will be permitted to assimilate and become White."[18] In other words, glossing over the complexities of racial issues leads to Latinos/as being almost entirely left out of the discussion.

Ignacio García is another scholar who has addressed the problem of the black/white binary: "In American scholarship there are only two major races and everyone else fits depending on their social or racial proximity to one side or the other of the racial poles." This binary, argues García, has caused scholars to hold the view that the topic of his research, *Hernandez v. Texas*, was neither a victory nor an important judicial decision.[19]

Perea's and García's criticisms of the black/white binary paradigm carry a great deal of weight. But it is easy to see where this model comes from. Policymakers and Mexican American activists of the 1930s worked within the paradigm, whether they realized it or not. For example, in his discussion of how the pre–World War II generation of Mexican American activists (many of whom were World War I veterans) differed from the post–World War II generation (most of whom were World War II veterans), Ignacio García discusses how the 1930s activists were the first to call themselves Mexican Americans and called "for civic responsibility on the part of barrio residents." In the black/white binary, they viewed themselves as white, although, as García states, "among themselves and their people, they were Mexican [and they] 'knew' it was really a different race." The activists of this generation were proud of their American citizenship and did not look to Mexico for their political and philosophical foundations. They emphasized citizenship and English and "demanded only opportunity without affirmative action."[20]

By contrast, García describes the post–World War II generation as wanting to break out of the black/white binary. They "had come of age in World War II, and liked to view themselves as 'Americans who happen to be of Mexican descent.' Thus, they were not interested in discussing identity or their particular place in American society." As native-born Americans, they knew they were entitled to rights as American citizens. They went even further in distinguishing themselves from Mexican nationals, allowing "the political boundaries of the border to become cultural and social borders that were added to class borders."[21] They saw both the Bracero program (which allowed for temporary entry of Mexican laborers into the United States) and illegal immigration as detrimental to the job prospects of Mexican Americans.[22] Ironically, in the 1930s, it was the nativists who sought to break out of the paradigm by classifying Mexican immigrants as anything other than white or black, in order to apply Section 13 of the 1924 Immigration Act (known as the Asian Exclusion provision) to Latinos/as.

For the purposes of this study, the variety of paradigms in use by the various factions in this account begs the overall question, then, of how whites and Latinos/as in general related to each other during the first 100 or so years after the Treaty of Guadalupe Hidalgo. Describing late nineteenth-century relations in one of the areas with the highest Latino/a populations, New Mexico, Laura Gómez describes two "competing narratives of race." The first she calls the "dominant view," which characterized Mexican Americans as unfit for self-government due to a perceived racial inferiority. The second she calls the "progressive view," which viewed Mexican Americans as "a more benign presence" but also assumed Mexican racial inferiority. Because the dominant view was, in fact, dominant, New Mexico's statehood languished for more than sixty years after US conquest of the territory. Since, as Gómez points out, both views are discriminatory in nature, discrimination followed.

One very compelling argument explaining the variety of paradigms in the debates over Mexican immigration, exclusion, and race in general is presented in a doctoral dissertation by Linda Noel. Noel outlines four strategies that white Americans used to deal with Mexican immigrants: assimilation, pluralism, exclusion, and marginalization.

> Exclusionists, who included Anglo American nativists and their political allies, envisioned an America in which only people of northern and western European heritage (who they presumed would have a middle-class status) would continue to be admitted into the nation. Assimilationists, including various types of reformers and their political supporters, had a broader vision for their ideal America, and viewed anyone with a pure European heritage as capable of entering the country and becoming American, providing that they agreed to forego their native language and customs in favor of the dominant Anglo American mores. Regardless of the newcomers' class status, these Americans believed that the new arrivals had the capacity to improve their economic position in society. Much like the assimilationists, pluralists, who primarily lived in the Southwest and claimed an European heritage, imagined an America populated by people with a pure European lineage. They disagreed, however, that these descendants, particularly those from Spain, should have to renounce their native language and culture. Instead, they believed that those who held a Spanish heritage were every bit as American, and perhaps more so, than those with English ancestors. Marginalization-

> ists, including agribusiness leaders, other major employers, and their political cohorts, dreamed of an America in which Anglo Americans would continue to be in charge of the nation, but in which people of various backgrounds, including those not deemed to be European or white, would be allowed to enter the nation to work in the lowest class jobs in society. These newcomers, then, would either enter only temporarily or remain permanently in jobs with no social or economic mobility. By the mid-1930s, this image of America was the one that prevailed.[23]

While Noel's four strategies are very helpful in explaining the motives of various members of Congress, the CJIC, and Mexican American civil rights activists, the State Department's strategy likely did not fit any of these models. Their agenda was largely one of maintaining positive relations with Mexico, and the *Andrade* ruling offended Mexico. Since the administration's policy of classifying Latinos/as as white had to be uniformly applied to both Mexican immigrants and Mexican Americans, the Mexican American civil rights movement benefited from its implementation.

While racial and cultural identity among Mexicans and Mexican Americans has received a great deal of scrutiny in academic literature, research into the origins of the US government's racial policies has only recently been increasing. The *Andrade* case presents several key components of this growing area of research. As an aspect of Mexican American history, this analysis provides a wider view of the effectiveness of Mexican Americans' role in this policy process. One early piece of scholarship that is quite relevant specifically to the *Andrade* decision is work done by Mario T. García, one of the first scholars to address the issue of "whitening" to obtain civil rights. In this early work, García made a few assumptions—reasonable assumptions, to be sure, as his work was cutting edge and lacked the broader background available today. In his 1984 article, García presented an analysis of the efforts by the Mexican American community of El Paso, Texas, to force the El Paso city health office, the US Census Bureau, and the Social Security Board to change their policies of classifying Mexicans as either "colored" or nonwhite. García credits the El Pasoans with pushing the entire FDR administration into adopting the "white" standard.[24]

Although there certainly is some truth to García's argument, it is an incomplete truth. García apparently was unaware of Knight's *Andrade* ruling, because his sources were unfamiliar with it. His main primary sources were documents contained in the Cleofas Calleros Papers at the University of Texas at El Paso. Calleros was unaware of the *Andrade* decision and the efforts of the State Department officials who were already attempting to manipulate racial classification policies at the time of the El Paso incident. In addition, while the El Paso members of the League of United Latin American Citizens (LULAC) were, in fact, successful in forcing a change in the Census Bureau's policy, Census director William Lane Austin later stated that the decision was made in haste. In August 1939, he was prepared to reverse that policy and return to classifying Mexican Americans as Mexican.[25] Only the efforts of the State Department prevented him from doing so. Therefore, while LULAC certainly made a major contribution to the FDR administration's overall policy implementation, they were not the driving force behind the planning or implementation as García suggests. This book argues that *Andrade* was the motivation behind that policy.

Another area of recent growth in scholarship is the role of the government of Mexico in Latino/a civil rights. Mexican Americans have one tremendous advantage over most other minority groups seeking civil rights: the proximity of Mexico to the United States. Although the Mexican government does not necessarily fight specifically for Mexican American civil rights, when it does fight to protect the civil rights of Mexican nationals in the United States, Mexican Americans are direct beneficiaries of any positive results of the process.

Here, too, we find early scholarship that made reasonable assumptions but lacked a broader picture due to the recent development of the subject matter. For example, the transnational aspect and the "whitening" aspect came together in an article focusing on Texas during World War II by Thomas Guglielmo. He raised both issues in great detail, and his arguments and conclusions are quite consistent with (and helpful to) this work.[26] However, at the time of his writing, like García, Guglielmo was unaware of the *Andrade* ruling and the fact that it was one of the origins of this binational effort toward what he terms Caucasian rights. In introducing his article, he wrote, "we learn that government officials began seriously considering the international ramifications of domestic race problems during World War II—not during the Cold War [as other scholars have suggested]."[27] He does mention the white racial classification policy that emerged from the *Andrade* ruling, but cites the El Paso–Census Bureau case (discussed by Mario García) as the origin of that policy. With knowledge of the government's response to the *Andrade* ruling, we can push back the beginnings of serious consideration by government officials an additional ten years.[28] With respect to the efforts to counter Judge Knight's ruling, the binational effort can also be labeled trilateral, because three major organizations were fighting this battle: the government of Mexico, the FDR State Department, and Mexican American civil rights activists.

Mexican and Latin American History

Because the State Department solicited the direct involvement of the Mexican Embassy, and because the government of Mexico took its own initiatives in this case, the events following Knight's ruling provide an excellent example of Mexican action in, and responses to, US political issues. Further, the circumstances exemplify the cooperation between the US and Mexican governments during the FDR years and show just how much Mexican Embassy officials (as opposed to Foreign Secretariat officials in Mexico City) understood the complexities of American politics.

As an example of the Good Neighbor Policy in action, the *Andrade* citizenship case provides an illustration of the FDR administration's dedication to developing and maintaining the reciprocity that characterized the ideals behind the policy. When the Mexican Embassy first learned of Knight's ruling, Ambassador Castillo Nájera assumed that the US government would provide no assistance to Mexico in responding to the decision. However, Assistant Secretary of State Sumner Welles quickly proved to the ambassador that the FDR administration's agenda was entirely congruous with Mexico's.

Immigration History

These events will be particularly interesting to immigration historians because they add a new dimension to the historiography of Mexican immigration issues. Although the direction of US policy toward Mexican immigration remained largely unchanged by Knight's ruling, the State Department's efforts to maintain the status quo provide a new perspective on how one branch of the FDR administration viewed the issue, especially when one considers the massive expatriation effort taking place in the border states at the very same time. This history also reveals a previously unknown situation where the nativist movement, in the waning years of its influence on policy, almost achieved success in closing the doors on Mexican immigration.

Overview

First, this work provides the historical and legal background necessary to understand the *Andrade* ruling. Much of the information presented in chapters 2 through 5 is a basic survey but remains essential to that understanding. Informed scholars may wish to skip the information about which they are knowledgeable, while reading the chapters that fall outside of their expertise. Student readers are, of course, encouraged to read all of the background materials.

In chapter 2, I examine the history and development of the US immigration and naturalization laws, the history of American nativism, and the movement's impact on that legislation until 1924. From there, this book focuses on failed legislative efforts on the part of the nativists toward Mexican immigration. In 1930 the US Congress came extraordinarily close to adding Mexico to the quota system. But those efforts failed. One of the commonalities in older immigration histories is an assertion that the 1924 Immigration Act was the pinnacle of the movement, and that the 1930 congressional debates were their desperate final efforts. However, the reality is that the nativists remained viable until at least 1938 but simply became less public in their tactics. One of the more successful of these nativist groups, the CJIC, was directly involved in the development of the legal precedent that Judge Knight handed down against Andrade's petition for citizenship.

Next, this book places the *Andrade* ruling within the overall domestic political context of 1935. It explores the New Deal and FDR's Good Neighbor Policy, both of which had a direct impact on how the State Department dealt with Judge Knight's ruling. One important aspect of the Good Neighbor Policy was the internal conflict between Sumner Welles and Cordell Hull. This work as a whole may serve to support the analyses of such scholars as Irwin Gellman and Benjamin Welles, who have brought these departmental problems to the attention of Good Neighbor scholars.[29]

Then, to understand the CJIC's final efforts, this work examines the racial thinking and politics of the 1930s. An ideology called eugenics played a role in the scientific thinking behind racial definitions of the era. In Europe and North America, the eugenicists used the science of the time to demonstrate the supposed superiority of the Anglo-Saxon race. It was also within that policy context that Mexican American civil rights activists had to operate. Some issues that Mexican Americans faced were that most white Americans associated them with Mexican immigrants, used *Mexican* to indicate a racial rather than a national identity, and, in some parts of the United States, implemented segregation against Mexican Americans just as they segregated black Americans. So to many Mexican American activists, obtaining civil rights also meant being racially classified as white.

One of the most important aspects of this work is the legal context out of which the *Andrade* decision arose. Until Judge Knight's ruling, Mexican nationals had been allowed to become US citizens, regardless of race. This was recognized because of a federal district court ruling, *In Re Rodriguez* (81 Fed. 337, May 3, 1897). Although it took time to build a precedent that would counter the *Rodriguez* decision, McClatchy and his CJIC demonstrated enough patience to do just that.

Judge Knight's ruling created a serious dilemma for the State Department. Chapters 7 and 8 are dedicated to how, and more important why, the State Department took steps to counter Knight's ruling, in terms of both the traditional and technocratic approaches. Finally, this work examines the implementation of the policy and its consequences along with the unintended consequences and failures of the FDR administration's policy.

2

Nativists and Immigration Law to 1924

> V.S. McClatchy hasn't got the hives.
> But he does get quite a bunch of money.
> Which is good enough as far as it goes.
> But Sacramento is still shuddering.
> When a king bee has no beehive he may turn to and start a hornet's nest of his own.
>
> *Los Angeles Times*[1]

ONE TREMENDOUSLY INFLUENTIAL FIGURE IN AMERICAN NATIVISM was Valentine Stuart McClatchy, who was born in Sacramento in 1857 (figure 2.1). His father had been co-owner of the *Sacramento Bee* newspaper, and when his father died, the other owner sold out to the McClatchy family. At that point, V. S. and his younger brother Charles Kenney (C. K.) became comanagers. C. K. handled the editorial side of the *Bee*, while V. S. handled the business end. Together, they built the newspaper into a western media giant.[2] The McClatchy Company is, today, a large media conglomerate with outlets in at least fifteen US states.

V. S. McClatchy seems to have been somewhat aggressive in his younger years. In 1896 he assaulted a "recently deposed" city clerk

Figure 2.1. Valentine Stuart (V. S.) McClatchy, 1923. Center for Sacramento History, *Sacramento Bee* Collection, 1983/001/20638.

after the former clerk made threats against McClatchy over some advertising bills that the *Sacramento Bee* sent to the city of Sacramento. To be fair, the former clerk did call McClatchy "an opprobrious epithet."[3]

By 1910, V. S.'s business acumen led him to challenge the practices of the Associated Press and the way it treated western newspapers. When the AP sought to keep the western papers from forming their own news-sharing organization, V. S. was elected to the AP board of directors and remained there until his brother bought out his share of the *Bee* in 1923.[4]

After 1915 V. S. McClatchy became a leader in the nativist movement. At a November 12, 1920, meeting, the Japanese Exclusion League of California chose McClatchy as its spokesman to confer with the House Committee on Immigration and Naturalization.[5] While V. S. was working on Japanese exclusion, he and C. K. began to disagree on the direction of the *Bee* newspaper chain. On August 18, 1923, the *Los Angeles Times* published an article detailing speculation on the pending split between C. K. and V. S. While both McClatchy brothers told reporters "I have nothing to say," the *Times* reported the major factor accelerating the already imminent split was that "anti-Japanese articles written by V. S. McClatchy, publisher of the Sacramento *Bee*, were rejected by the editorial department, presided over by his brother as editor, unless he paid advertising rates. Later, V. S. McClatchy is reported to have issued an order that all his brother's writings should be edited and certain matter deleted."[6]

Ultimately, C. K. and his family purchased V. S. McClatchy's holdings for a sum reported to be in excess of $1 million.[7] The modern McClatchy newspaper organization writes in its own history, "When the final break came in 1923, and C.K. wrested control, it drove a permanent wedge between the two brothers. When they met unexpectedly on a San Francisco street in February 1924, V. S. refused to shake his brother's hand."[8]

In its final, heavily sarcastic report on the conflict, the *Los Angeles Times* wrote, "The McClatchys were still determined to make America as wet as a Saturday night bathtub, to drive the Japs into the Pacific Ocean and elect Hiram Johnson to something, but they could not agree on methods nor could they join hands in a common cause." The final five lines of the article, the short poem at the beginning of this chapter, were quite prophetic, considering V. S. McClatchy's role in the 1924 Immigration Act and in the events detailed in this work. V. S. McClatchy played an enormous role in the impact of the American nativist movement on immigration and naturalization laws, which worked directly against Mexican immigrants at the time of the *Andrade* decision.

Early Immigration and Naturalization Laws

The earliest US immigration laws had no immediate limitations, racial or otherwise, until the Alien and Sedition Acts of 1798, which Congress allowed to expire after 1800. With the major exception of the Chinese exclusion acts, discussed later in this chapter, the first series of truly restrictive immigration measures were relatively minor in scope. These laws restricted only those whom most people would find unwelcome, such as prostitutes, convicts, lunatics, idiots, and those likely to become a public charge.[9] The first general immigration legislation that had nativist overtones was the Contract Labor Law, which restricted the importation of workers under contract. This law was a result of labor groups lobbying Congress to prevent the importation of cheap labor.[10] As this antilabor nativism grew and added other targets of restriction, it eventually resulted in the 1907 Dillingham Commission, the findings and influence of which are also discussed in more detail later in this chapter.

In contrast to immigration laws, naturalization laws had restrictions almost from the beginning. Article I, Section 8 of the US Constitution empowers Congress "to establish an uniform Rule of Naturalization," and on March 26, 1790, the US Congress passed the first US naturalization law. This law allowed only for the naturalization of "free white aliens after two years' residence in the United States."[11] The racial requirements remained unchanged until 1870, when Congress added "aliens of African nativity or African descent." This was done largely (as believed by Mexican Ambassador Castillo Nájera) "in order to satisfy the large black population of this country."[12] These racial requirements for naturalization were in effect in December 1935, when Judge Knight denied Timoteo Andrade's petition on the grounds that he was racially ineligible for US naturalization.

The next change in racial qualifications came with the Nationality Act of 1940, which added "descendants of races indigenous to the Western Hemisphere."[13] Several of the FDR administration officials who wrote this legislation were also directly involved in the administration's efforts to counter Judge Knight's ruling. This work argues that those officials wrote that part of the legislation as a direct result of the *Andrade* decision.

The Meaning of White *in Naturalization Law*

Richard W. Flournoy was one of the State Department legal advisers who worked diligently to counter Judge Knight's ruling against Timoteo Andrade, and was also one of the key authors of the 1940 Nationality Act. In a 1922 article that examined the legislative history of naturalization, Flournoy commented that one of the objectives behind the wording in the 1795 Naturalization Act was "to reduce the danger of granting naturalization and the rights accompanying it to vagrants, shifting aliens who had not taken root in our soil or really become identified with America, and who sought American citizenship merely for the advantages and protection which it conferred."[14] Flournoy's point of view is important because, in his writings, he shows himself to be generally conservative in his views of citizenship and naturalization, especially in terms of how loyalties to an expatriate's nation of origin may influence that person's loyalty to the United States. But in fighting Judge Knight's decision and ultimately helping to author the Nationality Act of 1940, which made Western Hemisphere natives eligible for naturalization in the United States, he showed himself to be in favor of Mexican immigration and removal of the racial barriers to naturalization of Western Hemisphere natives. Simply put, it appears that Flournoy believed that even those who did not meet the racial requirements as they existed prior to 1940 could become good, loyal US citizens.

Because the First Congress chose to use the words "White Person," many naturalization cases "forced the courts into a case-by-case struggle to define who was a 'white person.' More important, the courts were required in these prerequisite cases to articulate rationales for the division they were creating. [Judges] had to explain the basis on which they drew the boundaries of Whiteness. . . . In short, the courts were responsible for deciding not only who was White, but *why* someone was White."[15] In more simple terms, "law constructs race."[16] Two rationales predominated in court decisions on race: common knowledge and scientific understanding. In using law to define race, "rule-makers can and have altered the human behavior that produces variations in physical appearance. In other words, laws have directly shaped reproductive choices . . . by excluding people with certain features from this country."[17]

Nativism and the Growth of Restrictionism

Nativism can be defined as an "intense opposition to an internal minority on the ground of its foreign (i.e., 'un-American') connections."[18] The author of that definition, John Higham, further defined specific forms of nativism, saying, "through each separate hostility runs the connecting, energizing force of modern nationalism. [Each] nativism translates [its own characteristics] into a zeal to destroy the enemies of a distinctively American way of life."[19] Well before 1935, nativists had come to believe that anyone who was not from northwestern Europe was undesirable or inferior. They achieved success in their agendas of excluding Asians and restricting southern and eastern Europeans with the passage of the 1924 Immigration Act.

The two elements of immigration law that arose out of nativism, restrictionism and exclusionism, can generally be seen as the same. The main difference between the two concepts is that restrictionists are willing to allow limited numbers of "undesirable" immigrants, while exclusionists prefer to totally end all immigration of such elements.

Eras of Nativism

Prior to 1935, the United States experienced several eras of nativism, starting with Know-Nothing religious nativism, which was directed mostly at Irish Catholic immigrants prior to the Civil War.[20] Then political (antiradical) nativism rose in the 1880s. In 1885, Congress passed the Contract Labor Law at the urging of unions. American laborers were among the first to develop an anti-immigrant attitude, viewing the foreigner as a "cheap competitor, whose presence undoubtedly held down wages and bred unemployment."[21] Many Americans also associated immigrants with the radical movements of this period. Another important factor was the shift in immigration patterns that took place around 1880, toward southern and eastern Europe.

The crisis of the 1880s intensified in the following decade as the economy worsened into a four-year depression (1893–1897). Hatred of immigrants increased along with labor unrest, and both American laborers and employers blamed radical immigrants for their problems. The restrictionist movement gained some distinction when, in 1894, several well-known and respected Americans, including Senator Henry Cabot Lodge (R-MA), formed the Immigration Restriction League.[22] This group found congressional success in 1896 with its literacy test law, which would have worked mostly against immigrants from southern and eastern Europe, where illiteracy rates were high in comparison to other areas. However, President Cleveland vetoed the bill on the grounds that it was "a 'radical departure' from previous policy."[23] The restrictionists continued their efforts, which resulted in the formation of a commission to study the immigration problem.

The Dillingham Commission and the 1917 Immigration Act

The Dillingham Commission, which included three senators, three representatives, and three presidential appointees, surveyed several aspects of immigration to the United States and published forty-two volumes on its findings in 1911. This commission distinguished the old immigrants, who were "hardy pioneers who helped develop the United States," from the new immigrants, who were "latecomers who had migrated to cash in on American prosperity and had failed to assimilate with the older population."[24] Ironically, the Dillingham Commission said of Mexican immigration that it was of little importance because most were temporary immigrants who returned to Mexico after a short time.[25]

At the commission's recommendation, and after several more presidential vetoes, Congress passed the 1917 literacy test law, overriding President Wilson's final veto. Although this law did not target any specific nation or ethnicity, it did "erect the first substantial barriers to the legal immigration of Mexican workers. . . . To people from a poverty-stricken nation with a low educational level, the head tax and literacy requirements were formidable obstacles indeed."[26]

The 1921 Immigration Act

In the wake of World War I, the United States experienced one of its strongest periods of both nationalism and nativism. High postwar unemployment and fears of an "alien flood" helped the restrictionists. Their opponents stood silent, since their usual argument that there was a shortage of manual laborers held little merit. Postwar conditions bred the Immigration Act of 1921, which introduced the concept of restricting immigration through the use of quotas. According to the act, 55 percent of immigrants had to come from the "whiter" nations of northern and western Europe. Southern and eastern European quotas were almost 20 percent lower than the numbers actually arriving from those nations in 1920. Congress intended the 1921 law to be merely a temporary measure. After its passage, the fear of a postwar wave of immigrants decreased, and postwar unemployment dwindled as America entered the "roaring twenties."

Asian Exclusion and Racial Thinking Prior to the 1924 Act

Because they remained white under immigration and naturalization law, immigration restriction seemed the obvious choice to deal with southern and eastern Europeans, which nativist philosophy viewed as inferior. But when it came to Asians, western nativists sought a much simpler approach, as Asians were not classified as white.

CHINESE EXCLUSION. When the US Congress developed separate immigration policies for the Chinese, nativists had their quickest and earliest success. Obviously, Chinese immigrants did not resemble the traditional immigrant. Therefore, it came easy for lawmakers to exclude them, and many Americans found it easy to agree with xenophobes that the Chinese were a problem. Because of the California gold rush, mining and railroad companies imported thousands of Chinese immigrants, who were at first welcomed because they performed menial labor. However, due to post–Civil War economic depressions, an anti-Chinese movement began that reached its peak in the late 1870s.[27]

In a pattern being repeated today with undocumented Mexican immigrants, many anti-immigrant groups opposed the influx of cheap labor, arguing that foreign workers were willing to work for lower wages. In the case of the Chinese, the primary opposition to immigration came from labor unions. California passed its own exclusion laws, which probably would have proven effective, but the US Supreme Court overturned them on the basis that immigration was a federal matter. Congress's first attempts to pass a federal Chinese exclusion law met with presidential veto, but in 1882 President Chester A. Arthur signed an exclusion bill with a ten-year sunset clause. In 1892 it was renewed for another ten years, and then made permanent in 1904.[28]

JAPANESE EXCLUSION. With Chinese exclusion, employers turned to Japanese labor as a replacement. However, the exclusionists viewed the Japanese as a "yellow peril" and sought to apply similar immigration measures to them. Stopping Japanese immigration, however, would not be as easy. Shortly before Japanese immigration to the United States peaked, Japan had achieved the status of a world power and was in a position to put political pressure on the United States. California's political elite, under the guidance of the Japanese Exclusion League (formed in 1905), called for Japanese exclusion and boycotts of Japanese businesses. Also, several of California's congressional representatives consistently attempted to attach anti-Japanese measures to immigration bills.[29]

Compounding the problem in the eyes of Californians was the fact that Japanese laborers had a much different work philosophy than their Chinese predecessors. They formed cooperatives, pooled their resources, bought land, and ended up competing with their former employers.[30] As Japanese immigrants became farm owners, California passed the Alien Land Law in 1913. This prohibited aliens who were ineligible for citizenship from owning real property. This land law also did not solve the "problems," and as far as the California nativists were concerned, the situation only continued to worsen.

It was during this period, in 1919, that V. S. McClatchy became a public figure in the debates, focusing on economic rather than racial issues.[31] McClatchy began a publicity war against Dr. Sidney Gulick, secretary of the National Committee for Constructive Immigration Legislation. Dr. Gulick's organization was urging the House Immigration Committee to relax the federal laws banning Asians. Gulick sought a 5 percent quota on Asians based on the number already in the United States. McClatchy argued that California organizations opposed the admission of Japanese immigrants "on the ground that they were undesirable economically rather than racially."[32] Two months later, McClatchy brought US Senator James Duval Phelan (D-CA) into the battle. Phelan publicly declared that a bill sponsored by Senator Dillingham (R-VT) that would allow just such a 5 percent quota on Japanese immigration was really the work of Dr. Gulick, and Phelan accused Gulick of being "simply a Japanese agent." McClatchy added to Phelan's comments that Gulick was working with Japanese newspaperman K. K. Kawakami in developing the legislation.[33]

McClatchy later appeared before the House Immigration Committee and urged the members to consider deportation of Asians already in the United States. McClatchy argued that open immigration would result in the "United States being made a Japanese province."[34] He later gave similar testimony before the Senate Immigration Committee. Senator Phelan used McClatchy's testimony to propose legislation that would completely bar the Japanese, similar to the Chinese exclusion acts.[35]

Apparently, McClatchy had been doing such a good job of arguing the anti-Japanese case that late in 1920 the Japanese Exclusion League of California named McClatchy as its official spokesman.[36] As that spokesman, McClatchy then went about briefing local branches of the Asian exclusion movement and California politicians.[37]

In addition to his other duties as spokesman, McClatchy took it upon himself to keep the State Department in the loop. In 1921

McClatchy wrote a brief to the State Department on behalf of the Japanese Exclusion League, detailing the facts of Japanese immigration as seen through the eyes of California exclusionists. In this document, McClatchy argued that Japanese immigrants were taking over California's industry, farmland, and other economic sectors, and asked the State Department and the Harding administration to help push for legislation that would totally prohibit Japanese immigration.[38]

As the debates over what would become the 1921 Immigration Act came to a conclusion, McClatchy fired his last shots. He appeared before Congress on April 18 and presented four fundamental principles during this testimony:

1. Absolute exclusion of all Japanese for immigration purposes, detailed as both male and female, and laborers as well as landowners, shopkeepers, and professionals.
2. Exclusion should be managed by US officials, not Japanese officials, and should restrict immigration from nations other than Japan.
3. Sounding quite similar to modern advocates of stronger border enforcement, McClatchy demanded compliance by federal agencies with the US Constitution. He believed that those agencies might interpret treaties as superseding state laws such as California's Alien Land Law or as overruling naturalization statutes, such as those that prohibited Asians from being naturalized.
4. To protect the rights of Japanese already legally in California, and to afford them fair treatment under the law.[39]

Although McClatchy's organization failed to achieve total exclusion in the 1921 Immigration Act, during the debates that led to the 1924 Immigration Act, McClatchy's organization, which ultimately became the California Joint Immigration Committee, was instrumental in gaining the much-sought-after Japanese exclusion provisions added to the final legislation. From California's Alien Land Law, Congress borrowed the idea of making naturalization eligibility a criterion for other qualifications—in this case immigration.[40]

EUROPEAN EUGENICS AND "ETHNICITY." Despite lacking any obvious differences at a fundamental human level that would distinguish them from their northwestern counterparts, southern and eastern Europeans began to face a new form of racial prejudice based on the work of a growing number of eugenicists, who noted slight physical and not-so-slight cultural differences. In the 1920s, that prejudice worked its way into the American nativist movement. Although eugenics was strongest from about 1870 to 1940, it has roots deep in European history. By the Renaissance era, Europeans had already accepted the self-serving (and profit-serving) ideologies that defined Africans as inferior. In the post-1492 era, the fate of American Indians in both North and South America reflects the same European thoughts on race. However, the accelerated pace of scientific achievement in the eighteenth century contributed to the impulse to scientifically classify even minor differences across various peoples within the greater human race. The late eighteenth century saw many works contributing to that philosophy, including Johann Friedrich Blumenbach's *De generis humani varietate nativa* (*On the Natural Varieties of Mankind*, 1775), in which Blumenbach coined the word *Caucasian*.[41]

Charles Darwin's theories on evolution provided a foundation for eugenicists to further examine race in scientific terms. Once authors such as Herbert Spencer began to apply Darwin's theories to race, the idea of scientifically based racism began to gain popular acceptance. Spencer was the first to call Darwin's theories "evolution" and to use the term "survival of the fittest."[42]

Building upon Spencer, Madison Grant became the leading figure in this area. He brought several streams of race thinking together and published his ideas in *The Passing of the Great Race* in 1916. This new philosophy "attempted to elevate racial prejudice to the status of scientific theory."[43] The ideas that Grant wove together were based upon an emerging "race science" that had its foundations in the Darwinian theories and the later phases of the scientific revolution, and it divided those who were racially white into stratified subcategories. The concept of the Anglo-Saxon race had already emerged in the nineteenth century, and Grant argued that this race was the only group of people that was capable of producing great civilizations. In the United States the Anglo-Saxon race became identified with national pride, although it was not originally part of a formula for excluding or attacking "inferior races."[44] But in the period of racial nativism, Anglo-Saxons were considered to be far superior to the eastern European Alpine and southern European Mediterranean whites.

The old immigrants to the United States were, of course, part of the "racially superior" stock. Therefore, to the racial nativists, immigration was only becoming a problem with the shift in immigration patterns after 1880. Racially different immigration threatened America's social stability and would injure the nation, as the "inferior breeds" could not maintain American civilization in the eyes of eugenicists. These "scientists" viewed immigration in biological terms and argued that admitting "degenerate breeding stock" was a sin that the nation was committing against itself.[45] In the early 1920s, Grant's ideas grew in popularity as other authors repeated them, but with a "tone of crisis." In 1920, one of Grant's leading disciples, Lothrop Stoddard, wrote *The Rising Tide of Color*, which hypothesized that the brown, yellow, and other "inferior" races would overwhelm the white world.[46]

For the restrictionists, who were always open to new reasons to further limit immigration, this eugenics crisis proved to be quite appealing as it attracted new support to their cause at the height of the debates over the 1924 Immigration Act. Part of that new support came from northern intellectuals who now had an academic reason to validate racist thought.

The 1924 Immigration Act

In 1924, the US Congress passed the infamous Johnson-Reed Immigration Act. On the European side of the immigration debates, this act kept the quota principle of 1921, but lowered the quotas. On the Asian side of the debates, Congress implemented the McClatchy organization's Japanese exclusion provisions.[47] This culminated the legal development of racial identity in the United States and made *white* and *American* almost synonymous, while "foredooming Asians to permanent foreignness."[48]

THE WESTERN HEMISPHERE EXEMPTION. Western Hemisphere nations were exempted from the quota system. While many nativist groups (unions among them) favored restrictions on Latin America, southern and western restrictionist groups favored keeping immigration from Mexico open for economic reasons, arguing that "Mexican guestworkers were by definition temporary, powerless, and easily expelled."[49]

Further, these immigrants were neither formally included nor excluded from the provision requiring that all immigrants be eligible for naturalization. This lack of formal mention would leave a legal loophole that the California Joint Immigration Committee would ultimately attempt to exploit in its efforts to end Mexican immigration.

THE IMPACT OF THE 1924 ACT ON MEXICAN IMMIGRATION. During the debates over the 1924 act, Senators Willis (R-OH) and Harris (D-GA) proposed amendments to include the Western Hemisphere in the quotas, and warned of "a great influx of peons" if the "back door" to immigration was left open.[50] But even one of the leading restrictionists, Senator Reed, appealed to the idea of pan-Americanism to justify exempting the Western Hemisphere. Ironically, the 1924 Immigration Act had a tremendous impact in that it increased immigration from Mexico. Before 1876, there was little Mexican immigration to the United States, but it steadily increased during the period known in Mexican history as the Porfiriato (1876–1910). During this era, Mexico and the United States became economically intertwined, while the Porfirio Díaz regime (for whom the era is named) carried out land policies that displaced many of Mexico's peasants. This immigration further increased during the Mexican Revolution (1911–1920). The biggest boom, however, occurred because of the 1924 restrictions on European immigration, which greatly increased the demand for labor from Mexico. This was especially true in the southwestern United States, but also as far north as Michigan, Ohio, and Illinois.[51] Between 1890 and 1929, between 1 and 1.5 million Mexican immigrants entered the United States,[52] most arriving in the wake of the 1924 limitations.

For his part in the debate, V. S. McClatchy made no bones about his intention to use these statistics to his organization's advantage.

In 1933, with several years of data on Mexican immigration, McClatchy wrote of the success of the 1924 act in cutting immigration from Europe and of the resulting increase in both legal and illegal immigration from Mexico. He ended his note with a plea to his readers to demand congressional action.[53]

3

Mexican Restriction Debates, 1924–1930

IN AUGUST 1924, THE FOUR ORGANIZATIONS RESPONSIBLE FOR the Asian exclusion provisions of the 1924 Johnson-Reed Act united as the California Joint Immigration Committee (CJIC) to continue to fight groups that promised to battle for repeal of Asian exclusion. The four organizations were the American Legion, the Grange, the Native Sons of the Golden West, and the California office of the American Federation of Labor (AFL). In addition to representatives of the four organizations, members at large included C. S. McClatchy (secretary), former US Senator James D. Phelan, State Attorney General U. S. Webb, and V. S. McClatchy (who would later become executive secretary, and who continued to spearhead most of the committee's operations).[1] In addition to fighting to keep Asian exclusion, the CJIC sought to address the "weakness" of that act, Congress's failure to place Mexico on a quota.

Arguments over Mexican Restriction

At first there were only a few advocates of a Mexican quota in Congress. A few bills emerged in 1926, but they did not go very far. One reason that the issue took several years to peak is that even many of the major restrictionists did not support a Mexican quota. In March 1925 Pennsylvania Senator David Reed stated, "we are told that America 'is being swamped by hordes of illiterate Mexicans coming across the border in great numbers.' That is not true."[2] Despite the fact that the Western Hemisphere had been exempted from the quota system, Reed believed that literacy tests and head taxes would help to limit Mexican entry into the United States.[3]

Mexican immigration had actually peaked in 1924, at slightly over 89,300. In the years after the 1924 act, those numbers fell to about 50,000 annually. This figure was not much more than it had been in the first half of the 1920s. However, with the sharp decline in European immigration after 1924, the percentage of Mexican immigrants compared to others increased sharply. Table 3.1 shows annual percentages by region and illustrates this shift.

In addition, most restrictionists argued (correctly so) that illegal immigration added to the official numbers (in this period, Mexican nationals crossed the border illegally to avoid paying visa fees and head taxes, which totaled $18). These conditions led to the belief that the volume of Mexican immigration was extremely large and out of proportion to the number of European immigrants.[4] On the other hand, some scholars argue that the opposite was true, at least during the Great Depression. Those who have studied Depression-era repatriation efforts note that official numbers of Mexicans residing in the United States were higher than real numbers due to those efforts. No one kept statistics on those returning or being returned to Mexico.[5]

TABLE 3.1. Sources of Immigrants to the United States

Decade	*N. and W. Europe*	*S. and E. Europe*	*Canada and Newfoundland*	*Mexico*	*Other*
1851–1860	93.6	0.8	2.3	0.1	3.2
1861–1870	87.8	1.5	6.6	0.1	4.0
1871–1880	73.6	7.2	13.6	0.2	5.4
1881–1890	72.0	18.3	7.5	*	2.2
1891–1900	44.6	51.9	0.1	*	3.4
1901–1910	21.7	70.8	2.0	0.6	4.9
1911–1920	17.4	59.0	12.9	3.8	6.9
1921–1930	31.2	29.1	22.5	11.2	6.0
1931–1940	37.4	28.6	20.5	4.2	9.3

* Less than 0.1 percent.
SOURCE: Mary Anne Thatcher, *Immigrants and the 1930s: Ethnicity and Alienage in Depression and On-Coming War* (New York: Garland, 1990), 40.

After 1925 the Mexican restriction movement grew substantially, as did the opposition. The debates peaked in 1930. One weakness on the anti-immigrant side was that the various factions argued among themselves over whether to restrict immigration from the entire Western Hemisphere (including Canada), or if they should propose legislation that applied only to Mexico, or if they should simply leave the Western Hemisphere unrestricted.

Also, the anti-immigrant groups opposed powerful economic interests in the Southwest that desired cheap Mexican labor. Southwestern agricultural groups argued that stopping Mexican immigration would create economic disaster along the border. Finally, the restrictionists' efforts also faced opposition because the State Department sought to prevent any legislation that could be considered offensive to Mexico.[6]

Anti-immigration Groups and Their Arguments

One of the leading restrictionists on the House Immigration Committee was John Calvin Box of Texas. Representative Box may have thought he was promoting his constituents' interests in his efforts to restrict Mexican immigration, but his own words as they appear in the *Congressional Record* reveal his racism. During debates, Box called Mexican immigrants "illiterate, unclean peonized masses" who originated from "a mixture of Mediterranean-blooded Spanish peasants with low-grade Indians who did not fight to extinction but submitted and multiplied as serfs."[7]

In all likelihood, it was also "the Mexican question" that cost Box reelection in 1930. Box lost the Democratic nomination that year to Martin Dies Jr., and the *Los Angeles Times* credited Dies's addressing that issue as one of the main reasons that he defeated Box in the primaries.[8] But while Box was in Congress, he was instrumental in helping the nativist movements, including the new CJIC, almost achieve their goals. Box and the restrictionists had three major arguments as to why Congress should place Mexico on a quota system: economic issues (job loss among native-born Americans), racial differences (and the related social and cultural differences) between white Americans and Latino/a immigrants, and simple "legislative equality" between Mexico and the European nations that were already under the quota.

ECONOMIC ISSUES. During the floor debates on restriction bills in Congress, the economics argument often popped up when lobbyists from the AFL would argue that Mexicans were depriving Americans of jobs because they worked for lower wages and were often used by employers as strike breakers.[9] Representative Box supported labor's arguments, stating that Mexicans were accustomed to low wages and poor living conditions. This, he argued, allowed them to drive American labor to poverty, as American employers preferred to pay these low wages rather than raise wages to hire Americans.[10] When those who did hire Mexican labor argued that there was a labor shortage, nativists argued that if employers offered a living wage, such a shortage would not exist. Writing in the period, however, Dr. Manuel Gamio replied to the AFL's position by arguing that immigrants had to work for lower wages because the unions denied them admission; therefore they could not demand union wages from employers.[11]

Historical evidence supports Gamio's assertion. For example, to gain worker solidarity, Arizona mining unions banned Mexicans from their camps and made immigration restriction a priority in their early days. The result for Mexican workers was lower pay and segregation in housing and facilities.[12] The same holds true in California agriculture. The California office of the AFL was a member of McClatchy's CJIC. Later, Depression-era factors made Mexican labor that much less desirable. Californians "came to favor workers from Oklahoma and Texas over Mexican workers. . . . Even the literature of the time concentrates on the plight of the Oklahomans, lapsing into historical amnesia over the murder of Mexican workers."[13]

Several economic and labor associations debated among themselves the best way to restrict Mexican immigration. For nine months in 1927, the AFL leadership argued over the approach. Some endorsed restrictionist legislation from Congress. Others sought to consult with leaders of the Mexican Federation of Labor (likely the Confederación Regional Obrera Mexicana) to draft a treaty for both governments to consider that would put Mexican laborers on a quota system in the United States and vice versa.[14]

A compromise resolution emerged at the AFL's 1927 convention that asked Mexico to voluntarily restrict emigration to the United States and adopt its own quota based on the US formula. In return for a voluntary quota, the AFL would agree to allow Mexican workers already in the United States to join American unions with full membership rights. This would bring them up to union wage scale, which would also benefit American union members.[15] Secretary of Labor James J. Davis spoke at this meeting and called the 1924 act "the greatest piece of legislation enacted in 50 years," and said that the current wage scale prevailing in America (the highest in history up to that point) would not have been possible without the law.[16]

The compromise resolution had some powerful opponents. The California and Arizona State Federations, the International Seamen's Union, and the United Mine Workers continued to argue that Mexican labor was undermining American wage and living standards. The United Mine Workers' representative argued that Mexican labor was displacing American labor as far east as the Pennsylvania coal mines. In the final resolution, federation leadership promised that if Mexico did not agree to restrict emigration on their side of the border, the AFL would then go to Congress and ask for a quota.[17]

At its 1929 convention, only a few weeks before the infamous stock market crash, the AFL abandoned the compromise position that it had taken in 1927. Not only did it endorse a 2 percent quota on Mexico and Latin America, it also endorsed a platform asking that the existing quotas for Europe be cut in half again. The resolution adopted at the 1929 annual meeting stated that there were plenty of workers in America to handle the labor needs of American businesses.[18] That is quite an ironic statement considering the events that would follow very soon after the convention.

Agricultural interests were even more deeply split because of the obvious need for intensive labor in harvesting some crops, versus the minimal labor needs due to mechanization in others. At their 1927 meeting, the American Farm Bureau Federation argued heavily over the Mexican immigration issue. The southwestern states, with the backing of other western states, wanted open immigration from the Western Hemisphere because "they could not get American labor to do the work in sugar beet and vegetable fields that immigrants would." But New England farmers and dairy farmers opposed open immigration. Finally a compromise resolution was reached that simply requested a "congressional investigation before any additional immigration restrictions to nations of the Western Hemisphere are applied."[19]

After the Crash of 1929, as economic circumstances worsened, so did the arguments in favor of restricting Mexican immigration. C. M. Goethe, president of the Immigration Study Commission and member of the CJIC, argued that the Depression and increasing farm mechanization were new reasons for Congress to impose a Mexican quota. Goethe noted the jobless Mexican peons in California whose sole source of food was the garbage can: "Is it not a social crime against the people of Mexico as well as those of the United States to continue attracting Mexicans by the lure of high wages? The increasing use of machinery is more and more accelerating unemployment. There still are, however, brutally-minded employers, who yearn for yet more of these docile Mexican peons."[20] Finally, the Depression would even change minds in Congress. For example, Representative Arthur Free (R-CA), an ardent opponent of a quota during the major debates of 1930, submitted a bill in January 1931 that would restrict Mexican immigration for two years.[21]

RACIAL, SOCIAL, AND CULTURAL DIFFERENCES. The second major argument for restriction, racial, cultural, and social differences, was spearheaded largely by patriotic societies and eugenicist organizations. A group known as the Eugenics Committee of the United States advocated rigid enforcement of the existing laws, alien registration, and extension of the quota system to Western Hemisphere nations.[22] In the eyes of these organizations, even Mexicans who were racially white bore an inferior status, as they were of Mediterranean rather than Nordic stock. Those who were Mestizo or Indian were that much worse. Since Mexicans were, therefore, inferior to those inferior races that had already been restricted, they too should be added to the quota list. Yet others argued that Mexicans were in the process of reconquering the American Southwest.

Even academics embraced such arguments. Commenting on the 1924 quota act, sociology professor Frank H. Hankins of Smith College stated that although the laws were working well,

> they would never be efficient until they were applied to Mexico and Canada. The Spanish Mexican is the lowest in intelligence and physique of all our immigrants. They are the kind who will never contribute to our leadership classes, or artistic achievements, or whatnot. They merely serve to increase the proletariat. Since the quota laws the growth of immigration from Canada and Mexico has been such that last year they gave us one-half our immigrants, where formerly they gave us only 15 per cent of the whole.[23]

Another sociological argument contended that although Mexicans might lower costs for industry, they proved expensive to society, as they brought crime, disease, and public dependence, all of which outweighed the short-term gains. Simply put, "the Mexican immigrant was described as a social leper who would contaminate the American way of life."[24] By May 1926, Mexicans were entering the United States at a reported rate of approximately 9,000 per month. With these statistics in mind, quota advocates added another argument from the sociological perspective: Mexican immigrants did not seek US citizenship, which might improve their status in the United States. Instead, after seasonal work ended, many moved "into Western cities and live[d] in slums of the most vicious sort" rather than returning to Mexico.[25]

Even groups of Mexican Americans opposed immigration. They feared that the influx of "impoverished, uneducated Mexican peasants would reinforce and inflame the negative stereotypes Americans already held about Mexicans."[26] Finally, social and public health workers argued that the basic standard of living among Mexican immigrants could be raised for those already in the country if new immigrants were prevented from entering the country.[27]

Plain and simple racism marked the worst of those who adopted racial or cultural arguments. Restrictionists in Congress relied upon an official report written by economist Robert Foerster in 1925.[28] Writing for the Department of Labor, which backed the restrictionists, Foerster argued that 90 percent of Latin Americans were of Indian blood and were racially inferior to whites. Therefore, he proposed severe limitations on Latin American immigration. In many cases, social and economic arguments against Mexican immigration were "window dressing" intended to hide "outright racial prejudice."[29]

LEGISLATIVE EQUALITY. The third argument for a Western Hemisphere quota, legislative equality with the already restricted European nations, came mostly from Congress and members of the Coolidge and Hoover administrations. Addressing the United German Societies in New York City, Immigration Commissioner Henry Hull spoke of the "inequitable situation" and "unfairness" whereby Mexican natives could enter in unlimited numbers, while an American citizen with family still in Europe could not bring his "aged parents" into the country because of quota restrictions.[30] Secretary of Labor Davis also addressed legislative equality, in a roundabout way, saying of the 1924 Immigration Act:

> The fruit of this mistaken policy is already visible. Evasions and violations of the law are frequent. The alien smuggler, like the bootlegger of liquor, has become an institution. Not only does he smuggle in aliens, who have no legal right to be here, but he engages in those other illicit traffics, alcohol and narcotics. The only way to get rid of him, and with him the alien who makes use of our back door to efect [*sic*] entry into America, is to extend our immigration policy to all countries which are now exempt from it.[31]

Davis does not say how changing a law will stop those who are breaking an existing law, nor does he call for better enforcement of existing laws—just new laws.

Even Senator Reed, who had argued that the Western Hemisphere should remain excluded from quotas in 1925, eventually changed his mind based on the legislative equality argument. One section of the 1924 act allowed for three years of statistical research, and beginning with fiscal year July 1, 1927, the "National Origins" plan was to go into effect. By January 1927, most of the research had been done, and the new quotas were published. Beginning in July 1927 (pending a proclamation by President Coolidge), the quota for England and Northern Ireland would be substantially increased, while the quota for Germany, Free Ireland, and many other countries would be reduced. This drew new attention to the Mexican immigration question because of its nonquota status. In a January 1927 article based largely on interviews with Senator Reed, Representative Johnson and Secretary of Labor Davis, Mildred Adams wrote in the *New York Times*: "The invasion of the South by Mexican settlers in particular has tied a new knot in the immigration tangle. [Western hemisphere immigration] is increasing so fast that the experts are worried." She quoted Senator Reed as saying "the greatest defect of the present law is that Mexico is not under the quota restrictions. Action should be taken to extend the restrictions to her. I do not think, considering the drastic laws she has herself enacted, that she would object."[32]

Benjamin M. Day, commissioner of immigration at the Port of New York, warned that "if there was no limitation from [Mexico] a situation similar to the Japanese problem in California would likely result. 'I am astounded at the marked increase of Mexicans in the United States,' he said, 'and can see no reason why Mexico shouldn't come in the same category as European countries.'"[33]

By May 1927, Labor Department officials were reporting statistics showing an upsurge in Mexican immigration due to the 1924 Immigration Act. The report finished by stating that Representative Albert Johnson (R-WA), chair of the House Immigration Committee, would champion the new proposal.[34] Representative Johnson believed that the Labor Department's statistics would change public opinion in favor of restriction. Citing that data, he argued that legal Mexican immigration reached more than 65,000 in fiscal year 1926–1927, an increase of more than 7,000 over the prior fiscal year. Further, estimates of illegal migration from Mexico showed approximately 130,000 entrants.[35]

Pro-immigration Groups and Their Arguments

Like the groups that supported a quota, those that supported open immigration had various arguments. The two most common arguments included the other side of the economic argument, and maintaining positive foreign relations with Mexico. But often included in these arguments was a necessary counterargument to the nativists' racial and social point of view (although some ironically subscribed to the same stereotypes to make their arguments).

ECONOMIC ISSUES. The main point of the pro-immigration economic argument, provided by southwestern farmers, cattlemen, sugar manufacturers, railroad executives, and even livestock and mining representatives, was that Mexican immigrants provided an important labor source. They did jobs that whites were not willing to do (and therefore, were not taking jobs away from whites). Mexican immigrants, on the other hand, had no objection to performing such difficult work and had proven themselves to be reliable workers.[36] Agricultural representatives testified during the committee hearings that whites were unwilling to do "stoop labor" that Mexican laborers would, while railroad executives described the "section work" done by Mexicans as tedious, backbreaking, and degrading to American workers. As a benefit, they argued, by doing the undesirable tasks, Mexican workers helped "agriculture and industry to flourish, thereby creating attractive opportunities for American workers in the higher job levels."[37] Restriction, they argued, would therefore destroy the economy of the southwestern United States.

Charles Davis of the El Paso Chamber of Commerce, speaking for cotton growers from west Texas to California, argued that there were differences between southwestern cotton and southern cotton. Southerners still relied heavily on African American sharecroppers and tenant farmers, while southwesterners needed a large number of Mexican laborers for their cotton harvest. "With the quota restrictions in effect it would be almost impossible to gather the cotton crops of the Southwest, and cotton, which has become one of the staple crops in this section, would be a losing venture for the farmers on irrigated lands." Davis's racial attitudes showed when he pointed out that there were "few negroes in this section, and . . . there would be no one to pick cotton crops but the Mexicans who live on the American side of the border [i.e., Mexican Americans] and there [were] far below the number required for picking the local fields."[38] California fruit growers also argued the need for Mexican immigrant labor. Representing their interests, S. Parker Friselle said, "Ninety per cent of the farm labor used in California this season was Mexican. This Mexican labor problem is not one which we urge because it means cheap labor, but one that insures us man power." In reference to Filipino and Puerto Rican workers, Friselle noted that since both groups were US citizens, they could not be deported if brought to California. "The Mexican," he said, "is an alien and can be handled."[39]

The newspapers themselves went beyond simply reporting the issue and began an editorial war with representatives and with each other over restriction. The *Washington Post* favored restriction, while the *Los Angeles Times* took the lead among newspapers opining against a Mexican quota. When Representative Box announced that one of the first items on the congressional agenda after the holidays (January 1928) would be his bill to extend the quotas to the Western Hemisphere, the *Times* reported that such a quota would limit Mexican immigration to 1,500 per year, which could destroy California agriculture. The San Joaquin Valley alone needed 30,000 workers during harvests. California businessmen immediately protested Box's announcement. In a very profound argument, the *Times* presented California farmers' reasons why Mexican immigration should remain unrestricted:

> "It behooves every Californian . . ." said Dr. George Clements, head of the agricultural department of the Los Angeles Chamber of Commerce, "to pray that Congress may not pass this bill . . . because it is the unanimous opinion of all leaders in California agriculture that the sudden shutting off of the State's single reservoir of casual farm labor will bring about an economic dislocation bound to be felt in industry and finance.
>
> "California agriculture is not wedded to Mexican labor . . . because it is cheap labor. That cry raised against the Mexican worker is a fallacy. Mexican labor is far from cheap. White workmen, when they're available, work side by side with Mexican in the grape vineyards and cotton fields, and at the same wage for piece work."
>
> Dr. Clements gave the crucial place of labor in the California farmer's scheme thus:
>
> "There are around 135,000 farmers in our State. Of these 100,000 have under 100 acres: 83,000 under forty acres—and it is this latter group who are mainly responsible for our agricultural supremacy. The success of the farmer depends upon his handling of the crop to keep production costs as low as

> possible. His project is a one-man affair until his harvesting period is reached.
>
> "A hired man for the year is unnecessary. A single hired man at harvest is a cypher [a term commonly used to mean 'of no importance' in the 1920s]—he needs 10, 20 or 50—and he needs them quickly to get his crop off and into market. Fluid, casual labor is his only salvation; it is an absolute necessity. Suddenly cut off the single dependable source of that labor and your small farmer faces ruin."[40]

A few weeks later, the *Los Angeles Times* published an editorial titled "It Must Not Pass!" about the pending Box bill, which would have placed quotas on the entire Western Hemisphere. In this editorial, the *Times* editors agreed that fair treatment seemed reasonable, but adding Mexico would destroy the economy of the Southwest. It agreed that the economy would adjust in the long run, but the Box bill would be a needless disaster to that part of the country. The editorial argued that as more and more farms entered the machine age, fewer and fewer Mexican laborers would be needed. Further, those immigrants would naturally go home when they were no longer needed here, and Mexico would naturally also expand its agriculture, which would require more labor in Mexico. The editors then asked why businesses and civic organizations were not lining up with growers. Why did they favor restriction? They answered, "There's an Ethiopian in the woodpile" (an expression meaning that there was a hidden problem). The editorial pointed out that Easterners did not see the big picture. During the cold winter months, most farm products consumed in the east were grown in California and the Southwest. Therefore prices on fruit would skyrocket for easterners if they got their way on Mexican immigration.[41]

Even representatives from the same state and within the same party took opposing views on the issues. In February 1928, future vice president and Texas Democrat Representative John Nance Garner debated his colleague Box. Garner argued against quotas on Mexico, stating, "The Mexican constitutes no economic or social problem in Texas, where they are found in the largest numbers in this country." Further, he reiterated the argument that Mexicans did labor that white Americans would not do. Garner's district encompassed over 600 miles of the Texas-Mexico border, while Box represented a northern Texas district.

> "But we are trying to solve this problem from a national viewpoint rather than from the viewpoint of your district," cut in Representative Box. . . .
>
> "All right, then," replied Garner, "go ahead and restrict, but leave a zone 150 miles deep along the border where Mexicans can come in as at present. We have had them with us for 200 years in my country and we like them. We can't get along industrially and agriculturally without them. . . . Some of the most respectable people in the State are Mexicans of the better class."[42]

SOCIAL COUNTERARGUMENTS. In many cases, the social arguments posited in favor of the status quo truly countered the arguments made by the nativists. But in some cases, these groups were not much better than those who were supporting restriction. They did, in fact, refer to many of the same stereotypes in their arguments. Even those who recognized the value of Mexican labor often viewed Mexican culture as immoral, illiterate, evil, and childlike, among other degrading descriptions.[43] To those who favored Mexican immigration, "Mexicans represented little more than a huge, tractable labor pool to be exploited at the whim of American industry."[44] Some did support Mexicans as being racially acceptable; however, they often did so in comparison to Asians, Filipinos, and Puerto Ricans, whom they considered much more inferior than Mexican immigrants.[45]

Probably the most flagrant racism shown by those who favored Mexican immigration was in the fact that they preferred Mexican labor due to the passive nature of Mexican workers. Mexicans actually had little or no choice in being paid lower wages for harder work.[46] One Nueces County farmer told interviewer Paul Taylor that he "refused to hire white labor because 'We can't handle them as we do the Mexicans. . . . Whites cannot be as easily dominated, led, directed as the Mexicans.'"[47] Other farmers gave interviewers comments such as, "We find the Mexicans a very peaceful, timid people"; "They seem to know their place"; "They can be imposed on; the sheriff can go out and make them do anything." These quotes show that "employers of the Southwest favored unlimited Mexican immigration because it provided them with a source of cheap labor that could be exploited to the fullest possible extent."[48]

Racism even emerged in the shots fired between opposing media outlets. In the fight between the *Washington Post* and the *Los Angeles Times*, the *Post* published an editorial calling Mexican immigrants an "undesirable element" and calling for a quota.[49] In reply, the *Los Angeles Times* editorial staff asked:

> what do Washington editors know about Mexican immigration . . . ? Would not Los Angeles county, which has had long and ample experience as to this matter and in which there are at present more than 175,000 persons of Mexican birth, be better qualified to judge of Mexican merits or demerits when it comes to a consideration of such an "immigration problem" as Mexican residence in this country seems to present, than an editor living in the District of Columbia, where there probably are not so many as 500 Mexicans? Assuredly. And let it be said of the Mexican element in Los Angeles County that it is by no means undesirable, but distinctly desirable.

The editorial then goes on to discuss the economic need for Mexican immigrants in the railroad industry, as well as the desirability of pre-1848 "fine old families" (the Californios). It concluded with, "Before it publishes further tirades against Mexicans in this country the Post should dispatch a commissioner to California to study the first-hand facts of the situation."[50]

The *New York Times* also chimed in. Repeating what the *Los Angeles Times* wrote in response to the *Washington Post*, the *New York Times* commented on the issue:

> The border states "don't get" the anti-Mexican discussion, and much of the "international problem" about which Eastern dispatches devote complex interpretation is as foreign to those who come into contact with the Mexican people as is the smug statement of a Washington Editor who said, refer-

> ring to émigrés, "they are an undesirable element. . . ." What does Washington know about it, anyway? . . . As a matter of fact, this element is distinctly desirable. They are industrious and dependable. They give little trouble to the police, and their labor finds a ready market. Mexico, in most of the border towns, merely corresponds to "the other side of the street" in an Eastern community, and while Tia Juana lacks some of the elements of a New England village, Mexicali and Nogales are fine, well built, progressive communities.[51]

Later in the year, the *Los Angeles Times* used newly released statistics to argue that northwestern European immigration still remained predominant and that Mexican immigration would not harm America overall. But the *Times* did acknowledge that New Mexico, Arizona, Texas, and California had a disproportionate number of Mexican immigrants, which gave them a "burden of assimilation" formerly seen on the East Coast with Italian immigrants. The editorial implied that it was not an unfamiliar burden to Americans, and therefore should not be used as an excuse to restrict Mexican immigration.[52]

FOREIGN RELATIONS CONSIDERATIONS. As is often the case, economics and foreign relations ran hand in hand in the arguments over the proposed Mexican quota. Many antirestrictionists took their lead from the State Department, which even prior to Franklin Roosevelt's Good Neighbor Policy was advocating good neighbor relations with Mexico and Latin America. Secretary of State Frank B. Kellogg, serving under President Calvin Coolidge, opposed legislation placing any Western Hemisphere nation on the quota system. The State Department's primary concern may have been appeasing Mexican officials who were at the time threatening to expropriate American-owned oil companies.[53]

South of the border, presenting the Mexican government's perspective, the Mexico City correspondent to the *New York Times* reported "that Mexico would not object to the establishment of a quota on Mexican immigrants if it were based on something other than the Mexicans' alleged low standards of living and the like."[54] Americans in Mexico City, the correspondent wrote, argued in favor of determining America's needs first, and then establishing policy based upon those needs, not simply opening or closing the doors to Mexican immigrants.

Representing a somewhat official Mexican perspective, former president and presidential candidate Alvaro Obregón commented on the Box bill:

> Every Mexican laborer in the United States produces more than he consumes, thereby establishing co-operation for both private and public riches. Therefore there is no pretext, in the most rudimentary logic, for the restriction of Mexican immigration.
>
> Those who speak of Mexico's inferiority and undesirability are not aware of the desirability of Mexico's natural resources for exploitation by the United States capital. Restrictions of immigration would be advantageous to Mexico economically, but morally it would be depression and injurious to national sentiment.
>
> Mexico should, by the development of its own resources, provide work at home for all Mexicans, thus avoiding the necessity of their emigrating where they are well exploited, but badly treated.[55]

US State Department officials also helped present the Latin American perspective. John F. Simmons of the Visa Division filed a memorandum:

> Reports . . . from American diplomatic representatives in Latin American countries are practically unanimous in their statement that the application of quota restrictions to them could not fail to be interpreted by them as a radical departure from the traditional policy of this country toward Latin America and as evidence of unwillingness to continue to regard them as equals and neighbors having common problems, interests and aims.[56]

On the US side of the border, as early as 1927, Secretary Kellogg urged President Coolidge to take a strong stance against Western Hemisphere restriction, and continued to advocate against restriction in the following years. During that time, the State Department exercised considerable influence on immigration policy. Kellogg, too, testified before Congress, bringing both the foreign relations and the foreign investors' perspectives to the debates. Western Hemisphere nations benefited by receiving more than 60 percent of American overseas investment, and 34 percent of American foreign trade. Kellogg argued that restriction would damage America's own economic standing if these investments were threatened.

American businesses made many of the same arguments. At a Douglas, Arizona, commercial border state conference that represented businesses in both Mexico and the United States, the delegates endorsed a resolution not only opposing a Mexican quota but requesting Congress to remove the $10 visa charge and the $8 head tax imposed on Mexicans entering the United States. This group placed the issue within the context of trade, and both Mexican and American representatives agreed that negative changes in immigration policy would lead to negative consequences in trade relations.[57]

The foreign relations aspect of the congressional immigration debates also created an example of the political disunity that was common in presidential cabinets prior to President Franklin Roosevelt. While Labor Department officials (which included the Department of Immigration in that era) fought for restriction, State, Agriculture, and Interior Department representatives, including Secretary of State Kellogg, testified against any quotas on Mexico. Their arguments directly countered Labor Secretary Davis's.[58] In his testimony, Kellogg "told the committee that elements in European nations unfriendly to the United States would seize on enactment of such legislation as a means of fomenting anti-American feelings in Mexico."[59] The *Los Angeles Times* went so far as to (prematurely, perhaps) declare that because of the unified opposition of the remainder of Coolidge's cabinet, the Box bill was "laid away in the Congressional morgue."[60]

By July 1929, even Senator Reed would change his mind—again—and would oppose a Mexican quota. In switching back to the opposition, he (in part) cited diplomatic reasons. As of July 1, 1929, the national origins provisions of the 1924 Immigration Act went into effect, having been delayed by two years. This implementation was seen as a victory by Senator Reed, as opposition to the quotas grew after 1924, including opposition by President Hoover. Reed argued that the implementation of the national origins section was a victory over those who wanted to do away with the 1924 act altogether. With the State Department's efforts at restricting visas (discussed below), he had changed his mind about adding Mexico to the quota system. Reed additionally argued:

> May I say as a further expression of my own viewpoint with respect to the problem of immigration from Mexico, regarded by many persons as one of the most serious with which we are called upon to deal, that if we can enforce the existing laws it will not be necessary to put Mexico on a quota basis.
>
> I realize that this is by no means the unanimous judgment of those who have studied the subject. It seems to be clear, however, that if the border can be sufficiently guarded there will be no necessity for additional legislation at this time.

Finally, Reed concluded that maintaining the positive relations with Mexico begun under Ambassador Morrow was more important than adding restrictive measures.[61]

While maintaining those positive relations caused Senator Reed to back off Mexican restriction, that idea forced some in Congress who were "interested in fair play [and] who [would] not countenance doing anything to the neighbor at the south that is not done to the one at the north" to amend Representative Box's latest bill to "draw Canada into the fray." In response to those who would amend his bill, Box asserted, "this is . . . a rather futile argument inasmuch as we certainly have singled out Japan and China from the rest of the world. . . . We have the perfect right to do as we wish with regard to those entering our boundaries."[62]

As is often the case today, in all the arguments presented on both sides of the matter, both sides were obviously protecting their own interests, especially in an economic sense. Unfortunately, neither side showed much concern for the immigrants themselves. Historian Robert Divine commented on these debates:

> Most evident were the petty and narrow motives which inspired the antagonists. The supporters of restriction, posing as

> defenders of the American laborer and protectors of American society, seemed to be moved primarily by racial prejudice. Their opponents, ostensibly acting to prevent a serious dislocation in the nation's economy, appeared to be motivated by economic self-interest. Thus the Congressional hearings, which were held to acquaint congressmen with the basic nature of the problem they faced, turned into a bitter contest between forces of bigotry and greed which did little credit to the democratic process.[63]

By the end of Congressional Session 71-2, which ended in July 1930, even supporters of the bill began to shift their focus as the economy fell deeper into the Great Depression. One impact of that slide was that Mexican immigration slowed tremendously. The *Washington Post*, which had long supported the idea of a Mexican quota, published an editorial on August 10, 1930, stating that the need for such legislation had waned due to the efforts of the State Department to limit the number of visas for Mexican immigrants. The *Post* changed its focus from one of supporting legislation to backing the State Department's efforts and backing Representative Johnson's new agenda: "Instead attention could be given to unification and strengthening of the border patrol, so as to reduce the number of aliens who gain admittance to the United States illegally."[64] Here we see a major shift in agendas, from limiting immigration as a whole to simply curbing illegal immigration. This shift can also be seen on the other side of the debate, in the comments of quota opponent Representative Arthur Free of California, who stated in a radio address, "the whole question is enforcement of present law and not passage of more laws."[65]

The Legislative Process and the State Department's Administrative Efforts

Unlike most other groups involved in the restrictionist debates, the State Department was in a position to take direct action to carry out its agenda and influence the legislative process. Initially, State Department officials asked Ambassador Morrow to attempt to gain

Mexico's cooperation in limiting emigration to the United States. When this failed, the State Department took its own action. In a policy implementation plan that parallels the State Department's later efforts in the *Andrade* case, officials designed policies that they hoped would serve as a sufficient compromise and end the debates in Congress. In August 1928, Secretary of State Kellogg sent instructions to American consuls in Mexico ordering them to apply existing immigration standards in a more rigorous manner. First, the consuls began enforcing literacy qualifications. But more important, they began to enforce prohibitions against contract laborers and, for the first time since it was enacted, the "likely public charge" provision of the 1917 Immigration Act.[66] These two rules became a double-edged sword that allowed the consuls to deny visas almost at will. If an applicant stated that he had a job waiting in the United States, he could be denied a visa as a contracted laborer. If he did not, he could be denied a visa as likely to become a public charge.

Mexican immigration statistics provided by the US Census Bureau offer some illustration of the effectiveness of this policy (table 3.2). While the number of immigrants between 1921 and 1929 averaged more than 49,000 per year, in the period from 1930 to 1935 (the year of the *Andrade* decision), that average dropped to just over 3,700 per year. Depression-era economic factors also kept Mexican nationals from entering after 1930, which certainly con-

TABLE 3.2. Mexican Immigrants to the United States, 1921–1938

Year	*N Immigrants*	*Year*	*N Immigrants*
1921	30,758	1930	12,703
1922	19,551	1931	3,333
1923	63,768	1932	2,171
1924	89,336	1933	1,936
1925	32,964	1934	1,801
1926	43,316	1935	1,560
1927	67,721	1936	1,716
1928	59,016	1937	2,347
1929	40,154	1938	2,502

SOURCE: Adapted from US Department of Commerce, Bureau of the Census, *Historical Statistics of the United States, Colonial Times to 1970* (Washington, DC: US Department of Commerce, Bureau of the Census, 1975), Series C 89-119, Immigrants by Country: 1820–1970.

tributed to the declining numbers. Further, several groups in the United States carried out repatriation efforts that might have discouraged some immigration, although that would not be directly reflected in these numbers, as any records of the numbers of immigrants being returned are not included in this Census Bureau data.

While the State Department's actions can be seen as an effort to hinder the restrictionist movement and to keep Congress from offending Mexico, some scholars have viewed this issue differently. Abraham Hoffman saw them as a part of the restrictionist movement's own efforts:

> Further attempts at restriction through legislation were rendered superfluous by an important new development: Mexican laborers were no longer entering the United States. The victory that proponents of restriction finally achieved did not come to them by act of Congress. While restrictionists' attempts to secure a quota for Mexico were defeated, a partial success was achieved when consular officers, on orders from the U.S. State Department, began enforcing provisions of the Immigration Act of 1917 which in effect denied entry to most Mexicans who applied for visas.[67]

While Hoffman's arguments have merit in that the policy did indeed decrease Mexican immigration, the content of the congressional debates, newspaper reports, and State Department documents clearly indicates that the State Department's chief concern was US-Mexican relations, not helping the restrictionist movement.[68]

Later in the debates, in April 1929, State and Labor Department officials began a discussion over the restriction issue that reinforced the State Department's resolve to continue with its administrative approach. Unlike the FDR and subsequent presidential administrations, in which "the strong presidency" united cabinet officials on policy agendas, the cabinet officers in the administrations of Roosevelt's Republican predecessors took opposite sides. The Labor Department supported the restrictionists, while the State Department argued that the agenda would interfere with positive Latin American relations. Also, both departments lacked clear guidance on the issue from the Republican presidents. According to Assistant Secretary of State Wilbur J. Carr, "President Coolidge, though understood to be unfavorable to the proposed [restrictionist] legislation, gave no instructions . . . to either Secretary and publicly took no definite stand upon the subject."[69]

Communication between the two departments began after Labor Secretary Davis sent a letter to Representative Albert Johnson suggesting two potential solutions to the Mexican restriction debates. First, Davis suggested that Congress appoint a binational commission with Mexico to explore the immigration issue and find a solution acceptable to both countries. A more practical solution, suggested Davis, would be to simply end the debates by passing the legislation that would place Mexico on the same quota restrictions as the European nations.[70]

Davis copied this letter to the State Department and, in response, State Department officials responded that both paths were unacceptable. The first violated the basic premise that immigration had always been considered a domestic policy issue.[71] The idea of foreign representatives influencing American legislation simply went too far. The reason that the State Department opposed the second alternative, of course, was to prevent offending Mexico. To further its arguments against the quota legislation, the State Department again touted its success in implementing its own policies. Before those orders had been issued, the State Department had issued 5,000 to 6,000 visas per month to Mexican nationals. That number fell to just over 2,000 per month afterward.[72]

These policies, which were implemented just before Coolidge left office, worked so well as a restrictionist tool that both the Hoover and FDR administrations continued them, and ultimately even applied them to immigrants from other nations.[73] It has been argued that the success behind this policy rested in the fact that it provided an effective remedy to the situation without creating ill feelings by labeling Mexicans as "undesirable."[74] Despite its success, it failed to pacify the restrictionists, and the debates continued in Congress from 1927 until 1930. The State Department's success only added a new element to the debate, as Congress began to argue the merits of the quota system versus the success of the administrative enforcement.

Very soon after the passage of the 1924 Johnson-Reed Immigration Act, and as the Sixty-Eighth Congress was closing (March 1925), Senator Reed stated that it was not necessary to place Mexico on a quota system.[75] Reed's attitude was likely a reason that restriction was not much of an issue in the Sixty-Ninth Congress (December 1925–March 1927). However, early in the first session of the Seventieth Congress, Senator William J. Harris (D-GA) sponsored a bill to add the Western Hemisphere to the quota. This bill coincided with Representative John C. Box's bill in the House, which would have placed Mexico alone on a quota. Therefore, Harris decided to amend his bill to make it consistent with the Box bill. Both houses began to debate the issue in early February 1928.[76]

Anticipating extensive debates over the Box bill, Representative Johnson, chair of the House Immigration Committee, obtained permission for the committee to meet while the House was in session. Hearings were scheduled to begin on the 15th and were initially expected to last two weeks, with one week each dedicated to opponents and proponents. Representative Box asked for a month, stating, "at least four or five weeks will be required" to hear all of the testimony. However, the hearings did not get off to the start that Box and Johnson had planned. The opening date was postponed at the request of the State Department, because the United States and several Latin American nations were meeting in Havana, and having the US Congress discuss a Western Hemisphere quota would be seen as a slap in the face to those nations. But, with the end of the Pan American conference, the House opened hearings on the 21st.[77]

When the hearings began, the major issue was not whether to exclude Mexican immigrants, but whether to exclude both Mexican and Canadian immigrants. Representative Clarence MacGregor (R-NY), argued that the bill should apply only to Mexico as it would interfere with over $600 million in annual sales from the United States to Canada. Henry Ward of the Immigration Restriction League also argued in favor of a Mexico-only bill. To Ward, it was a matter of "cheap labor" versus "better citizenship."[78]

Attacking the businesses who favored open borders, Representative Box said that the committee should "consider the views of 'the millions of people back in the border States who are not appearing here,' [instead of] listening to the arguments of paid representatives of large farming interests and chambers of commerce. 'A few men,' he asserted, 'will make more noise before the committee than 1,000,000 back home who have no financial interest to bring them here, and who are not represented in Washington by legislative agents.'"[79]

By March 1928, Representative Box may have begun to face the reality that his restriction bill would not pass during the current session. But during the testimony, many of those who opposed a quota stated that they did favor more rigid enforcement of the existing laws. Representative Box took advantage of those suggestions, and on March 2 he introduced a new bill that would more than double the number of Border Patrol agents on the US-Mexico border. Opponents of his quota bill publicly stated that they supported this new one. The news media speculated that Box had concluded that his quota bill was dead, but Box denied that he was doubtful of a quota bill passing, saying of his Border Patrol bill, "If the bill introduced by me applying quota restrictions to Mexico . . . [is] enacted, additional forces will be necessary."[80]

Near the end of the first session in late March, Box asserted that he had new evidence that would contribute to his fight for a quota. When asked if he would reopen the hearings to present the evidence, he answered simply that they had never been closed.[81] Apparently, the only new evidence that he had to present was an attack on the State Department. In "reopened" hearings on April 5, Box "assail[ed] the State Department for opposing the bill." He stated that the "regulation of immigration [was] 'purely a domestic affair subject to the wisdom of Congress,'" and that "the State Department had no business 'meddling' in the consideration of his bill and asked that the committee 'pay no heed to its leadership.'" Finally, Box stated that the hearing would be the last, although the record would be kept open to receive additional evidence.[82] Finally, as the session drew to a close, Representative Johnson, chair of the committee, stated that there was not enough time left to move forward on the Box bill, but that the issue would be revisited in the following session, to begin in December 1928.[83]

The intersession between the first and second sessions of the Seventieth Congress was an election season, and the Mexican quota issue dominated the headlines. Senator Harris and Representative Box swore to renew the fight for a quota bill. Representative Johnson promised an even more restrictive bill, one that would only allow a one-for-one exchange: Mexicans would be allowed to immigrate only in a number consistent with the number of Americans who emigrated to Mexico, which was fewer than 2,000 per year.[84] All of these issues hit the newspapers again in early November, just before the election.[85]

After the election, Representative Johnson tried to have a presession meeting to resurrect the quota issue, but only five members showed up, preventing any official action because the committee lacked a quorum.[86] When asked about the closed-door nature of the attempted intersession meetings, Johnson stated that he opposed open hearings because of the "irresistible demand" for a quota bill from across America. Quota supporters blamed the open meetings during the first session for the demise of the bill. Johnson declared that closed meetings would begin as soon as a quorum of the committee returned to Washington, DC, for the next session of Congress, which was set to open on Monday, December 3, 1928.[87]

During this recess and after the election, the State Department publicized the program that it began in August to more strictly enforce visa fees and the double-edged contract labor and "likely public charge" laws. This enforcement proved quite successful, and even by the end of that November the number of legal documented border crossings was reported reduced by 25 percent. The State Department reported that it would continue the policy as Congress geared up for the coming session.[88]

Early in the second session, both Senator Harris and Representative Box reintroduced their quota legislation. Harris's bill sought quotas on the Western Hemisphere as a whole, while Box's sought one on Mexico only. But when the Senate Immigration Committee reported the Harris bill out of committee, it had amended it to be consistent with the Box bill in the House. The Box bill, on the other hand, did not receive the same quick treatment as the Harris bill because of opposition to a Mexican quota on the part of southwestern agricultural interests.[89]

Meanwhile, due to the success of curbing immigration on the State Department's end, Secretary Kellogg called a special meeting of all US consuls in Mexico to give instructions for even more rigid enforcement of rules requiring examination of potential immigrants. With the appointment of Dwight Morrow as US Ambassador to Mexico, US-Mexican diplomacy began to move in a much more positive direction. Kellogg saw the quota debates as a potential sticking point in those good relations. He wanted to eliminate the "need" for such legislation as much as possible through administrative action.[90] The Seventieth Congress ended without any legislation coming forth.

As President Herbert Hoover took office, and the Seventy-First Congress began, Representative Box very quickly resubmitted his restriction bill. By this time, the need to maintain positive relations with Mexico had caused Senator Reed to back away from a Mexican quota, and this was also the point where Box's opponents brought up the issue of "fair play" by "draw[ing] Canada into the fray" to defeat the bill entirely.[91]

During the first session in July 1929, the national origins quotas of the 1924 Johnson-Reed Act went into effect. Shortly after, members of the House Immigration Committee publicly stated that the Box bill needed to be reconsidered because it would have applied quotas to Mexico based on population estimates from 1924, rather than those used to implement the national origins quotas of 1929. Their basic approach to the bill was to ask, "Should the new National Origins system be applied to Mexico, or should Mexico be dealt with independently, as were Japan and China in the 1924 Act?"[92] This was likely just a stalling tactic, as the session ended without further consideration of any restrictive legislation. However, it is also possible that attention was diverted from the issue during the last days of the session due to the October 1929 stock market crash.

Session 71-2 began in December before any real impact of the impending Great Depression could be felt. As it began, Representative Johnson announced that he would propose a restriction bill that would limit the Western Hemisphere to 50,000 annually. He believed that most of these immigrants would come from Canada and Mexico, and since the quota would be a large one, "the restriction will not be offensive to Canada, Mexico or any other country of the Western Hemisphere."[93]

Still attempting to suppress legislation, the State Department issued a report on the results of its administrative enforcement efforts, which had begun more than a year earlier. By then the State Department said that entries from Mexico had "been reduced to 434 a month, and that the so-called 'Mexican problem' [was] no longer to be regarded seriously."[94]

Apparently giving in to pressure for "legislative equality," Representative Box dropped his insistence on a Mexico-only bill, and on January 13, 1930, proposed a bill similar to Representative Johnson's that would limit the Western Hemisphere to 50,000 immigrants annually. Box cited recent rising unemployment caused by the stock market crash as yet a new reason to restrict the entire Western Hemisphere, including Canada.[95] Despite the apparent growing support (and the growing economic crisis), the State Department continued to attempt to thwart the legislation. Testifying before the committee, John F. Simmons, chief of the visa section, and his predecessor, Monet B. Davis, both argued that restriction would be unnecessary because of the State Department's enforcement efforts. Simmons further asked that the committee consider all diplomatic and business interests while debating the bill.[96]

During the 1930 debates, public attention focused on the House Immigration Committee, with almost none being given to what was happening in the Senate. With little notice before the fact, the Senate Immigration Committee approved a restriction bill that would apply to Latin America but would exclude Canada and Newfoundland. This came as quite a shock to the Washington press corps. Laurence Benedict of the *Los Angeles Times* wrote that this was done "with virtually no discussion and with only four members present" and after chairmanship of the Committee passed from California Senator Hiram Johnson (who opposed restriction) to Senator Arthur Gould (R-ME). Senator Harris (D-GA) obtained two proxy votes in favor of the bill to attain a quorum at the meeting. Harris's bill would be even more restrictive than the Box or Johnson bills then being studied in the House Committee. Benedict continued:

> The meeting was called for the purposes of considering [another] bill . . . and no mention was made that the Mexican-

> restriction bill was to be called up. Apparently only friends of the measure were notified and five minutes before the meeting Chairman Gould told newspaper correspondents that the Mexican question and that of general restriction on this hemisphere would not come up. Despite this, the first thing the committee did was to vote the favorable report on the Harris bill. It was one of the neatest bits of railroading that veteran observers have seen in a Congressional committee room in many a moon.[97]

While the whole Senate considered the Harris bill, the House Immigration Committee continued testimony on the Johnson bill, and in late February that committee reported out a revised bill that would allow 76,064 immigrants rather than the original 50,000. The major change was in Canadian numbers. The new bill would allow 67,556 from Canada and Newfoundland and only 2,900 from Mexico. Other nations in the Western Hemisphere would be limited to a minimum of 100, with larger countries having a quota as large as 586.[98] Benedict reported that, like the Harris Bill in the Senate ten days earlier, this bill was reported out with "tricky methods." Chairman Johnson assured Representative Arthur Free (R-CA), the only opponent of the bill who was present at the time, that no action would be taken that day. Free then excused himself from the meeting. "Within an hour of [Free's] departure, the bill was ordered reported to the House by unanimous vote of members present. Representative Free refused to comment on the incident tonight, but was plainly angry."[99]

Several executive departments quickly issued protests against the House bill after it was reported out of the Immigration Committee. The Federal Farm Board protested based on the necessity of Mexican labor in southwestern farming. The State Department reiterated its protests based on the potential impact of American investors in the Mexican economy if the government of Mexico decided to retaliate through embargos or boycotts of American manufacturing. But even with regard to Canada, the State Department pointed out that it had a tradition of dealing with Canada as if it were not even a foreign nation because Canadian and American interests were basically the same.[100]

Representatives Arthur Free (R-CA), Samuel Dickstein (D-NY), and Bird J. Vincent (R-MI) filed a series of minority reports protesting the Johnson bill. The reports cited the State Department's successes in limiting visas from Mexico as a reason to end legislative efforts. The reports pointed out the danger of offending Mexico, as it was the main target of the restrictionist efforts. In his report, Dickstein cited lack of enforcement of the literacy requirements and stated that if border inspectors would step up enforcement, immigration from Mexico could be substantially curbed.[101]

As the end of the second session drew near, all indications were that the House Rules Committee would not allow the Johnson bill to come to the floor of the House. The most likely immigration bill to pass Congress was the McNary resolution in the Senate, which asked the president to establish a commission to study Western Hemisphere immigration as it related to American farm labor needs.[102] State Department officials backed the McNary plan. Acting Secretary of State Cotton argued that "enforcement rather than legislation" should be sufficient to restrict immigration.[103]

But on April 10, 1930, both houses of Congress restructured the immigration restriction argument based on new data on the emerging Great Depression. Senator Harris presented new figures that showed over 7 million unemployed, "many of them veterans of the World War."[104] On May 13, 1930, the Senate passed the Harris bill. It would have limited Mexican immigration to 1,900 per year (a 2 percent quota). The bill passed fifty-one to sixteen. Most of the sixteen opponents were Republicans.[105] Almost immediately, Representative Box "rushed to the House hopper with an identical measure" in hopes that the House Immigration Committee would speed it to a floor vote.[106]

Reporting on the Senate vote, Laurence Benedict described the procedure as "unusual" and "as slippery as the way the measure was originally jimmied out of committee." Senator Copeland asked that the bill be restored to the calendar and stated that he had no intention of it being considered for a vote. It was approved without opposition, at which point Senator Harris declared that he wanted the bill disposed of and substituted a single clause applying the quota to Mexico in place of the "badly bungled bill which had been recommitted." Harris's amendment of the bill then passed the Senate.[107]

State Department officials requested time before the House Immigration Committee in response to the Senate passing the Harris bill and Representative Box submitting it in the House. Assistant Secretary Cotton appeared to testify about the potential diplomatic setbacks that such legislation could cause. Box, however, was convinced that his bill would pass the committee unless the State Department officials managed to "'change a lot of votes.'"[108]

Taking the debates to the public, at a dinner of the American Eugenics Society, Representative Albert Johnson (R-WA) stated that the House would accept the Senate bill on Mexico as a forerunner to total Western Hemisphere restriction, arguing that the majority of the American people wanted further restrictions: "The house committee will accept the Senate proposal only because the House proposal to restrict immigration in all of the countries of the Western Hemisphere created consolidated opposition from too many minorities to be handled just at present. Later we can try for further restriction."[109]

While protests continued from the Hoover administration and the government of Mexico, House leaders were making efforts to keep the Harris-Box bill from reaching the floor, because it was likely that if it did, the House would pass the bill. Both Box and Albert Johnson stated that they would ignore any official protests made by the government of Mexico to the State Department. Box said, "'I don't know what the committee will do, but immigration is a purely domestic question and we have never permitted a foreign country to dictate our policies.'"[110]

On May 22, 1930, the House Immigration Committee reported the bill out. The committee hearing lasted only about half an hour. The report also asked the rules committee to give the bill special status to go straight to the House floor. The committee vote took place only after Chairman Johnson visited with President Hoover in hopes of getting a promise of a signature. Johnson was rumored to have reported to the committee that Hoover would not veto the bill if it passed the House, although Johnson publicly denied the rumor. The general consensus among supporters and opponents alike was that if the House leadership allowed the bill to reach the floor, the House would pass it.[111]

Just as they had in the past, Representatives Free (R-CA) and Dickstein (D-NY) filed minority reports on the Harris bill stating that it would serve no purpose but to offend Mexico. They advocated continuing the State Department's administrative efforts and increasing the size of the Border Patrol. That same day, Representative Johnson sponsored a bill that would increase the size of the Border Patrol as well as the pay scale for Border Patrol officers.[112]

Meanwhile, the Senate Agriculture Committee reported the McNary resolution out on June 11, 1930. The resolution asked President Hoover to establish a commission to study southwestern agricultural labor issues in lieu of restricting Mexican immigration. The McNary resolution was an effort to thwart the Harris-Box Bill and prevent it from coming to a vote in the House.[113] Ultimately, the resolution passed the Senate, but in the House of Representatives it was pigeonholed for the session when it was sent to the House Immigration Committee, where Chairman Johnson "promptly sat down on it."[114]

Not giving up on the issue, toward the end of the second session, House Immigration Committee Chairman Johnson took advantage of the deepening crisis of the Great Depression to sponsor a new immigration bill. His proposal would have amended the 1924 act, cutting the existing quotas in half, while adding Western Hemisphere nations to the quota system (basically a revamping of his prior Western Hemisphere legislation). Johnson stated that he did not believe it would pass the current session, but that the measure was necessary as unemployment continued to increase substantially since the stock market crash of October 1929.[115] Session 71-2 ended on July 3, 1930, just as the party primaries for the 1930 midterm congressional election were heating up. In September, the State Department released its August figures for Mexican immigration. The report stated, "there is nothing in the Mexican question further to agitate any member of Congress, no matter how hard up he may be for an issue in some district or State remote from the border and from a clear conception of the matter."[116]

In the interim between the second and third sessions, Representative Box lost his primary bid for renomination. In reporting on Box's defeat, the *Los Angeles Times* also speculated that the other leading restrictionists, Chairman Johnson and Senator Harris, were both in a fight to win renomination as their parties' candidates in the general election.[117] However, Johnson won renomination and reelection in 1930, but lost reelection in 1932. Senator Harris won renomination and reelection, but died in office in 1932.[118]

On December 1, 1930, Session 71-3 opened. Because of the worsening economic crisis, representatives deposited over 200 immigration bills in the legislative hoppers of the US Congress. The three most prominent were the Harris-Box bill, which remained alive in the House, and two new proposals that were identical to each other, one submitted by Albert Johnson in the House and the other by David Reed in the Senate (the two authors of the infamous Johnson-Reed Immigration Act of 1924). The new Johnson-Reed bill would suspend immigration totally for two years. This bill was a response to the fact that virtually every nation was beginning to restrict immigration in the face of a declining economy.[119] In the House, the Johnson side of the bill very quickly passed the House Immigration Committee.

Even Representative Free, who had opposed a Mexican quota in 1930, submitted a bill that would restrict Mexican immigration to 1,180 per year for two years, would restrict all other immigration by 90 percent, and would allow 500 Filipinos per year to the mainland, although it would not restrict Filipino immigration to Hawaii.[120] The Free bill passed the House Immigration Committee.[121]

Ultimately, President Hoover had the final say on the Harris-Box Bill, and did so without having to exercise the veto. He exerted his influence with the House Rules Committee and stopped the bill from reaching the House floor.[122] Although there was a great deal of activity on the issue during the third session, no Western Hemisphere immigration bills reached President Hoover's desk.

Ironically, although Hoover himself stopped any restrictive legislation, the most restrictionist of the media outlets, the *Washington Post*, praised the administration for being the proactive branch of government on the issue. After the Seventy-First Congress ended, the *Post* reported, "Congress failed to provide additional protection for American workmen at its last session, but the administration is making up for that failure." The *Post* was simply reporting on the existing efforts by the State Department to use the likely public charge law to help restrict immigration.[123]

Session 72-1 began on December 7, 1931. The new Congress, however, brought back some old ideas. Very quickly, the idea of a Mexican quota returned to the forefront. The two major objections, the idea that it would be an affront to our neighbor and that it would cut off a needed labor supply, "appear now to have lost most of their weight due to the economic depression and the necessity of preserving all possible jobs for native citizens." As was typical in economic hard times, white Americans did find themselves willing to do the stoop labor that "only the Immigrant" would do before. Further, President Hoover suggested that the administrative restrictions that the State Department had been following up to that point be codified into law.[124]

As the session continued, the idea of a Mexican quota gained strength. The Senate Immigration Committee reported out another Harris bill that would have applied a quota to Mexico.[125] But several senators stated that they wanted to know the position of the State Department before voting on the bill, as they were well aware that the State Department had, in past years, opposed the measure.[126]

On the House side of the debates, California and other southwestern agricultural interests continued to urge the House Immigration Committee to refrain from passing a Mexican quota. They pointed out that under the State Department's efforts to enforce the likely public charge rules, the doors had been closed as necessary during the Depression, but if a bill were passed, those doors would remain closed when the economy recovered, which would harm future farm needs. However, if Congress refrained from passing such legislation, then when the economy recovered, the administrative rules could be relaxed to meet the needs of southwestern farmers.[127]

After 1930, legislation that focused on Mexico or only on the Western Hemisphere never reached the floor of the House again. In 1931, after the Democrats gained the majority in the House, Samuel Dickstein, an antirestrictionist, became chair of the House Immigration Committee.[128] Dickstein's chairmanship and the fact that every president from Coolidge to FDR opposed restriction effectively put an end to the idea of legislating Mexican immigration restriction.

However, as is shown later in this work, those who opposed Mexican immigration still faced one branch of government that was in the hands of the restrictionists. The CJIC, which had successfully excluded Asian immigration under Section 13 of the 1924 Immigration Act, decided that the federal courts might be able to apply that section to Mexican immigration as well, and close the doors to Mexican nationals. They just needed a legal precedent, and a cooperative judiciary, to do so.

4

Good Neighbors and New Dealers

PRESIDENT ROOSEVELT'S GOOD NEIGHBOR POLICY AND HIS NEW Deal both became significant factors in the outcome of Judge Knight's ruling against Timoteo Andrade. The Good Neighbor Policy shaped the State Department's agenda of reversing the ruling, and the New Deal refined the policymaking approach (administrative law) that brought about an effective solution. The general policy approach of the Hoover administration strongly supports an assumption that had Knight's ruling occurred under Hoover, then the outcome surely would have been very different, although this can only be conjecture. Herbert Hoover did have a good neighbor agenda with Latin America, and he did oppose adding Mexico to the quota system. But those agendas certainly would not have caused his administration to take any effective action to counter Knight. Under Hoover, neither a proactive good neighbor policy nor the extended use of administrative law would have been in place.

The Good Neighbor Policy

One of the key architects of FDR's Good Neighbor Policy, Sumner Welles (also known as Benjamin Sumner Welles), also played a major role in the State Department's efforts to counter Judge

Knight. After graduating from Harvard University, Welles entered the Foreign Service, and at only twenty-eight years old he became the chief of the Latin American Division. He held that post from 1921 until 1925, under the Harding and Coolidge administrations. After he left the Foreign Service, Welles remained involved in both Latin American affairs and domestic politics. When FDR became president, he appointed Sumner Welles to the position of assistant secretary of state for Latin American affairs.

After World War II, historians debated whether or not FDR's Republican predecessors should receive credit for laying the foundations of the Good Neighbor Policy. Some called the era of nonintervention during the Harding through Hoover years a start, while others argued that nonintervention was not enough to constitute a foundation for the policy. It was simply an end to old policies of using force in Latin America. The Good Neighbor Policy came into existence only when Roosevelt supplemented nonintervention with "positive measures designed to help the Latin Americans develop their economies and raise their standards of living."[1] Others said that what distinguished the Good Neighbor Policy from the Republican good neighbor attitude came from Roosevelt's idea of reciprocity.[2] Another suggestion was that Roosevelt's policies were "a set of actions and reactions to unique circumstances" that did not exist in the Republican period.[3]

The Republicans: Good Neighbors?

While the Republicans probably do not deserve credit for the Good Neighbor Policy per se, they do deserve credit for ending most military interventions. Hoover especially was "responsible for redirecting US policy away from what the nation has always done poorly—military occupation—and toward what it does exceptionally well—business."[4] As president-elect, Hoover toured nine Latin American countries to show his interest in regional issues. During this trip, Hoover received warm welcomes in these countries. Despite Hoover's obvious efforts to establish hemispheric hospitality, his policies were overshadowed by the international impact of the Great Depression, which struck in the first year of his presidency. And, as has been shown earlier, the Republicans sided with the

Mexican point of view during the Mexican immigration debates in Congress.

The Republicans and US-Mexican Relations

The way the three Republican presidents handled US-Mexican relations shows that their administrations put a much stronger emphasis on the protection of American interests there than in any other Latin American nation. President Harding had inherited difficult relations with Mexico from Woodrow Wilson, who had twice sent troops into Mexican territory during the Mexican Revolution. The situation only worsened under Harding, because of the hardline policies set by administration officials who feared that Article 27 of Mexico's 1917 Constitution would threaten American investments. Article 27 gave the Mexican government the right to expropriate any land that did not serve the "public interest." It also gave the government the subsoil rights to all private property, and, most important, it prevented foreign nationals from owning land unless they were willing to be treated as Mexican nationals and would promise not to invoke the protection of their home government in land disputes.

Because Mexico was in the final throes of its revolution, Harding did not trust Mexican President Alvaro Obregón, who had taken power only shortly before Harding assumed office. Although Harding had an agenda of working with most Latin American nations in a positive manner, he allowed his cabinet secretaries to set administration policies toward Mexico. Harding administration officials sought to withhold diplomatic recognition to force Obregón to protect US citizens from Article 27. However, Herbert Hoover, as commerce secretary, stood in favor of recognition for economic reasons and managed to gain influence with Harding in state affairs. He argued that recognition of Obregón would improve Mexico's economy and therefore would benefit the United States and its investors.

In 1923, Calvin Coolidge ascended to the presidency at Harding's death, and the following year Plutarco Elías Calles succeeded Obregón. Coolidge's secretary of state, Frank B. Kellogg, influenced by Assistant Secretary Robert E. Olds, sought positive relations with Mexico. Olds was open-minded and had an enlightened approach. After Coolidge appointed Ambassador Dwight Morrow, one of the most well-known US ambassadors ever to serve in Mexico, the team of Kellogg, Olds, and Morrow normalized relations between the two nations.

In addition to having Kellogg and Morrow, Coolidge had retained Herbert Hoover as commerce secretary. As he had done under Harding, Hoover continued to advocate friendly relations for economic reasons. It is clear that with respect to Mexico, the Republicans sought to normalize relations while protecting American interests. The relations established by the Republicans certainly did give Roosevelt some foundation for positive relations with Mexico.

Roosevelt Assumes Office

Upon assuming office, the Roosevelt administration did not alter existing Latin American policies overnight. In fact, in coining the term "Good Neighbor" during his first inaugural address, FDR was referring to how he intended to conduct his administration's foreign relations as a whole. Roosevelt built his State Department around Cordell Hull, a southern Democrat who had been a strong supporter of Roosevelt since the 1920s. This selection helped to bring other southern Democrats into the New Deal coalition.[5] However, Roosevelt did not allow Hull to build the department on his own. Roosevelt also selected Hull's subordinates, including Sumner Welles. Roosevelt's selection of Welles created stress within the State Department, as a personality conflict arose between Welles and Hull. Hull resented Welles's personal relationship and better access to Roosevelt. However, Welles proved quite capable of guiding US policy toward Latin America for the following decade, until the personal conflict between Hull and Welles became irreconcilable, and Welles resigned.[6]

Of the political actors involved in the formulation of Roosevelt's Latin American policy, only Welles had any experience, and it was outdated. It was not long, however, before the administration began to develop its own policies, which came directly from Roosevelt, Hull, and Welles.

Roosevelt and Mexico Before Andrade

Because of the history between the United States and Mexico, Sumner Welles had to develop an approach to relations that would respect Mexico's desire to keep the United States from meddling in its internal affairs but still protect the rights of American citizens living and working in Mexico. Assisting Welles in this process was Ambassador Josephus Daniels, whose approach to Mexico was similar to that of the assistant secretary.

With Mexico, Welles focused on the one issue that had plagued US-Mexican relations at least since 1914 (when US troops occupied Vera Cruz): Mexico's sovereignty. Roosevelt and Welles took extensive measures to assure Mexico that, as the Good Neighbor Policy promised all Latin American nations, the United States would not interfere in Mexico's domestic politics. Welles had been so successful, in fact, that on the morning of the very day that senior officials in the State Department and the Mexican Embassy learned of Judge Knight's decision, Ambassador Castillo Nájera concluded a telephone conversation with Welles "by saying that in his considered judgment, relations between Mexico and the United States had never seemed so promising as at this moment."[7]

The New Deal and Administrative Law as Public Policy

The State Department's efforts to counter Judge Knight's decision came at a time of tremendous change in both American politics and federal government policymaking practices. Many scholars argue that the New Deal lasted only five years, from 1933 to 1938, and in fact came in "spurts in 1933, 1935, and, least important, in 1938."[8] After that, the New Deal tapered off. While that may be true, the way the US government develops and implements policy in general has changed because of the way New Dealers approached policy. The majority of these policymaking changes occurred just before Judge Knight rendered his decision, and they are reflected in the variety of ways that State Department officials approached the problem.

The bureaucracies established during the early months of Roosevelt's first term exemplified his efforts to achieve simple economic recovery. Those initiatives were largely improvised. Because most skilled public administrators had come into their positions during the previous twelve years of Republican leadership, FDR had to "create an entirely new government."[9] Congress created these new agencies, but they were operated through changes in government policymaking. "The charm of the New Deal was not at the level of political visibility but hidden in the agencies and subagencies."[10] While FDR did not invent administrative policymaking, a fact clearly demonstrated by the Republicans' State Department and their policies aimed at preventing Congress from passing restrictive legislation, New Dealers substantially expanded and vigorously refined the practice.

The Growth of Administrative Law

The 1930s marked the growth of power of the executive branch at the cost of the power of the legislative and judicial branches. For the purposes of examining the State Department's response to Judge Knight, this study contextualizes that shift in power by comparing two prevalent theories in policy studies, the democratic or "liberal theory tradition" and the technocratic or "progressivist theory tradition."[11] According to democratic theory, "the legislator shall make the law. The judge shall apply it to the disputes brought before him."[12] And the executive enforces the law. In other words, this is the traditional constitutional separation of powers and equal access to due process in an adversary system of justice that the framers of the Constitution created in 1787. The technocratic theory, on the other hand, places policymaking and justice in the hands of administrative and technocratic experts working for the government. These experts are also supposed to work on behalf of those who cannot afford to pay for legal services required to defend their rights under the traditional model. Both models had coexisted even before the FDR administration. But the two philosophies "came into sharpest conflict during the New Deal era of the 1930s," when the technocratic tradition made its greatest gains as the standard policymaking philosophy.[13]

In the early twentieth century, the complexity of American society grew beyond the ability of Congress to respond quickly and decisively enough to deal with the types of regulatory problems that emerged. This legislative weakness increased during the era of the Great Depression, when "only by wholesale delegations of legislative power to the Executive . . . could the demands of economic emergency be met."[14] Further, the legislature lacked the technical expertise needed to deal with such issues.[15] These conditions helped contribute to the shift to the progressive technocratic model, which concentrates governmental power in the hands of technical experts who are supposed to be above political partisanship.[16]

The Depression allowed New Dealers to develop the concept of the "strong presidency," in which the president became "the Chief Legislator, whose legislative program was to be enacted by a dutiful and disciplined Congress."[17] For example, many of the laws passed by the New Deal Congress in Roosevelt's first 100 days were "essentially enabling act[s]," and "which policy options were followed, which groups would be satisfied, would depend on the way the Act was administered."[18]

To accomplish the goals of the New Deal, the administration had to find ways to change and to work around the existing economic, political, and legal systems in the United States. Administrative law scholars have written of the New Deal:

> The architects of the welfare state had a characteristically narrow and negative conception of the role of law in government. To them, law evoked a system of rigid constraints that paralyzed initiative and prevented effective action to solve the problems of society. Government had to be freed from undue legalism, relieved of the burdensome formalism of legal procedure. It needed broader discretion in making and interpreting public policy.[19]

In addition: "Procedural innovations were seen simply as a means to be measured in instrumental terms; that is, did they help in achieving legitimate agency goals? Experimentation in . . . rule making practices was the rule of the day."[20] And finally: "What was unprecedented was the delegation of extensive powers to a peacetime president. . . . As in war, executive orders replaced detailed congressional acts."[21]

New Deal Critics

Although FDR had critics on the left who believed that he did not go far enough to break down the old economic system,[22] conservatives remained the most vocal critics of the New Deal. Conservative opponents believed that the growth of administrative law would destroy the government's obligation to answer to the people, would weaken individual power, and would reduce American citizens to servile subjects. The rule of law, they argued, is intended to curb the power of government, and constitutional divisions of power are intended to prevent minority factions from seizing government and using it to control the lives of individuals.[23]

The conservatives maintained two fundamental arguments. First, the authority delegated to Congress by the people cannot, in turn, be delegated to another. In administrative law, Congress creates agencies that have the power to create rules and regulations. Therefore, Congress, whose authority is granted by the people, entrusts that authority to these administrative agencies. Second, administrative law removed court protection from the people, because administrative agencies not only developed rules and regulations but enforced them and adjudicated conflicts that arose from that enforcement. This constituted a "combination of function," a violation of American constitutional principles.[24] The "narrower the discretion officials enjoy in the implementation of policy, the fewer are the opportunities for interested parties to challenge and influence existing policies."[25] This argument stated that since all functions of policymaking, implementation, and adjudication rested under one authority, administrators could operate without legal scrutiny, therefore potentially denying citizens their right to due process.

The most powerful conservative critics of the New Deal were the federal judiciary. The majority of these judges had been appointed when the concept of laissez-faire economics dominated American capitalistic thinking, and they were a product of that thinking. The concept of the constitutional system of separation of powers went hand in hand with that economic philosophy, and to them, Roosevelt's New Deal programs operated counter to both of those philosophies. This conflict "led the judiciary to try to 'nullify the new deal.'"[26] The main question raised by the courts was how much power the legislature could delegate to administrative agencies, and under what conditions.

Since the New Deal era, the roles of the three branches of American government have changed. Congress now reacts to policy proposals, rather than making policy, while "administrators are given broad grants of legislative power that can be exercised independently or subject to congressional *oversight*."[27] But in the period when administrative law was still developing, when the State Department dealt with the *Andrade* ruling, the courts were fighting the New Deal and trying to protect Congress's traditional role.

Robert Jackson, Roosevelt's attorney general (1940–1941) and later a Roosevelt appointee to the US Supreme Court (1941–1954), wrote that "'hell broke loose' in the lower courts. Sixteen hundred injunctions restraining officers of the Federal Government from carrying out acts of Congress were granted by federal judges" in 1935–1936.[28] Within two years, the New Deal came under the scrutiny of the Supreme Court. New Dealers were concerned that the conservatives on the Supreme Court would find such legislation unconstitutional, and, beginning in 1934, their fears were realized.[29] The Supreme Court struck down several pieces of New Deal legislation. On a single day, May 27, 1935 (known as Black Monday to New Dealers), the Supreme Court ruled three separate New Deal programs unconstitutional.[30] In one case, *Panama Refining Co. v. Ryan* (293 U.S. 388, 1935), the Supreme Court determined that Congress could not delegate its authority over interstate commerce to the executive branch. In *A. L. A. Schechter Poultry Corporation v. United States* (295 U.S. 495, 1935), the court ruled that "Congress is not permitted to abdicate or to transfer to others the essential functions with which it is . . . vested."[31]

In March 1937, after winning his first of three reelection campaigns, Roosevelt decided it was time to respond to the Supreme

Court's opposition "by asking Congress for the authority to appoint an additional justice for each member of the Court who had held his position for at least 10 years and had reached the age of 70, until the Court reached a total of 15."[32] He called the plan a reform measure. But it was obviously an effort to appoint pro–New Deal justices. But he sprang it on Congress and "defended it by hypocritical arguments, and then pushed it by every political trick, every type of ruthless pressure and cunning he possessed."[33]

This issue gave Roosevelt's silent opponents a reason to speak out. Roosevelt eventually backed down and Congress ultimately defeated the "court-packing plan." But another reason he backed down is that the Supreme Court also began to side with the New Deal. The standard narrative of how this happened says that Roosevelt eventually dropped his efforts after Justice Owen Roberts, who usually sided with "the four horsemen" (the four hard-line conservatives), voted to uphold a minimum wage law from the state of Washington. A month later, one of the four horsemen, Justice Willis Van Devanter, retired. After March 1937 the Supreme Court began to side with the New Deal philosophies and the power that the administration exercised over Congress. This change to judicial acquiescence, known as the "switch in time that saved nine," gave the administration a tremendous edge over the Supreme Court. Recent scholarship questions that standard narrative, but the argument is not over whether or not it happened, but over how and why it happened. The only issue that is important to the analysis of the *Andrade* ruling is that the change in favor of New Deal legislation did, in fact, happen. "Virtually all scholars accept that it did."[34]

Over time, Roosevelt had the opportunity to appoint a majority of the justices, adding to the Court's deference toward the New Deal.[35] In addition, Roosevelt appointed a large number of lower court judges. Congress also added to Roosevelt's power over the judiciary with the Judiciary Act of 1937, which required three district court judges to agree to an injunction against the federal government, rather than allowing a single judge to grant one. This change in the relationship between the three branches of American government was essential to the State Department's efforts to prevent another *Andrade*-type ruling from the federal judiciary.

Judicial Acquiescence to the Roosevelt Administration

The period following the "switch in time" is known as the period of judicial acquiescence. The courts could not develop a constitutional argument that would support New Deal legislation, so as a whole they simply deferred to Congress (and to the president by default, since the legislature had already deferred to the executive) and "accepted legislative delegations and administrative intervention in the economy and society."[36] After the switch, several challenges to New Deal legislation that went before the Supreme Court were decided in favor of the administration. Essentially, the courts accepted a doctrine necessary to survive the Great Depression and allowed for those who "knew the facts" (the FDR administration) to make appropriate decisions.[37]

5

Mexicans, Mexican Americans, and Civil Rights

IN ADDITION TO FDR'S POLITICAL AGENDAS WORKING IN TIMOTEO Andrade's favor, social currents were also working in favor of both Mexican immigrants and Mexican American civil rights activists. Two of these issues dealt directly with racial classification, the first of which was an effort to define the race of Latin Americans.

The Politics of Race and the Other Side of Eugenics

Several arguments had originated in Latin America, where racial theorists began to develop interesting interpretations of eugenics. While European and North American eugenicists used "science" to prove the "superiority" of the Anglo-Saxon race, Latin American (particularly Mexican) eugenicists used the movement to redefine race. The Mexican political elite viewed themselves as racially white but incorporated the concept of *mestizaje* (referring to being of both Spanish and Indian heritage) and racial equality into their racial thinking. The Mexican people, on the other hand, tended to take the philosophies of *indigenismo* (a movement to defend the indigenous peoples from oppression) and *mestizaje* literally, and showed pride in being part Indian. This pride, in fact, became one of the points of contention in Andrade's petition.

While northerners relied upon eugenics to further subdivide white ethnicity (see discussion in chapter 3 under the section Arguments over Mexican Restriction), Latin American intellectuals adapted certain aspects of eugenics in their own arguments about racial classifications in their countries. Although the racial theories that dominated both North America and Latin America from the mid-1870s to the mid-1920s were waning in the 1930s (a fact that contributes to the ultimate success of the State Department over the California Joint Immigration Committee), they still held enough sway to contribute to the nativists' efforts to restrict and exclude immigration from Mexico. In fact, these theories would not be totally denounced by scientists "until the Nazis began to . . . undertake massive extermination of the 'inferior' races."[1]

The racial status of Latin American (especially Mexican) populations has long been debated. In the modern context, based on genetic theory, racial definitions are based upon genotype (genetic characteristics) rather than phenotype (physical characteristics based on the interaction of a person's genotype and environment). This, of course, puts all "races" on a relatively equal footing because a genetic analysis of race shows that we are all the same, and that the differences between Indians, mestizos, whites, or any other race are insignificant. Modern science tells us that the racial differences that can be found around the world "have resulted from mutations, natural selection, and genetic drift . . . , and have been maintained by geographic isolation."[2] In the social context (that is, racial constructs and racism), "the arbitrary assignment of moral values to Whiteness and Blackness is contingent on particular psychohistorical events. Thus . . . in contemporary critical terms, racial meanings are socially constructed."[3] Put another way, "races are not preexisting natural entities but social groups produced out of unequal power relations and discriminatory practices."[4] Therefore, in terms of genetics, miscegenation has made no real impact upon the world. Outside of those artificial models, there are no superior or inferior races, as we are all of one blood.

Unfortunately, at the time of the *Andrade* decision, that older "race science," eugenics, was still a prevalent mode of racial thought in the world. Those nineteenth- and early twentieth-century ideas of race, combined with theories such as social Darwinism, helped to justify economic and political stratification, and ironically, "made it possible . . . for mestizos and mulattoes—by identifying themselves with white elites as against Indian or black majorities—to accept theories that justified white domination over 'colored' populations."[5] In considering our own thoughts on race relations today, we should never ignore the fact that we are all of one blood. But for the purposes of this study we must refocus our attention on the predominant racial theories to which the intellectuals of that era (and more important to this study, the policymakers) turned for answers.

Even the State Department records show evidence of this. About three months prior to Judge Knight's decision regarding Timoteo Andrade, the State Department referred a question about racial classification to the Smithsonian Institution. A University of Texas research assistant named Grace Benjamin sent a request addressed directly to Cordell Hull requesting information on how to describe race and ethnicity. Miss Benjamin had gathered data from 140,000 households in Texas divided it into "three groups, all of them mutually exclusive in the eyes of the community."[6] She was hoping that the State Department could provide her with some way to distinguish the Mexicans and Mexican Americans from the Anglo Texans without offending the Mexican people. Assistant Secretary R. Walton Moore informed Miss Benjamin that the State Department was not in a position to offer advice in the matter but had forwarded her request to the Smithsonian.[7] Moore's reply bears a certain irony, considering that within the next two years, the State Department would develop and implement a policy that would classify Mexicans and Mexican Americans.

In the reply from the Smithsonian, the chief of the Bureau of American Ethnology suggested to Miss Benjamin the use of "Anglo-American" for whites, "Afro-American" for blacks, and "Ibero-Americans" for both Mexican nationals and Mexican Americans. This bureau chief noted, "While this classification may not be very precise racially speaking, it is obvious which groups are meant and is balanced in such a way that offense should not be given to any of the groups. Anthropologically speaking, the great majority of the Mexican population is of pure American Indian extraction, but it is presumed that it would be desirable to avoid this implication."[8] Grace Benjamin's research was eventually published by the University of Texas as *Texas' Children: The Report of the Texas Child Welfare Survey* in 1938.[9]

Latin American and Mexican Perspectives on Race

South of the border, racial theorists had to contend with the issues of miscegenation and the northerners' perceptions of American Indian "inferiority," combined with the fact that the northerners viewed even Spanish blood as inferior to theirs. One of the leading scholars to tackle the issue of racial identity was José Vasconcelos. He was considered one of the most brilliant minds in Mexico. Vasconcelos was educated in Mexico City and had earned a law degree by the age of twenty-three. One of his goals as President Obregón's secretary of education was to bring the rural peasants into mestizo society.[10] In his most famous writing, *La raza cósmica* (*The Cosmic Race*), Vasconcelos "accepted the 'superiority of whites but not their arrogance,' alleging that Mexicans would not be mighty and strong till they felt themselves 'to be as Spanish as the offspring of Spain.'"[11]

In dealing with the history of race in Mexico, Vasconcelos had an interesting array of circumstances to synthesize into a racial theory. In colonial Mexico there existed literally dozens of racial classifications in a caste system that "rigidly regulated race until the late 1700s. [And since race] determined social position, there was not much vertical mobility."[12] Whites were at the top and the offspring of an African parent and an Indian parent occupied the lowest rung of colonial Mexican society.[13] The colonial powers sought to maintain a separation between the Indians and the Spaniards, and power was associated with racial identification. Over time, however, the barriers separating one racial category from another eroded, and the caste system became secondary to an emerging economic class system. Under the Plan de Iguala in 1821, legal racial classifications were eliminated, although these classifications continued to be used for some time thereafter. Further, although all Mexicans were considered equal before the law by the beginning of the Porfiriato (1876), the Mexican Census Bureau still used racial labels.[14] A stigma associated with being of mixed race still remained in 1876.

The Latin American mestizo and the southern US mulatto faced similar circumstances in their respective cultures. To the "superior" white, those of mixed blood were "conceived as a threat against the established political, economic and social order."[15] These groups also marginalized themselves. Not only were they rejected by their white parental stock, but they often refused to associate with members of their nonwhite parental stock because even they considered their non-white relatives to be inferior.

THE PORFIRIATO. Despite legal equality in Mexico, the Porfiriato (1876–1910) was one of the most racist periods in Mexican history. Mexico's mainstream intellectual elite, the *cientificos*, borrowed ideologically from both social Darwinism and positivism to justify Porfirio Díaz's social programs, and offered Díaz a convenient quasi-scientific justification for the ruthless exercise of power. Under the positivist banner of "Order and Progress," Díaz moved to create an atmosphere in Mexico that would attract foreign investment. Of course, a modern, progressive nation, where "backward" Indians had no say in its direction, would be most attractive to outsiders. During this period, Mexico also attempted to attract European immigrants, "so as to obtain a cross with the indigenous race, for only European blood [could] keep the level of civilization . . . from sinking."[16]

The Díaz era in Mexico coincided with a eugenics movement across Latin America. Like American and European evolutionists, those in Mexico and other Latin American nations were "concerned with beauty and ugliness, purity and contamination, as represented in race." Mexican eugenicist Alfonso Herrera believed that laboratory science would help humans achieve "'supreme beauty . . . , intellect, and virtue.'"[17] Mexico in particular was seen as backward because of its large numbers of Indians and mestizos. In general, Europeans viewed this hybridization as one of the main causes of Latin America's developmental problems.

These European views left Latin Americans in an intellectual dilemma, because the Latin American elite viewed themselves as a part of European civilization and sought closer connections to European nations in political and social issues. However, they had to face the reality of the racial heterogeneity of their societies.[18] This left Latin American intellectuals sensitive to these judgments, and they began to ask if the racial intermixture really was a sign of inferiority and a cause of national decay, or whether hybridization, once it leads to a homogeneous national race, could be an asset rather than a liability.[19] With those questions in mind, the early twentieth-century Latin American eugenics movement began to evolve in a manner that would help to answer the European racial critics, especially in the period after the Porfiriato and the revolution.

THE REVOLUTION. Any streams of racial thought that were current in Mexico during the Porfiriato were put on hold during the military phase of the Mexican Revolution, which began in 1911 and lasted until 1920. However, the issues over which the revolutionaries were fighting, combined with the new Latin American eugenics, contributed heavily to the emergence of a new line of racial thinking in Mexico in the 1920s. Some scholars have argued that the "elimination of racism and the rehabilitation of the Indian were central, even *the* central, elements" of the revolution.[20]

While this may be debated, the official ideology of race in Mexico certainly changed substantially in the postrevolutionary period. The political and intellectual elite who assumed power under the leadership of Alvaro Obregón set about reversing the racist philosophies that had dominated the Porfirio Díaz regime. However, their ideas exhibited a reverse racism that was "every bit as intellectually flawed as that of those whom they opposed."[21] The most persuasive of these postrevolutionary philosophers, José Vasconcelos, began to develop the concept of *indigenismo*, which became not only the official ideology but a cultural icon in Mexico. Although it resulted in anthropological and archaeological studies, and romanticized the role of Indians in Mexican culture and history, it did little to actually celebrate Indian culture. Nor did it acknowledge their role in the revolution. "*Indigenismo* was a construction of the Indian by the white elite, and one that carried with it no profound commitment to social reforms."[22] It was, in fact, the revolutionaries who "quelled the last Yaqui revolt with an efficiency [that] Don Porfirio would have envied."[23] Revolutionaries believed that rather than contributing to the revolutionary nation building, Indians were more of an obstacle because they were not loyal to the revolution and lacked the essential attitude of citizenship.

The followers of the *indigenismo* philosophy sought to "mestizo-ize" the Indians. Ultimately, the "rehabilitation" of the Indian following the revolution was not a celebration of the Indians but a recognition of the Indians' contribution to the building of the nation and to the shaping of a stronger, new race through intermarriage. This new race, hypothesized by Vasconcelos, was called the "Cosmic Race." It was through this ideology that Mexico responded to the European eugenicists' criticisms of racial intermixture. The Cosmic Race became the national race of Mexico, and the "carrier of 'the national culture of the future.'"[24] Vasconcelos, who served as minister of education under Alvaro Obregón, wrote *The Cosmic Race* in 1924. In his work, he stated that Latin America would be the stage for the rise of a new age, dominated by this Cosmic Race of mestizos. Rather than being backward, as European and North American eugenicists had argued, the mestizo would be the ultimate stage in race formation. All races would be fused in this formation, bringing racial unity to the world. This would occur in Latin America, of course, because it was the one region of the world where all races came together, and the one region where this racial fusion had already begun.[25] Pure Indians certainly did not fit into this philosophy, thus creating the need to incorporate them into mestizo society.

Vasconcelos's main audience was the Mexican people themselves. The ideology was an attempt to unify them, regardless of their race, and to solidify the victory of the Obregonistas as a national victory, thus ensuring the end of the military phase of the revolution. One of Vasconcelos's contemporaries, Luis Cabrera, argued that the mestizo was essential to this unification, and that the Indian element must be dissolved into the mestizo element.[26] Important to the international aspects of Vasconcelos's and his contemporaries' writings was the fact that they did not reject the science upon which the eugenics movement was based. They simply reinterpreted it to suit their goals.[27]

While Vasconcelos and other intellectuals recognized the mythical proportions of this ideology (in fact, he even repudiated it in the

1930s), Mexicans in general took *mestizaje* at face value, "as though a commitment to the mestizo meant an actual acceptance of all and every race in the nation."[28] However, the cult of *mestizaje* had three flaws that worked against these popular beliefs:

1. The philosophy was imposed on the Indians from the outside.
2. It asserted that Indians could be acculturated in an enlightened fashion such that the positive elements of Indian culture could be preserved, while the negative elements were eliminated.
3. The philosophy actually reproduced the racist assumptions that it was meant to counter.[29]

By the 1930s, with the ideology developing around these three flaws, and with the possibility that the United States would apply the quota system to Latin America, Mexican eugenics realigned itself more with the traditional model. Even Vasconcelos accepted some of the rationale behind North American restriction, recognizing that Mexico, too, had restricted or excluded certain races from immigrating. However, he cited economics as the main reason, as well as the idea that races unfamiliar to Mexicans (such as Asians, eastern Europeans, and blacks) would disturb the process of national unification that the revolution had started. It is more likely, however, that Mexico was exercising the same kind of nativist philosophy as was the United States in the 1930s. "Some wanted to make sure that only the fit entered to mix their blood with the new Mexican type that was in formation."[30]

This particular attitude showed itself even in relation to Judge Knight's ruling on Andrade's naturalization petition. Two days after Knight rendered his decision, one Mexico City newspaper editorialized in support of the ruling:

> Judge Knight has full authority to interpret the laws of his country, and even to have rendered his decision without basing it on any law, . . . but the argument for the decision in question is not legal but biological. The criterion of the United States with respect to immigration is that it must strengthen the Saxon characteristics of the country. If we had

> a patriotic criterion and thought of conserving the characteristics of our race, we would not so readily grant citizenship to a large number of people of race totally unassimilable with our own, as we are wont to do. Judge Knight is right in considering that the purity of his blood is endangered by the mixtures with Indian blood which might result from the admission of Mexicans into his country, and with greater reason, for the same considerations, we should support, protect and encourage the immigration only of races analogous to our own. The protest of Mexico which, according to dispatches, will be made as a result of this incident, will be ineffectual (*inoficiosa*). Every country has a right to admit or reject the racial elements that it pleases according to its convenience. What we should see in it is an example for our own conduct.[31]

Mexican racism was not only aimed at blacks and Asians. Even with respect to Mexico's own Indian population, the revolutionaries and reformers "perpetuated stereotypes and labels that justified or rationalized the treatment of Indians as objects of state intervention rather than historical actors in their own right."[32]

THE 1930S. How, then, did Mexican intellectuals and government officials define the race of their nation's inhabitants in 1935? Even in Mexico, there is not, nor has there ever been, a firm definition. The definition of "Indian" ranges from one extreme to another, depending upon who is doing the defining. The "*indigenista* spokespersons" have always included anyone who was not pure European in the category "Indian."[33] However, the Mexican government defined only those who spoke a native language as "Indian," which, in 1910, included only 13 percent of the inhabitants of Mexico.[34] Those who spoke Spanish were considered either white or mestizo. This, therefore, was a very narrow definition of Indian that included as few people as possible.

Since this study deals with official perspectives, the narrow definition used by Mexican authorities provides the framework necessary to understand the goals and objectives of both the Mexican and US governments in the period after the *Andrade* decision. This perspective also helps to define the essential philosophy behind the views of most Mexican nationals toward race in 1935; they believed that although they had Indian blood (referring to the proud Aztecs of the past), they were not Indians (referring to the poor peasants and peons of their own time).

Mexican Americans, LULAC, and Civil Rights Activism

While the Latin American perspective on race worked in favor of Mexican immigrants and Mexican American civil rights activists, a second racial classification question came directly from the civil rights activists themselves. Ironically, however, it did not glorify their indigenous roots. The desire for equality in civil rights demanded a certain level of separation between Mexican Americans and immigrants. So for Mexican Americans, obtaining civil rights also meant denying their Native American roots and being racially classified as white. Mexican American activists had been fighting for that recognition long before Judge Knight rejected Andrade's petition.

Three Mexican American civil rights activists, all founding members of the League of United Latin American Citizens (LULAC), directly involved themselves in the congressional debates over a Mexican immigration quota, as well as the issue of racial classification, and therefore indirectly in the Andrade situation. They were Alonso S. Perales, J. T. Canales, and Ben Garza. Together the three would testify against quota legislation (in opposition to LULAC's official position) during Representative Box's efforts to apply quotas to Mexico. Alonso Perales was the youngest of the three, in his early thirties at the time of the congressional debates over a quota. Like many in his generation, Perales served in the army during World War I.[35] He became a lawyer in 1926 and used his legal talents to become an advocate for Mexican American civil rights.[36] José Tomás (J. T.) Canales came from an elite *tejano* family and was also an attorney.[37] The first president of LULAC, Bernardo (Ben) F. Garza, was only a few years older than Perales. Unlike his two colleagues, Garza was not an attorney but a working-class *tejano* with a sixth-grade education.[38] But like Perales and Canales, Garza fought tirelessly for Mexican American civil rights.

By 1935, the Mexican American community in the United States had begun to establish a functional civil rights movement. Many of the initial efforts focused on school desegregation. The first successful court case took place in Tempe, Arizona, in 1925.[39] But in 1931, activists in Lemon Grove, California, achieved a much more notable school desegregation victory. School officials insisted upon segregation and built a small school in the middle of the Mexican community, arguing that Mexican students needed to be separated until they learned to speak and read English. In the hearings, Lemon Grove Mexican American students took the stand and demonstrated an advanced knowledge of English, as well as other general academic skills. In March 1931, the courts found for the Mexican American community and ordered the desegregation of Latinos/as in Lemon Grove.[40]

However, the most powerful organization in the Mexican American civil rights movement emerged in Texas. This was LULAC, founded in 1929. By 1933, there were chapters throughout the Southwest and in several eastern states. LULAC was a middle-class organization. Its driving goal was to instill a conservative, middle-class set of values based on achievement and personal accountability. One irony of this philosophy was that even white America had lost faith in traditional middle-class values during the Depression.[41]

White American Perspectives and Race Relations

While there certainly is no single view of Mexicans held by white people across the United States, there are commonalities. The "Mexican American race" has been called "off-white" due to the nature of their collective naturalization under the Treaty of Guadalupe Hidalgo, which "suggested Mexicans had white status given that, at the time, naturalization was limited to white persons. Thus, Mexicans' collective naturalization in 1848 promoted a *legal* definition of Mexicans as 'white.' Tensions around Mexican Americans' racial status arose because this legal whiteness contradicted the *social* definition of Mexicans as non-white."[42] One of the foundations of white–Latino/a race relations was created by an 1828 US Supreme Court decision that distinguished between US "federal citizenship" and "state citizenship" and said that "those citizens who held *only* federal citizenship . . . had the protection of the Constitution . . . , but they did not have political rights."[43] The Mexicans annexed in the Treaty of Guadalupe Hidalgo fell under such a classification.

Regionally, white views of Mexican Americans are as different as the regional white cultures themselves. In the greater Chicago area, there appears to have been far less discrimination and racism in the era of the *Andrade* decision than in the Southwest and Texas. "In essence . . . by the 1930's the ambiguity in Mexicans' racial image began to help Mexicans, allowing them to actively manipulate and alter whites' perceptions."[44] Part of this perception may stem from the possibility that people in the Chicago area "were much more likely than their counterparts in Texas and the Southwest to look to federal racial classifications as a guideline for their own dealings with Mexicans. When they did so, they received anything but a clear answer about Mexicans' racial identity, and they certainly did not find a firm juridical basis for classing Mexicans as non-white."[45] Of course, such a basis would not have existed prior to *Andrade*, and even that was quashed thanks to the State Department.

In Texas, the situation changed over time. In the early statehood period, many Mexican Americans still owned land, and there was a large upper class. However, that upper class disappeared in northern Texas by 1900 due to efforts by Anglos to dispossess Mexicans. This process culminated in south Texas in the early twentieth century as Anglo newcomers dispossessed Mexican Americans through the commercialization of farming. To those newcomers, who had no personal memories of any positive Anglo-Mexican relations or wealthy Mexican Americans, most Mexicans appeared to be nothing more than peons. Or, put another way, to most Anglo Texans, by 1900 "a Mexican was simply a Mexican."[46]

Across the desert Southwest and California, drastic changes occurred, largely due to changes in immigration patterns following the 1924 Immigration Act. In Los Angeles, prior to 1920, "Middle-class Mexicans [refugees from the Mexican Revolution] lived on the outskirts of the barrios or among white Euro-Americans. [But] by the 1930s, Mexicans were typically listed as members of the 'red' race, or just 'Mexicans,' on census forms and on birth and death certificates."[47]

In the mining regions of Arizona and New Mexico, Mexican and Mexican American workers were generally segregated, prohibited from joining the same unions as whites, and paid far less for doing the same work. But in Tucson, Mexican American attitudes toward racial or ethnic unity tended to be somewhat different than in other parts of Arizona: "Although Tucson's Mexican elite were concerned about racism, they looked upon *la plebe*, the people, in barrios such as Tucson's Barrio Libre, the Free Zone, with disapproval and sometimes contempt. Their indifference to the interests of working-class Mexicans made it easier for US ranchers, farmers, merchants, mine owners, and railroads to exploit them."[48] Further, "Tucson's first Mexican newspaper . . . condemned workers' societies as consisting of 'idle and depraved people who wanted a repetition of the [1789] Revolution in France.'"[49] Meanwhile, Tucson's Mexican elite, while championing their culture, did not question capitalism or its exploitation of working-class Mexicans. In one case, a Tucson-Spanish language newspaper did address white disparagement of Mexican Americans. But the newspaper did so because there were "not just thousands but millions of Mexican men and women, who could 'boast of as clear and fair complexion as may be found' in the United States."[50] Overall, however, Tucson's Spanish-language newspapers tended to be a bit conservative, "instrument[s] of the better off Mexicans."[51]

Phoenix and Tucson have always had very different cultures, and their approach to race relations reflects that:

> Friendly House, a Phoenix organization with substantial Mexican American support, was designed to help immigrants but mostly emphasized teaching immigrants to become domestic workers, learn English, and improve personal hygiene. It lauded employers' efforts to deport immigrant troublemakers who sought to organize strikes. These assimilationists wanted to Americanize the immigrants as a way of ensuring that the latter would conform to Anglo American cultural and class norms.[52]

Despite Friendly House's efforts, only a few days after Judge Knight denied Andrade's petition, Phoenix-area Mexican Americans launched a protest over discrimination and segregation aimed at their children. The Phoenix-area Junior Chamber of Commerce planned a Christmas event that would have had separate events and a separate Christmas tree for Mexican American children. Here, too, Mexican Americans used the "whiteness" argument in their demands for civil rights. One line of the protest document read, "Because our children are of the Caucasian race, they deserve the same considerations as white children." In this event, we can also see the differences between Phoenix and Tucson. The protest further stated, "In Tucson, fortunately, . . . we have no complaints as we do in Phoenix, as they recognize the worth of Mexicans."[53] Nearly a year later, and in response to the El Paso racial classification incident of October 1936, the Tucson Spanish-language newspaper *El Tucsonense* editorialized on racism in Texas, stating that "in Arizona, New Mexico and California, race relations have continued to improve day by day."[54]

Wherever they were in the country, when the Depression came, minorities were not the only people to suffer, but, unlike poor whites, their problems were compounded by racial bigotry. To Americans of the 1920s and 1930s, racial bigotry was much more justified than cultural bigotry. In other words, it was easier to hate Mexicans and blacks than it was to hate "poor white trash."[55] By the Great Depression, Anglo attitudes had largely lumped Mexicans in with blacks: "In short, the Mexican problem had nothing to do with integration or assimilation; rather, it was a question of locating another inferior race in American society. There was general agreement, in Texas and elsewhere, that Mexicans were not a legitimate citizenry of the United States. . . . A comparison with the 'Negro problem' seemed natural."[56] Further, "Anglos rarely distinguished between Mexicans and Mexican Americans and painted a picture of 'Mexicans' as an economic and cultural threat to America."[57]

The 1924 Immigration Act also helped shape that racism. As the number of immigrants from southern and eastern European nations dwindled, more and more employers turned to Mexican immigrants for cheap labor, which angered those who competed against Latinos/as for jobs. A shift took place in racial identification because of the 1924 act. Race and nationality (ethnicity) for whites became decoupled so that persons originating anywhere in Europe would simply be considered white. But for Asians and Latinos/as, race and nationality became conjoined. One of the consequences of this was that "Mexican" became "a wholly negative racial category, which comprised both Mexican immigrants and Mexican Americans in the United States."[58]

Even Mexican scholars in the 1930s had a similar view of white American racism. Dr. Manuel Gamio did considerable research on Mexican emigration to the United States and wrote that American racism dated back to the time "when white Americans first came into contact with Indians, Spaniards, and Indo-Spaniards in the frontier regions immediately after these states were annexed to the American union."[59] Unlike some LULAC members, who believed that discrimination was not racial but was a white American reaction to Mexican immigration, Gamio argued that the discrimination was indeed racial. He pointed out that in the United States, discrimination declined for second- or third-generation Germans or Italians, as compared to the continued discrimination against Mexican Americans, regardless of how many generations their families had been in the United States.

Ironically, however, Americans were fascinated with Mexican art and culture at the same time. Diego Rivera was very well known in the United States, for example. How could Americans appreciate such things while displaying such an extreme intolerance for Mexican immigrants? The answer lies in the culture of the Depression. First, "things Mexican" in Mexico did not compete with Americans for jobs. Mexican immigrants in the United States did. Second, Mexican culture was created by "educated, 'presentable' Mexicans," while those who immigrated were "uneducated, unrefined, untrained laborers."[60]

Those laborers, both US born and Mexican immigrants, suffered under "a particular type of cultural aggression" aimed at Americanizing them. This effort, however, was not meant to assimilate them into American culture. It was an attempt to weaken Mexican culture, identity, and language for the purpose of advancing Anglo political domination and economic exploitation.[61] This Americanization included punishing schoolchildren who spoke Spanish, and reinforcing North America's "cultural superiority" over Mexico.

Mexicans Americans and Mexican Immigrants

The relationship between Mexican Americans and Mexican immigrants has always been strained. In the restrictionist debates, many Mexican Americans took the side of the restrictionists because they feared that the influx of immigrants would reinforce the racial stereotypes that white Americans held about Mexican Americans. Immigrant Mexicans returned the resentment because Mexican Americans looked down their noses at them. However, with the rising bitterness of white Americans toward both groups during the Depression, Mexicans and Mexican Americans were left continually asking whether they should "cooperate with one another . . . to build ethnic solidarity, or had a half-century of political separation created unbridgeable . . . cleavages between them?"[62] Working-class Mexican Americans were more empathetic toward the immigrants than were the middle class. Even though the working class competed directly with the immigrants for jobs, they often worked side by side and saw issues, especially white racism, from the same perspective.

However, the segment of Mexican American society that made itself most visible, the middle-class LULAC members, continued to stand against immigration for their own political well-being. When *tejano* groups founded LULAC in 1929, they decided to focus their civil rights efforts on Mexican Americans and to exclude noncitizens. The original groups that founded LULAC did include several immigrants, and during the unification conventions the resident Mexican nationals protested against the motions to allow only US citizens to be members of the new organization. The founders believed that to develop the political clout needed to create social change, they must have a membership composed solely of American citizens. After all, government "authorities . . . did not respect or fear groupings of noncitizens."[63]

Further, the LULAC leadership believed that it made little sense for them to organize to protect their civil rights if the border remained open to Mexican immigration. In 1929, Secretary of Labor James J. Davis commented:

> Influential Mexican leaders in the Southwest are now advocating a quota for Mexican immigrants, and state that their reason for doing so [is] that "a regulated number for each year will enable Mexican leaders to develop protective and self-help organizations among the lower class of immigrants, who are now, it is claimed, being exploited. Large influxes of peons prevent the leaders among the Mexicans from developing an *esprit de corps* among the masses."[64]

LULAC even went so far as to claim that white discrimination against Mexican Americans originated not from racism against Mexican Americans but from the white reactions to Mexican immigrants entering the United States.[65]

Mexican Americans and Civil Rights

As immigration from Mexico increased, white Americans generally continued to view Mexican Americans in the same light as the immigrants. In fact, by the 1920s, whites commonly viewed the word *Mexican* as a racial classification rather than a national identity. Mexican Americans, of course, fell into this category with Mexican immigrants. These perspectives contributed to the resentment that already existed between Mexican Americans and Mexican immigrants, as Mexican Americans often blamed the immigrants for white attitudes. It also contributed to the Mexican Americans' desires to be recognized by white America as citizens, not immigrants, who therefore should be treated differently than those who had only recently arrived in the United States.

The intermediate position of Mexican Americans between whites and Mexican immigrants, and their separatist approach to obtaining civil rights, has opened up the "Mexican American generation" to criticism. One political model, however, helps to explain why the LULAC generation followed this course. In any generation, a large body of individuals represented by a "guiding minority" becomes the essence and historical definition of that generation. In this case, a vocal minority, the middle-class Mexican Americans who wanted to identify with white society, set the agenda for the whole of the Mexican American civil rights movement.[66] This struggle has been labeled a fight for "Caucasian Rights," which was a calculated "decision to fight for white rights for some, rather than equal rights for all."[67]

Another view of this generation is that "elite Hispanics have traditionally claimed for themselves and their communities White identities. From the 1930s through the 1950s, for instance, Mexican community leaders in the United States challenged segregation not on the grounds that it was wrong per se, but by arguing that they were White, thereby initiating a persistent trend in which certain Latinos/as seek assimilation through claims of Whiteness."[68] Related to that point of view was the attitude of that generation toward African Americans and their struggle for civil rights. One LULAC official in 1936 "encouraged members to 'tell these Negroes that we are not going to permit our manhood and womanhood to mingle with them on an equal social basis.'" Further, "Mexican Americans frequently supported the denigration and segregation of blacks."[69]

The late 1920s and early 1930s saw the largest US-born generation of those who were generally classified as Mexican, contributing to the first politically active and civil rights–oriented generation of Latin American peoples in the United States. These sentiments were particularly strong in Texas, where large populations of Mexican Americans, *tejanos*, had been US citizens since Texas entered the United States in 1845. *Tejanos* resented whites dismissing them as "mere Mexicans" and categorizing them with the recent immigrants, especially since they and most of their parents, and even grandparents, were native-born US citizens.

In addition, many had served in the US military during World War I, which certainly entitled them to the respect and dignity accorded to their fellow US citizens. This generation would no longer allow themselves to be treated as second-class citizens. In October 1924, San Antonio attorney Alonso S. Perales defined the early civil rights movement by stating that Mexican Americans did not wish to beg to become a part of Anglo-American society, but simply wanted, he said, "equal opportunity in our struggle to make a living, and equality before the courts. In a word, we ask for justice and the opportunity to progress."[70]

In the 1920s, lower-middle-class *tejanos*, many of whom were war veterans, founded several organizations such as the Sons of America, the Knights of America, and the League of Latin American Citizens.[71] For two years, these scattered Mexican American groups met, considered consolidation, and finally, on February 17, 1929, came together as LULAC. Unlike previous groups that advocated cooperation between citizens and immigrants, LULAC focused on the needs of the citizens. They sought assimilation into American society and culture, as well as to educate their membership in their rights as citizens. It was this separatist ideology that even caused LULAC to support the immigration restrictionists in Congress.

Ironically, although LULAC's official position during the 1930 Box bill debates supported restriction, three of LULAC's founding members took advantage of the committee hearings to attempt to push their civil rights agenda and, in so doing, came out against the Box bill. Alonso Perales and J. T. Canales testified together on January 29, 1930, and Ben Garza testified on January 31. While they did not, in principle, object to the intent of the restrictionist Box bill (which was consistent with LULAC's position), they did object to the abusive enforcement of existing immigration laws. Further, they feared that restriction would threaten Mexican Americans if immigration authorities enforced these new laws with the same kind of disregard for the rights of Mexican Americans that they applied to existing laws. Canales, an attorney from Brownsville, Texas, cited several cases in which US citizens had been deported, even after their citizenship was proven. New restrictions would only make it easier for authorities to abuse and deport US citizens who were unaware of their rights.[72]

Alonso Perales allowed the committee to believe that he did not oppose the bill in principle. He stated, "if the sponsors of this bill . . . can prove that the Mexicans—that is those from Mexico—are a menace to the American workingmen . . . then I say all right; good luck to you, more power to you."[73] This remark, however, can easily be read as a brazen, contemptuous comment intended to let the committee know how he really felt about the bill. Perales then stated that he believed that the restrictionists' efforts had little to do with economics and more to do with racism. Perales also went before the committee to defend his race. Rather than testifying, he entered a prepared statement into the record that cited several accepted authorities on racial politics who could not prove that Latinos/as were an inferior race (although even Perales accepted their assertion that "the intelligence of the white race is of a more versatile and complex order than that of the black race").[74]

Although Canales, Perales, and Garza left the impression in their testimony that they represented LULAC in Washington, the LULAC leadership in Texas sent a telegram to the House Immigration Committee:

> [We] wish to inform you that any testimony that may be offered to-day or to-morrow . . . by J.T. Canales, . . . Ben Garza, . . . and Alonso S. Perales . . . is not [an] official act of the league nor has it ever been discussed, indorsed, or supported by the general membership or any division thereof. . . . Please advise Mr. Perales . . . of the full contents of this telegram, as we wish to make it a matter of record in the league.[75]

The league, of course, did not wish the House Immigration Committee to be left with the idea that LULAC opposed restriction.

One aspect of Canales's and Perales's testimony was a defense of both Mexicans and Mexican Americans as descending from advanced civilizations. Canales pointed out that in the American Southwest, which was once northern Mexico, "You find there the white people, and they did not mix with the Indians, because the Indians at that time there were savages, like ours; whereas the Indians in the central part of Mexico were civilized."[76] Perales elaborated further, stating that the Indians of central Mexico were not savage like those of the American Southwest but were highly developed Aztecs, Toltecs, and Zapotecs, who helped to lay the foundations of modern Mexican culture.[77] Therefore, the Mexican American was either descended from the Spanish settlers who had not intermingled with the "savage" Indians of the Southwest, or was a modern mestizo who came from the best elements of the Spaniards and the highly civilized central Mexican Indians. In this respect Perales was, of course, borrowing from the Mexican philosophy of *mestizaje*.

LULAC AND "WHITENING." Part of the move to assimilate into Anglo-American society involved "at least partial denial of Mexican identity, which was accomplished by [claims] to 'Spanish descent' and mixed European descent."[78] This "whitening," however, evolved within the Mexican American civil rights movement over time. When Perales first defined the Mexican American ideal in October 1924, he stated, "We do not desire to renounce our race. On the contrary, we are proud to carry Mexican blood in our veins."[79] However, because of the realities faced by Mexican Americans, and the fact that white America associated them with noncitizen Mexicans, the movement began to develop this philosophy of whitening. In simple terms, Mexican American civil rights activists believed that the key to obtaining civil rights was to be considered racially white (seeking Caucasian rights). One effort to whiten themselves was to emphasize that as Latins, they had roots in ancient Rome. And Romans, after all, had contributed much to the development of Anglo-Saxon culture. So, as descendants of both Latins and Spaniards, they had a legitimate claim to whiteness.[80]

One of the LULAC's founding concepts was an effort to become Americanized in hopes of becoming acceptable to white society. This, of course, is also one of the main criticisms of the LULAC founders: this generation was accommodationist and "sold out" its ethnic background. However, LULAC's founders can also be defended from this accusation.[81] Far from being accommodationist, they have been viewed instead as relentless in their fight for first-class citizenship. Their critics view history through a modern lens, and therefore see their efforts as assimilationism, rather than a struggle to achieve equality. To understand the LULAC founders' approach, it is important to understand that they were Americans who had few political or social ties to Mexico. Therefore, they had little choice but to integrate into US society and to work within the American system to obtain full civil rights.[82] In short, Mexican Americans were taking the most pragmatic approach to obtain as much for their people as they could under the circumstances of the 1930s.

The Impact of the Great Depression

To summarize the issues at the time of the 1929 stock market crash, Congress was debating the future of Mexican immigration, the restrictionists were on the verge of getting a Mexican restriction bill out of committee, and the newly founded LULAC was pushing a civil rights agenda, but only for US citizens of Mexican origin. And with the exception of a few members in a leadership role, LULAC supported the restrictionists in Congress.

The Great Depression tipped the scales dramatically in favor of the restrictionists. After the crash, white American attitudes toward both Mexican immigrants and Mexican Americans changed for the worse. Mexican workers were singled out as scapegoats for American unemployment, and several American cities "organized campaigns designed to oust Mexican workers from their communities."[83] Small farmers, labor unions, and racists in general began to seek restrictions on immigrants from Latin America. A large number of white Americans actually believed that getting rid of Mexican workers would create jobs, which would help to end the Depression.[84] Furthermore, American business interests created some of this anger to divert the attention of unemployed and hungry white Americans from the emerging Depression.[85]

At the same time, welfare agencies began cutting Mexicans from their rolls, Mexican workers were among the first fired from their jobs, and the US, state, and local governments deported somewhere near half a million,[86] including many native-born Mexican Americans, most of whom were the children of adult deportees. Almost another half a million "voluntarily" repatriated to Mexico, many being coerced into doing so. However, over 50,000 received help from the government of Mexico in their efforts to return home, and clearly did voluntarily repatriate.[87] In total, the number of Mexican (and Mexican American) repatriates totaled somewhere near 1 million people.[88]

LULAC's Successes: El Paso and the Social Security Board

Despite the setbacks of the early Depression era, LULAC continued to teach Americanism, fight for civil rights, and fight against discrimination, and was quite successful at achieving its goals. The organization attained several legal victories in Texas, organized voter registration drives, and "began to chip away at the structure of the *de jure* segregation of Mexican American students" in Texas's public schools throughout the 1930s and into the early 1940s.[89] Segregation, of course, was unwarranted as far as Mexican Americans were concerned, as they were members of white society.

One of LULAC's greatest successes, an incident that had immediate beneficial consequences for the State Department's efforts to counter Judge Knight's *Andrade* ruling, was its efforts to fight the Census Bureau's efforts to classify Mexican Americans as "colored." In addition to being lumped in with blacks as nonwhite, a new theme had emerged in Anglo-Mexican relations: "Mexicans are dirty."[90] This applied not only to hygiene but was also a characterization of skin color and "inferiority." On October 5, 1936, El Paso city registrar Alex Powell and the city health officer, Dr. McCamant, announced that the city would begin classifying Mexicans as colored on birth, death, and other civil records.[91] The two city officials stated that they were simply following a US Census Bureau policy that required the reclassification of Mexicans from white to colored. The main reason for this order was to separate infant mortality rates of Mexicans and Mexican Americans from those of whites. El Paso city officials welcomed this new Census Bureau policy because they had been trying to sell the city as a major southwestern health resort. The high mortality rate among statistically white infants was embarrassing to city officials. In addition, "diseases such as diptheria [*sic*], smallpox, tuberculosis, typhoid fever and influenza" were common in south El Paso, in the barrios where the Mexican populations lived.[92] Like the infant mortality rates, these diseases had been included in white health statistics before the reclassification.

Both LULAC and the Mexican American unit of the Veterans of Foreign Wars protested against the El Paso reclassification. The leaders of these groups consisted of lower-middle-class Mexican Americans and Mexican nationals. This policy, of course, posed a major threat to the "Caucasian rights" efforts of LULAC. The protest was headed by El Paso attorney Frank Galván, who was also the president-general of LULAC at the time. Another leader, George Rodríguez, complained to the State Department, citing the negative consequences the decision would have for US-Mexican relations. The *Eagle Pass Daily Guide* in Texas issued a similar protest. The author of the article suggested that Powell should be fired because of his lack of understanding of pan-Americanism. After all,

Vice President Garner had only recently opened the Pan-American highway, and Western Hemisphere nations were currently meeting in Buenos Aires to promote hemispheric peace. The *Daily Guide* article asked, "How could the Delegate from the United States [at the Buenos Aires Conference] explain the attitude of the official Powell, if, before this American Congress, the Delegate from Mexico informs the assembly that in Texas, Mexican people are considered the same as 'colored people,' and does this place other Latin Americans at the same level as that of the black?"[93] *El Tucsonense* (Tucson, Arizona) carried a similar article, stating that indignation was spreading in Chihuahua due to this ruling, and that residents south of the border were organizing El Paso boycotts "to exert commercial influence."[94]

The primary mover behind the protests, however, was Cleofas Calleros, a member of the National Catholic Welfare Conference in El Paso. Calleros argued that the term "colored" was entirely inappropriate to Mexicans, as the only racial classifications that should be used for Mexicans were white, Indian, or mestizo. Others echoed Calleros's sentiments and denounced the use of "colored" to racially characterize Mexican nationals, stating that it was just as inaccurate as using the word "Mexican" itself as a racial description.[95] "Only the ignorant confused race with nationality."[96] Several editorials appeared in local newspapers, most arguing that Mexicans, because they were Spanish, were whites, and that Anglo whites were being racist.[97] One letter to the editor of the *El Paso Herald-Post* went so far as to blame the "influx of 'white trash' into Texas" for the problems Mexican Americans faced.[98]

Powell and McCamant initially stood their ground in the face of the protests, citing the Census Bureau as the source of the reclassification. McCamant told the protesters that they needed to take the issue up with the Census Bureau. Finally, the Mexican American community sought an injunction with the Sixty-Fifth District Court. Community leaders actively encouraged citizens to go to the courthouse and provided free transportation for those willing to go. In the face of such community activism, the city officials backed down, and the court dismissed the case.

With the victory over the El Paso city officials, Calleros and Galván turned their attention to the Census Bureau. As president of LULAC, Galván issued a notice to all councils on October 8, 1936, urging them to take the matter to their respective congressional representatives.[99] In a reply to Galván and Calleros, Alonso Perales stated that classification was not perceived as a problem in San Antonio, where city officials used "white" for Caucasians, "Mexican" for Mexican Americans, and "colored" for African Americans. No one protested San Antonio's classifications, he said, "because we persons of Mexican descent . . . are very proud of our racial extraction and do not wish to convey the impression that we are ashamed to be called Mexicans."[100] However, San Antonio members were offended at being classified as "colored" by the Census Bureau and agreed to participate in Calleros's efforts. With the help of Perales and the San Antonio council of LULAC, the El Pasoans raised the issue with several influential politicians. Perales, along with three other San Antonio LULAC representatives, personally delivered a resolution to their representative, Maury Maverick, that convinced Maverick to sponsor their cause. Maverick immediately sent the following telegram to William Lane Austin, director of the Census Bureau:

> I understand that Americans of Mexican or Spanish lineage are classified as "colored." They, and the inhabitants of the Southwestern states in general, consider this as a final insult and on behalf of those people, I protest against said insult if it is true. Please telegraph me if it is true so that we may discuss the issue in more detail and more extensively. I thank you for an immediate response in regards to correcting this policy.[101]

Maverick immediately followed up the telegram with a letter to Austin repeating and detailing his and LULAC's protest. Maverick suggested that the Census Bureau either use "white" or, if truly needed for the statistical separation of Mexicans from the white population, "other White—Mexican."[102] Further protests came from El Paso representative R. E. Thomason, New Mexico senator Dennis Chávez, and the district attorney for the city of Laredo, a Mexican American named John Valls.

Mexican officials also protested the El Paso classification. Ambassador Francisco Castillo Nájera sent his own protests to Census director Austin, and, in Mexico City, Deputy César Lara launched an initiative in the Chamber of Deputies to ask President Lázaro Cárdenas to formally protest the policy.[103]

On October 15, 1936, Census Bureau director Austin issued a circular that read in part:

> The Classification by color or race must be as follows:
> a.- white
> b.- Negro
> c.- All other
> The text and the tables (either by note at the head of the table or by footnote) must state definitely that the classification white includes Mexicans. Mexicans are whites and must be classified as *white*.[104]

In addition, Austin assured the protestors that the transgression would not be repeated and "blamed the controversy on an 'error' the Division of Vital Statistics made in not following the established classification . . . that Mexicans were whites."[105] Three years after this reclassification, Austin said of the El Paso incident:

> The . . . decision . . . to group Mexicans with the white population was made with haste under the pressure of a number of protests. The protests arose chiefly against a practice in vogue in the Division of Vital Statistics publications which divided all births and deaths into two groups, white and colored. It was natural that protests should have arisen from Mexican groups to be classified as colored because the word was misinterpreted to mean Negro. This defect was eliminated and, in fact, it was in the process of elimination before the protests arose in the first place.[106]

Whatever the origin of this racial classification policy, it ultimately proved quite useful to the State Department's agenda vis-à-vis Judge Knight's *Andrade* ruling.

The Mexican American leadership followed up their successes in El Paso and with the Census Bureau by continuing to protest further classification incidents. Within a month of the El Paso incident, El Pasoan Cleofas Calleros again contacted Perales to inform him that Mexicans were classified as nonwhite on the new Social Security Board's employment forms. Item twelve of the form read: "If you are either white or Negro, place a check mark in the proper space. For other than white or Negro, write out color or race to which you belong in the space provided. Typical examples are: Mexican, Chinese, Japanese, Indian, Filipino, etc."[107] The El Paso–San Antonio group again enlisted the help of their congressional representatives. Representative Maverick and Alonso Perales visited with the local office of the Social Security Board where the district manager, Oscar Powell, agreed to take up the issue with his superiors in Washington. In addition, the Houston Latin American Club contacted Texas's two senators, Tom Connelly and Morris Shepard, as well as their representative, Joe Eagle. Eagle wrote directly to the Social Security Board, stating that he supported the protest of Houston's Mexican American community.[108]

Perales wasted no time in getting the word out in the Spanish-language press that Mexican Americans should ignore the example in item twelve and should mark themselves as white on the Social Security forms. Apparently quite irritated by the Social Security Board's classification, Perales cited several state and federal laws regarding the racial classification of whites, blacks, and Latinos/as, as well as the Census Bureau's recent ruling that Mexicans and Mexican Americans should be classified as white.[109]

The Social Security board ultimately let those involved know that Perales's anger was a bit premature. Within a couple of days, Representative Maverick received a reply from both the commissioner of internal revenue and the executive director of the Social Security Board stating that when the Census Bureau had changed its policy, the Social Security Board had already printed over 40 million employment forms, and it would have been impossible to reprint them in accordance with the new policy. The Treasury Department promised to publicize the fact that Mexican Americans should check "white" on that form.[110]

6

The Andrade *Decision*

TIMOTEO ANDRADE WAS BORN ON JANUARY 24, 1897, IN LAGOS, Jalisco, Mexico (figure 6.1). At the age of eighteen, and in the midst of the Mexican Revolution, Andrade immigrated to the United States, crossing into El Paso, Texas, in June 1915.[1] As the United States entered World War I, and as would be expected of any immigrant seeking to become a US citizen in time of war, he registered for the draft. Exactly one week after World War I ended, Andrade married Sara de la Cruz, a fellow Mexican national who had immigrated late in 1915. At the time of the 1920 US Census the family lived in Tucson, Arizona.[2] At some point in the next year, they moved back to Texas, then to Galesburg, Illinois. By 1924, Andrade had moved his family to Buffalo, New York, where some of his descendants still live today.[3] During most of that time, Andrade worked in the restaurant business.

Prior to becoming a federal judge, John Knight served as district attorney in Wyoming County, New York, spent four years in the state assembly, and then moved over to the state senate (figure 6.2). From 1924 until his resignation from the state senate in 1931, Knight served as president pro tem.[4] He had earned an AB degree from the University of Rochester in 1893, and in 1896 he entered the bar through the common law practice of "reading the law." Knight had become a favorite of the New York Republican Party, and in January 1931, after Federal Judge John Hazel of the Western District announced his retirement, both state and national Republican leaders selected Senator Knight to replace him. Knight received a recess appointment from Herbert Hoover on March 18, 1931. Hoover for-

Figure 6.1. Timoteo Andrade, 1929. Citizenship Petition of Timoteo Andrade.

mally nominated Knight on December 15, 1931, and the Senate confirmed the nomination on January 6, 1932.[5]

Knight's nomination was steeped in controversy. Erie County Republicans, who had the largest representation in the Western Judicial District, objected to the appointment of someone from outside their county to the bench. This group went so far as to send various delegations to visit with President Hoover at the White House to urge that an Erie County resident be appointed to fill Hazel's position.[6] Further controversy arose when "unnamed persons" charged that Knight had interests in hydroelectric companies that would conflict with his duties as a federal judge. An investigation disproved these allegations.[7]

Timoteo Andrade and Judge John Knight met in one of the most ordinary ways that "common people" meet face to face with the political elite, in a routine legal procedure. But what Andrade expected to be routine ended up being far from ordinary. His naturalization petition became the focus of a powerful lobbying group's attempt to change the face of immigration to the United States.

The four organizations that formed the California Joint Immigration Committee (CJIC) were directly involved in obtaining Sec-

Figure 6.2. Federal Judge John Knight, 1931. © Buffalo and Erie County Historical Society, used by permission.

tion 13 of the 1924 act, having combined forces in 1923 to represent California's interests in the debates.[8] By 1935, the CJIC's representatives included James K. Fisk of the American Legion (committee chair); Paul Scharrenberg of the State Federation of Labor; John T. Regan, grand secretary of the Native Sons of the Golden West; Charles M. Goethe, president of the Immigration Study Commission (committee treasurer), Ulysses S. Webb, attorney general of the State of California; and V. S. McClatchy (committee executive secretary). After the success of Asian exclusion, the committee turned its attention toward excluding both Mexican and Filipino immigration, which had been exempted from both the quotas and racial exclusion. Even before the failure of the Mexican quota bills in 1930, the committee began working on developing a legal precedent that would apply the exclusionary provisions of the 1924 Immigration Act to Mexican immigration.

The CJIC chose John Knight to help develop a judicial precedent in regard to naturalization because of the failures of the restrictionists in the eastern United States to find a legislative solution to the perceived Mexican immigration problem. The easterners had attempted to pass legislation to apply the quota terms of the 1924 Immigration Act to Mexico. But after the 1930 election put Democrats in charge of the House, Representative Dickstein's chairmanship of the House Immigration Committee, combined with President Hoover's opposition to quota legislation, put an end to the restrictionists' efforts. This obliged the California exclusionist groups, which had successfully excluded Asian immigration under Section 13 of the 1924 Immigration Act, to find a way to apply that section to Mexican immigration to totally close the doors to Mexican nationals.

Perhaps reflecting upon the fact that the federal judiciary had created the existing "Mexican situation," McClatchy pursued a judicial, rather than a legislative, approach. Until Judge Knight's ruling, the judiciary had allowed Mexican nationals to become US citizens, regardless of race. The precedent for this had been set in 1897 in the case of Ricardo Rodríguez (*In Re Rodriguez*, 81 Fed. 337, May 3, 1897), in which natives of Mexico were found to be entitled to US citizenship because of the collective granting of citizenship in the Guadalupe Hidalgo and the Gadsden Purchase treaties.

Although it took time to build a precedent that would counter this 1897 decision, the CJIC demonstrated enough patience to do just that. Once they had a firm legal theory that they believed would exclude Mexican immigrants, the committee's executive secretary, V. S. McClatchy, recruited Judge Knight and naturalization examiner John Murff to test the legal foundations of the case law with respect to Mexican immigrants.

The Background of the *Andrade* Decision

According to McClatchy, Herbert Hoover's first secretary of labor, James J. Davis, issued an order "declaring all Mexicans, regardless of race, eligible to American naturalization."[9] This supposed order came in the form of a February 1929 memorandum to Representative Albert Johnson, chair of the House Immigration Committee. To counter this order, the CJIC first sought a legal opinion from one of its own members, California Attorney General Ulysses S. Webb. Webb, declared that "indians or red races in Mexico, constituting the bulk of the population in that country [are] ineligible for American Citizenship and subject to immigration restrictions excluding them as immigrants to the United States."[10] Second, the committee protested the ruling to Davis and later to his successor, William N. Doak, who became secretary in 1930. Late in 1931, committee member John Regan exchanged letters with Doak, arguing Davis's order. Doak replied that Davis's statements had not been an order, but simply an acknowledgment of existing circumstances. He told Regan, "'with relation to Mexicans, I presume you know that the courts have held them to be eligible for naturalization.'"[11] Secretary Davis was, in fact, defining this issue for Representative Johnson. Rather than saying "regardless of race," Davis had stated that Mexicans are "generally spoken of as belonging to the white stock . . . [if they] speak Spanish, and our Government, in its relations with the Mexican people, has uniformly recognized them as belonging to the white race."[12] Fundamentally, Secretary Davis was first "evading the issue of Mexicans' race" and then arguing "that Mexicans' eligibility for citizenship didn't depend on their race."[13] This position basically lent credibility to CJIC's point of view that Labor Department officials were, perhaps, of the opinion that Mexican immigrants were not white. If they were indeed of this opinion, they could not state it, as that could be used to apply Section 13 to Mexican immigrants.

The Rodriguez *Decision*

The court decision that allowed for the naturalization of Mexicans, to which Doak had referred, was *In Re Rodriguez* (81 Fed. 337, May 3, 1897). This precedent came from the District Court for the Western District of Texas. In this case, two Texas attorneys, A. J. Evans and T. J. McMinn, contested Ricardo Rodríguez's naturalization petition on the grounds "that he is not a white person, nor an African, nor of African descent, and is therefore not capable of becoming an American citizen."[14] Evans and McMinn had an ulterior motive for their objections. Their efforts were an attempt to disenfranchise *tejanos* and deny them the right to vote. They believed that if they proved that Rodríguez was ineligible for naturalization, then by default, those who had become citizens through annexation and treaty would also be recognized as illegitimate citizens.[15]

Issuing his opinion, District Judge Maxey noted that "the treaty of Guadalupe-Hidalgo . . . incorporated many thousands of Mexicans into our common citizenship, [but] the question of the individual naturalization of a Mexican citizen is now for the first time . . . submitted for judicial determination."[16] The question at issue was whether Evans and McMinn were correct that Rodríguez did not qualify as a "free white person." Maxey noted that Rodríguez "trace[d] his descent from neither the Spaniards nor Africans." Rodríguez claimed, as far as he knew of race, to be "a pure-blooded Mexican."[17]

Judge Maxey solicited opinions from members of an independent committee regarding the eligibility of Mexicans for naturalization. The arguments of two of these members, T. M. Paschal and Floyd McGown, appear in the court records. In his brief, Paschal discussed the issue of naturalization by treaty, answering to Evans and McMinn's claim that all *tejanos* were illegitimate citizens. He pointed out that foreign citizens who remained within territories annexed by the United States since the Louisiana Purchase had been granted US citizenship. More important, three separate treaties that incorporated Mexican populations into the United States gave Mexican nationals US citizenship: Texas annexation, the Treaty of Guadalupe Hidalgo, and the Gadsden Purchase. Paschal continued, "[Although] no treaty exists . . . by virtue of which the applicant may claim the right or privilege to become naturalized . . . these [treaties] are of great importance as to the main question which is at issue in this case, viz. as to the eligibility of the applicant for naturalization, because of the ethnological feature involved in the case, or in other words, because he is not a 'white' man."[18] Finally, Paschal argued that trying to define "white person" was simply splitting hairs and that the court should look at the legislative intent behind the naturalization laws, which he believed applied to all persons descended from Europeans, even those of racial intermixture. Therefore, he argued that important precedents had been set by the prior naturalization of Mexican nationals through the three treaties, and these measures allowed for the further naturalization of Mexican expatriates.[19]

The court's second independent commentator, Floyd McGown, saw things from a much more black-and-white perspective, so to speak. He determined that under a simple interpretation of the naturalization laws, Rodríguez did not meet the racial criteria for naturalization.

Although their opinions differed with respect to Rodríguez's racial eligibility, Paschal and McGown both agreed: "it does not appear . . . that [Rodríguez] has even a fairly approximate knowledge of the form or general structure of our government," and even "if he were a white person, his utter ignorance of the principles of our constitution would defeat his application."[20] Even Judge Maxey noted in his statement of facts that Rodríguez seemed to be "very ignorant and illiterate" in both English and Spanish.[21]

In opposition to Rodríguez, Evans and McMinn cited four cases in which nonwhites had been denied naturalization as precedents for their argument: *In re Ah Yup* (1 Fed. 223); *In re Camille* (6 Fed. 256); *In re Kanaka Nian* (21 Pac. 993); and *In re Saito* (62 Fed.

256). Judge Maxey responded to these four cases first by discussing the context of *In re Ah Yup*. At the time of this case, Congress had recently debated both Chinese exclusion and the addition of "persons of African descent" to the naturalization statutes. Maxey quoted Judge Sawyer from *Ah Yup*, who said, "it is clear from these proceedings that congress retained the word 'white' in the naturalization laws for the sole purpose of excluding the Chinese from the right of naturalization." This quote alone removed *Ah Yup* as a potential precedent for denying Rodríguez's naturalization, as Rodríguez certainly could not be considered Chinese.[22] With respect to all four cases, in fact, Maxey pointed out that they applied to individuals of a specific race and therefore could only be strictly interpreted to apply to future applicants of those races.

Consequently, of the four cases, only one could potentially be applied to Rodríguez. That was the case of *In re Camille*, decided by the Circuit Court for the District of Oregon in 1880. This decision dealt with Frank Camille, who was born in British Columbia to a white Canadian father and a Canadian Indian mother. Presiding over the *Camille* case, Judge Deady also cited *In re Ah Yup* and borrowed from it Judge Sawyer's "ordinary sense" definition of "white person." Deady argued that this definition did not include the "red race of America."[23] In addition, as to Camille's racial intermixture, Deady cited an Ohio case that found "a person nearer white than black or red was a white person . . . , but that where the colored blood was equal to or preponderated over the white blood, the person was not white."[24] On these grounds, Deady denied Camille's petition for citizenship.

Ultimately, however, in deciding Rodríguez's eligibility, Judge Maxey followed Paschal's logic that the racial argument was "splitting hairs" and therefore ruled that *In re Camille* also did not apply to Rodríguez. Maxey wrote in his ruling, "If the strict scientific classification of the anthropologist should be adopted, [Rodríguez] would probably not be classed as white." He continued, "If debarred by the strict letter of the law . . . , is he embraced within the intent and meaning of the statute?"[25] To answer these questions, Maxey followed Paschal's second line of reasoning, that the three aforementioned treaties, although applying to a collective population rather than to individual petitioners, set a precedent that Mexican nationals do fall within the intent and meaning of US naturalization laws. Maxey ruled that the meaning of "white male inhabitants" in the treaties remained at question, while "it is entirely clear, whatever meaning may be attached to those words, that the language of the acts explicitly recognized Mexicans who remained in the ceded territory . . . as citizens of the United States."[26]

Maxey also deemed that an 1868 treaty between the United States and Mexico reinforced this precedent. Although the treaty was terminated on February 11, 1882, Maxey referenced it "for the purpose of indicating the construction placed upon our naturalization laws."[27] However, Judge Maxey may have been stretching the existence of said treaty for the benefit of the case. In this treaty the two nations simply agreed to recognize their own expatriates who had been naturalized in the other nation as citizens of that nation. Neither nation made any reference to recognizing its own naturalization laws. Through some legal meandering, Maxey interpreted this treaty as an indication that Mexicans fell within the meaning of the US naturalization laws.

Ultimately, Maxey ruled that Mexicans, even of Indian descent, "came within the meaning and intent of the Naturalization Laws, and that Mexicans, as a class, had been recognized by the United States Government as embraced within the Naturalization Laws."[28] Or, put another way, "The essential logic of *Rodriguez* was that Mexicans were *white enough*, despite not being truly white."[29] With respect to Paschal's and McGown's objections that Rodríguez was ignorant of the Constitution, Judge Maxey cited the fact that Rodríguez had been a moral, law-abiding resident of San Antonio for ten years. This, to some degree, indicated to Maxey that Rodríguez at least understood the principles of the Constitution, and therefore he granted Rodríguez's petition.

Sometime after Knight's decision, State Department legal adviser Richard W. Flournoy assessed the *Rodriguez* decision to determine how it had granted Mexican nationals the right to naturalization in the United States. He stated that the issues presented in that decision were unclear, and that "in this case nationality and race appear to be hopelessly confused so that it is of little value."[30] However, Flournoy, who likely saw the issue entirely from a legal perspective, might not have considered the possibility that Judge

Maxey was acting entirely for political reasons in granting Rodríguez naturalization. Maxey's political motivation is evidenced by the fact that he overlooked Paschal's and McGown's objections (and his own doubts) about Rodríguez's constitutional knowledge and granted the petition anyway.

The Committee's Objections to Rodriguez

After receiving Doak's reply referring to *Rodriguez*, Regan directed the issue to McClatchy, who had effectively argued the committee's agenda in 1923–1924. McClatchy certainly was not happy with Doak's answer, and in response he argued that the provision excluding those ineligible for citizenship

> was urged as a logical and inoffensive solution to the Japanese immigration problem. It was intended by its promoters to apply, without discrimination and without specifying any race, to all members of the yellow, red and brown races, constituting half the population of the globe. . . . The provision was presumed to apply to Mexican Indians as members of the red race. Even the special privilege accorded in the 1924 act for entrance without quota of all citizens of free states of the Western Hemisphere would undoubtedly have been construed, in light of court decisions, as applying only to those not barred because of ineligibility to our citizenship.[31]

The *Rodriguez* decision had another critic as well. In 1935, George W. Gold published a legal article addressing racial requirements in general and discussing the eligibility of natives of several nations around the world. In his discourse on *Rodriguez* and Mexican immigration, Gold stated, "the conclusion reached in this case . . . is wrong." Gold reminded the reader that even Judge Maxey had recognized that Rodríguez would not be classified as white. He argued that, with this in mind, Maxey should have realized that the intent of the Treaty of Guadalupe Hidalgo was not to allow all Mexicans to become US citizens but to "avoid assuming a vast territory that would for some time thereafter be populated, almost entirely, by alien residents."[32]

Like Judge Maxey in the *Rodriguez* decision, several legal authorities agreed that the meaning of "white" was ambiguous, especially with respect to the Mexican population. Secretary Davis had already informed the committee:

> It is the view of this Department that native Mexicans cannot be denied permanent admission . . . because of . . . race. The Mexican people are of such a mixed stock and individuals have such a limited knowledge of their racial composition that it would be impossible . . . to classify or determine their racial origin. Thus, making an effort to exclude them from admission or citizenship because of their racial status is practically impossible.[33]

Even the courts had differed in opinion as to the meaning of "white," especially in terms of whether it should be defined in layman's terms or by "the science of ethnology," which itself could not furnish a satisfactory answer.[34]

McClatchy, however, argued that there was indeed a satisfactory answer, and referred Doak to California Attorney General Webb's 1929 opinion that had been published in the *Los Angeles Times*. Webb had argued the issue in the context of two subsequent US Supreme Court decisions, *Ozawa* and *Thind*.[35] McClatchy pointed out that the *Rodriguez* decision involved "no higher court than a U.S. District Court" and avoided dealing with the issue of race.[36] The two later rulings, he argued, very clearly defined "white race" with respect to naturalization law.

Ozawa v. United States

In *Takao Ozawa v. United States*, 260 U.S. 178 (1922), the petitioner's attorneys argued that the intent of the First Congress in 1790, in using the words "free white person," was to exclude black slaves and American Indians from citizenship. Since "white" originally meant "not Negro or not Indian," and "free" stopped having meaning in the statutes after the abolition of slavery, these words must not exclude those of the Japanese race from naturalization.[37] This argument would mean that the 1870 addition of "aliens of African nativity or African descent" would have completely opened the doors to all immigration, except for Native Americans.

Solicitor General Beck, arguing for the United States, countered Ozawa's attorneys, stating that legislators of 1790 surely knew that "white" applied to Caucasians, such as themselves, and had intended naturalization to apply only to those who shared common manners, culture, language, and appearance.[38]

Rendering the Court's opinion, Justice Sutherland ruled against the argument that the first legislature intended "free white person" to be an antithesis to "Negro slave," mostly because every legislature that had altered the law since had kept the same wording even after the US Civil War, and after the clause admitting Africans was added. Sutherland stated, "the provision is not that Negroes and Indians shall be *excluded* but it is, in effect, that only free white persons shall be *included*."[39] Who then were "free white persons"? Justice Sutherland did discard "free," in agreement with the petitioner's attorneys that it was a recognition that slavery had once existed. However, in defining "white persons," Sutherland cited *In re Ah Yup*, as well as several subsequent decisions (three of which were also cited in *Rodriguez*[40]) where judges had consistently defined this to mean "only a person of what is properly known as the Caucasian race." Further, he acknowledged that the meaning of even "Caucasian" was debatable, but it did offer a racial zone that clearly excluded Japanese and other Asian races.[41]

United States v. Thind

The Court's ruling in *Ozawa* formally defined "white" as Caucasian, defined the existing naturalization laws as allowing only Caucasian and black immigrants to be naturalized, and therefore excluded Asians from naturalization. The following year, Solicitor General Beck and Justice Sutherland took on the shadowy issue of the meaning of "Caucasian" in *United States v. Bhagat Singh Thind*, 261 U.S. 204 (1923). Thind, an East Indian, claimed eligibility for naturalization on the grounds that he was of high-caste Hindu stock, which had been classified by certain scientific authorities as of the Caucasian or Aryan race.[42] He initially received his US citizenship, but over the objection of the naturalization examiner. Government representatives filed an appeal, seeking to cancel the naturalization certificate on the ground that Thind was not a white person. In an opinion that reads like a supplement to *Ozawa*, Sutherland further narrowed the definition of "white." "What we now hold is that the words 'free white persons' are words of common speech, to be interpreted in accordance with the understanding of the common man, synonymous with the word 'Caucasian' only as that word is popularly understood. As so understood and used, whatever may be the speculations of the ethnologist, it does not include the body of people to whom the appellee belongs."[43]

In a *Federal Bar Association Journal* article, State Department legal adviser Flournoy summarized the *Thind* decision: "[T]he term in question [white person] was not intended to be used as an equivalent of 'Caucasian' or 'Aryan,' and . . . the first Congress did not have in mind any scientific, ethnological classification, but merely intended that naturalization should be restricted to persons of the same racial stock from which the first settlers of this country came, that is, white Europeans."[44] Ironically, five years after writing these words, Flournoy would be one of the key bureaucrats fighting to keep the *Andrade* ruling from applying *Thind* to Mexican expatriates, whom even he recognized were not "white Europeans." It was likely this legal understanding that, as is shown in subsequent chapters, caused him to fight for the legislative option over the administrative law alternative.

A Mexican Test Case?

McClatchy used *Ozawa* and *Thind* to argue with Doak that Mexicans, too, should be excluded. But with respect to Western Hemisphere natives, he acknowledged that a specific test case had not yet come before the Supreme Court. He fully believed, though, that these Supreme Court decisions, if applied to Mexican immigrants, would override the *Rodriguez* decision, and that if the Labor Department initiated a test case, then the Supreme Court would rule consistently with *Ozawa* and *Thind*.[45] However, finding a test case might prove difficult, simply because naturalization examiners did not question Mexican naturalizations because of the terms of the *Rodriguez* decision. And since the Hoover administration had fought the restrictionists, it certainly was not about to assist the exclusionists in the same endeavor by contesting a Mexican national's naturalization petition. Both Secretary Davis and Secretary Doak refused to find a test case in the situation.[46] Therefore, it fell upon McClatchy and his allies in the CJIC to set the precedent by launching their own test case.

The Committee Plans Its Next Move

With Doak's refusal to appeal a Mexican naturalization petition through the federal court system, McClatchy and the committee members set about researching other legal precedents and facts to further support their position.

In 1934 the California attorney general's office argued the *Morrison* case before the US Supreme Court.[47] Although not a naturalization case, it was indeed a product of one committee member's efforts (Attorney General Webb), and the committee readily used the Supreme Court's findings in *Morrison* to help develop the legal arguments that it eventually used in the *Andrade* decision.

Morrison v. California

The *Morrison* case was a criminal prosecution regarding California's Alien Land Law, which made it relevant to the racial prerequisite to naturalization. The Alien Land Law used the naturalization statutes to determine eligibility to own land in California. The defendants, Morrison and Doi, were convicted of conspiracy to violate this law by placing Doi, who did not meet the racial requirements for US citizenship, in possession of agricultural lands. The legal issue decided in this case "was the invalidity under the due process of law clause of the Fourteenth Amendment of a procedural provision of the Alien Land Law of California."[48] The defendants won their appeal on the grounds that the land law put the burden of proof upon the defendant, because those accused of violating the law were forced to prove their citizenship or eligibility to become citizens as a defense. The one aspect of the appeal that has direct bearing on the racial issue is that defendant Doi, a Japanese national, was of mixed Anglo and Japanese ethnicity. Physically, Doi appeared to be Anglo, which further benefited Morrison (a white man) because Morrison may not have been aware of Doi's racial ineligibility and therefore could not have conspired to violate that aspect of the statutes.

Although the Supreme Court overturned the convictions in the case, the justices took advantage of Doi's racial heritage to establish new case law with respect to naturalization, an issue that was totally irrelevant to the procedural issue under appeal. The opinion, written by Justice Cardozo, widened the definition of ineligibility for citizenship by stating that exclusion is not "limited to persons of the full blood. The privilege of naturalization is denied to all who are not white (unless the applicants are of African nativity or African descent); and men are not white if the strain of colored blood in them is a half or a quarter, or, not improbably, even less, the governing test always being that of common understanding."[49]

The opinion drifted even further from the issue of the appeal when Justice Cardozo hypothesized about the potential injustice that might be done to others in Morrison's position, should they deal with those who appear to be white but are not. Almost casually, Cardozo pointed out that just as Doi was of a racially mixed background, so too were Mexicans. Although Mexicans were brought into the decision for purposes of comparison, Cardozo's discourse on the matter brings the overall racial agenda into extremely sharp focus, where he appended what appears to be a simple tangential footnote to his hypothesizing:

> Indians not born in the United States . . . are ineligible for citizenship. There is a strain of Indian blood in many of the inhabitants of Mexico as well as in the peoples of Central and South America.
>
> Whether persons of such descent may be naturalized in the United States is still an unsettled question. The subject was considered in *Matter of Rodriguez*, 81 Fed. 337, but not all that was there said is consistent with later decisions of this court. *Ozawa v. United States*, and *United States v. Thind*, *supra*. Cf. *In re Camille, supra*.

> Mexicans have migrated into California in increasingly large numbers; and there have developed racial problems which have been considered by official bodies.[50]

Practically out of nowhere, the appeal of a routine criminal prosecution suddenly addressed the issues of *mestizaje* and Mexican immigration, and sent a clear message to anyone who was following the issue in 1934: if McClatchy's test case reached that Supreme Court, Mexicans would be excluded. With the Morrison decision in place, the CJIC had only one more move to carry out to gain exclusion of Mexican immigration. McClatchy had to find his test case.

Knight, Murff, and McClatchy: A Nativist Conspiracy?

In his search for a test case, McClatchy found two potentially willing officials who could implement the committee's legal theory. Together with acting naturalization examiner John Murff, who appeared willing to ignore the Rodríguez precedent,[51] federal Judge John Knight, of the Western District of New York (Buffalo), was willing to implement the *Morrison* footnote in a naturalization case. In the later months of 1935, McClatchy and his allies apparently "went to Examiner Murff and to Judge Knight . . . , putting pressure on them to rule against the naturalization of Mexicans of Indian blood."[52] On November 9, 1935, a few weeks after delivering the argument developed by the committee to Judge Knight and naturalization examiner John Murff, McClatchy wrote to Judge Knight to ask if he had yet had the opportunity to decide anything regarding any Mexican nationals.[53] As of that date, Knight had not. But slightly over a month later, Knight and Murff finally acted.

The Decision

On December 11, 1935, three Mexican nationals went before Judge Knight seeking naturalization: Timoteo Andrade, Porfirio Bravo, and Francisco Velez. Appearing on behalf of the Bureau of Immigration and Naturalization were district director Arthur Karnuth and acting naturalization examiner John L. Murff. None of the petitioners had legal representation.

On that fateful day, Andrade did not become a US citizen. At the hearing, Examiner Murff moved to dismiss the petition on the grounds that Andrade was racially ineligible, based on Andrade's affidavit that he was "of Indian and Spanish blood in equal proportions." Knight upheld Murff's objection, and the first precedent he cited was *Morrison v. California*, and Justice Cardozo's seemingly innocent footnote that read: "There is a strain of Indian blood in many of the inhabitants of Mexico as well as in the peoples of Central and South America. Whether persons of such descent may be naturalized in the United States is still an unsettled question." Judge Knight continued, in his own words, "The question is now raised as to an alien of one-half Indian blood."[54] In an opinion that bears striking resemblance to Cardozo's treatment of *Morrison*, Knight cited practically verbatim the CJIC's opinions on *Ozawa* and *Thind*.

In addition, Knight cited *In re Camille* (6 Fed. 256), one of the cases that had been rejected by Judge Maxey in the *Rodriguez* decision. *Camille*, again, was the case of a Canadian Anglo-Indian in Oregon where the judge held that the "red race of America" did not meet the definition of "white" and "that where the colored blood was equal to or preponderated over the white blood, the person was not white."[55] Finally, almost as an afterthought, Knight said only one thing about *Rodriguez*, the decision that had, for so long, been the reason Mexicans had been allowed naturalization: "*In re Rodriguez*, 81 F. 337, is not consistent with the later decisions of the Supreme Court."[56]

Soon after Knight handed down his decision, McClatchy issued a press release in which he proudly, but prematurely, announced: "The U.S. Federal Court at Buffalo, N.Y., John Knight, Judge, has declared Mexican Indians ineligible to American naturalization and therefore inadmissible as immigrants."[57] McClatchy also took the opportunity to attack former labor secretaries Davis and Doak in the release. First he made note of their order allowing Mexican immigration regardless of race and then remarked that the 1930 census indicated that 360,000 Mexicans were living in California, "most of [whom] had been admitted since 1924 and under the Davis order."[58]

With this, McClatchy had his test case. At that point, he could take no further action. He could only hope for one of two scenarios. First, it was possible that other judges would follow through with this new ruling, thus reinforcing the precedent and forcing the State Department to deny immigration visas to Mexican nationals. The other possibility, which is what the committee had been working to achieve, was that pro-Mexican forces would help Andrade appeal this decision, hopefully as far as the US Supreme Court. As has been shown here, with the exclusionist majority in the Court, Mexicans would then be legally defined as falling within the same excluded category as Asians.

The Consequences of the Decision

The most obvious consequence of Knight's decision, and ironically the one that never occurred, was that it should have closed the doors to Mexican immigration. However, the efforts of the State Department, the Mexican government, and others (detailed in the pages that follow) prevented that from happening. Because the administration ultimately managed to neutralize Knight's decision in 1937, this case may be viewed as merely a blip in the historical timeline, and possibly irrelevant in the larger scheme of immigration policy and history. However, for a brief time, the potential for a major policy change did exist because of Judge Knight's ruling.

While the potential impact upon immigration may have gone unrealized, this case did have a very real effect on two other issues, the first of which was US-Mexican relations. State Department officials noted that a "deplorable effect on relations between the United States and Mexico would result if it became the policy of the United States to exclude Mexicans."[59] The State Department, citing Mexican census figures, estimated that 29.6 percent of Mexicans were Indians and 59.33 percent were mestizo, which, if the *Andrade* ruling held, would make them ineligible to immigrate to the United States. These percentages were larger for much of the remainder of Latin America.[60]

Unintended Consequences: Mexican Americans

The second area where the decision had an actual effect was Mexican American civil rights. Long before Knight rendered his judgment, civil rights activists had been struggling to be recognized as part of the white race. This decision had the potential to totally destroy those efforts. If the precedent were allowed to stand, if Mexican nationals were to be legally defined as nonwhite, then by default Mexican Americans would also fall under that racial classification.

This fact was noted by attorney Walter Barry, who frequently consulted with the Latin American Chamber of Commerce in Los Angeles, in a letter to Julian Velarde, the president of the Chamber. Barry noted how the situation would affect land-owning Mexican Americans and Mexican nationals in the state of California. Because of California's Alien Land Law, many of the title deeds of the time had a provision that read: "It is provided and covenanted with a covenant running with the land, that no part of said premises shall ever be sold, leased, occupied by or conveyed to a person of any race except the Caucasian or White race."[61] In other words, Mexicans and Mexican Americans who owned land in California could easily be dispossessed as a result of Judge Knight's ruling.

Velarde, realizing the potential of this problem, forwarded Barry's letter to Mexico's foreign relations secretariat and offered his assistance to do everything possible to help defend against this dangerous precedent.[62] Despite Velarde's good intentions, the Mexican government rejected his help. Ambassador Castillo Nájera apparently saw little need for "the useless meddling of the so called 'Latin American Chamber of Commerce' of Los Angeles (an institution whose achievements are far from satisfactory)."[63]

In addition to the situation with the California Land Law, the legal definition of Mexican Americans as nonwhite would have disastrous consequences for LULAC's desegregation efforts in south Texas. While LULAC had some success based on the fact that Mexican Americans could be considered white, segregation of nonwhites was still legal in 1935. Finally, being legally defined as nonwhite had the potential to change the perspective of white Americans for the worse. Many white Americans often had an attitude that "nonwhite" was synonymous with "noncitizen." To a group of Mexican Americans who sought to assert their rights as American citizens, this could be a major threat to their way of life.

Conclusion

Looking at the origins of Judge Knight's decision, the evidence clearly shows that the CJIC wielded a great deal of power among nativist organizations. California Attorney General U. S. Webb, a member of the committee, had a hand in the *Ozawa* decision, which formally declared Asians ineligible for US naturalization in 1922. The committee as a whole played a major role in the passage of the 1924 Immigration Act, which barred those ineligible for naturalization from immigration. And as the analysis of *Ozawa*, *Thind*, and *Morrison* shows, the California group was deliberately working to build a precedent to exclude Mexicans. Had they acted more quickly, or had the political mood in the United States not shifted against their position during the 1930s, the committee certainly would have succeeded in barring Mexican immigrants with the *Andrade* decision.

The CJIC thoroughly researched the legalities of the 1897 *Rodriguez* decision and found a way to overturn that ruling. In that respect, they simply had to have their own precedent affirmed by the US Supreme Court, because the *Rodriguez* decision was a ruling of a lower federal district court. However, the State Department's efforts to control the outcome of Knight's decision proved very effective in preventing it from realizing its full potential and ending immigration from Mexico.

7

Efforts to Thwart the Andrade *Decision Using the Traditional Approach*

WHEN THE *ANDRADE* CASE CAME BEFORE THE STATE DEPARTMENT, Richard Wilson Flournoy Jr. was an obvious choice to assign to the issue. He was an acknowledged expert on nationality and citizenship, having written several legal articles on the topic.[1] Flournoy had been a US delegate to the Conference on Codification of International Law at The Hague in 1930, where he wrote one of the protocols related to dual nationality and military obligations. He was also a professor of international law at National University in Washington, DC.[2] Flournoy would be a key figure in the State Department's efforts to counter Judge Knight's ruling.

Word of Knight's decision traveled fast. The story hit the Associated Press (AP) newswire that night, and the morning editions of the *New York Times* and the *Buffalo Courier-Express*, among others, carried the story on December 12.[3] Mexican newspapers also carried articles detailing the incident, including a copy of the AP story in Mexico City's *Excelsior*.

Initial Reactions

Although Knight's decision was immediately publicized, State Department officials in Washington were slow to react. On December 12, American consul Alexander Sloan translated the *Excelsior* article and sent a copy to Washington from Mexico City, but it did not reach the State Department until December 19.[4] It was not until December 13, two days after the ruling, that J. F. Simmons of the Visa Division summarized the *New York Times* article for Secretary of State Cordell Hull. He also reported that he had made preliminary inquiries with the deputy commissioner of immigration and naturalization.[5] Simmons did not make this report to Secretary Hull, however, until he received confirmation from the commissioner's office that Andrade had indeed been denied citizenship. Seeing the situation from his vantage point in the Visa Division, Simmons was primarily concerned about whether his department would continue to issue visas to those seeking to enter the United States from Mexico. He did not seem to anticipate a foreign relations incident.

Mexican officials reacted much more swiftly. The honorary Mexican consul in Buffalo, Leon Lancaster, copied the article from the *Buffalo Courier-Express* to the consul general in New York City, Enrique Elizondo.[6] However, Elizondo already knew of the decision through the *New York Times* article. Like Lancaster, he had copied that article to his superiors at the Mexican Embassy in Washington, DC, as well as to the Secretario de Relaciones Exteriores (SRE) in Mexico City. Unlike Simmons, Elizondo did see the international relevance of this decision. He knew that this was only the beginning of a significant situation. In his first communiqué he stated, "I communicate this to you so that our government can consider its next steps, since, in accordance with American laws, only people eligible for naturalization may be admitted as immigrants to the United States. If they refuse Mexicans the right of American citizenship, then they also exclude practically our total population the right to immigrate to this country."[7]

The Mexican ambassador, Francisco Castillo Nájera, quickly brought the matter to the attention of his superiors in Mexico City. First, he spoke by telephone directly to secretary of foreign relations, Eduardo Hay, on the thirteenth. In this conversation, he requested and received permission to allow the consul general in New York to hire attorneys and to initiate an appeal before the Federal Circuit Court of Appeals (Second Judicial Circuit) and, if necessary, to the US Supreme Court. Second, Castillo Nájera received permission from Mexico City to release the following to the American press:

> A press dispatch published yesterday in New York announces that a Federal Court in the State of New York denied the petition of three Mexicans for citizenship because they have a strain of Indian blood. The same reliable dispatch adds that the opinion would make Indian blooded Mexicans ineligible for admission to the United States as immigrants. The Mexican Government has instructed its Consul General in New York [to] protest against the spirit of said decision and to officially appeal against it.[8]

In his report summarizing the telephone conversation, Castillo Nájera wrote to the secretary, "My original idea certainly was to protest [to the US State Department], but I know that they would tell me to first exhaust all legal options."[9] Ironically, only the day before, on December 12, Castillo Nájera concluded a telephone conversation with Assistant Secretary of State Sumner Welles "by saying that in his considered judgment, relations between Mexico and the United States had never seemed so promising as at this moment."[10] Although Welles returned the sentiment in the telephone conversation, little did Castillo Nájera know that Welles was about to prove his sincerity. Before long, State Department officials contacted the embassy staff to ask them not to follow the legal appeals procedures, so that both nations could find a mutually agreeable solution to the situation before Knight's ruling became solidified in an appeals court and then potentially a US Supreme Court ruling.

The Mexican Embassy's press release quickly made its rounds, appearing in the *New York Times* and in Mexico City's *El Nacional* on Saturday, December 14.[11] Castillo Nájera had given the press release directly to the *Times* and apparently had also spoken with a *Times* reporter. The article that appeared not only stated that Mexico would protest "the spirit" of the decision but also mentioned that Castillo Nájera had talked by telephone to Mexico City and to the consul general in New York, and that any further news would be coming from the consul general's office.

The State Department and the SRE: Two Governments, One Goal

On Saturday, December 14, sometime after reading the article in the *New York Times*, Edward L. Reed, chief of the Division of Mexican Affairs in the State Department, called upon Dr. Luis Quintanilla, chargé d'affaires of the Mexican Embassy, and asked what the nature of the protest against the spirit of Knight's decision would be. Quintanilla answered that the protest would be part of the planned appeal, which opened the door for Reed to discuss that situation. Reed wrote of this conversation:

> I remarked that it was the opinion of officials in the Labor Department that the decision in question would be sustained on appeal. I also said that . . . it was our impression that this decision would not necessarily have to be considered as binding in regard to the admission to the United States of immigrants of Indian blood. I pointed out, however, that if an appeal to the higher courts were taken and the . . . decision was confirmed, the responsible authorities of this Government would then have no choice but to be guided by the decision.[12]

Quintanilla acknowledged that Mexican officials already knew this but said that the Mexican government felt it had no other alternatives. However, he promised that the ambassador would provide full cooperation if the State Department could suggest any other ideas.

Finally, after a question from Reed, Quintanilla stated that he believed the situation had received very little attention in the Mexico City press and that the Foreign Office would likely agree to help keep the matter quiet in the future. After the meeting between Reed and Quintanilla, press coverage did indeed end in both countries.

The State Department took further efforts to quiet the controversy over Judge Knight's decision. With the help of the Labor Department, administration officials stopped the publication of the decision in the *Federal Reporter* to avoid making the decision too conspicuous. Also, the Labor Department agreed to warn its field officers not to repeat Murff's objections, which it termed a "mistake" that was not consistent with the department's policy toward the naturalization of Mexican nationals.[13]

International Cooperation

Simultaneously, State Department officials and Enrique Elizondo, the Mexican consul general in New York, worked at trying to convince Judge Knight to postpone putting his signature on the decision, an act that made the opinion an official ruling. Elizondo received word from Honorary Consul Lancaster that the consulate's attorney would work with Knight to postpone the signature,[14] while Sumner Welles and Labor Department officials began putting pressure on Knight for the same reasons.[15]

On December 18, Ambassador Castillo Nájera reported to Mexico City, detailing discussions between embassy and State Department representatives the day before. Both the ambassador and Assistant Secretary Welles participated in these talks. Mexican officials made the meaning of the protest against the spirit of the decision clear. They wanted Americans to know that Mexico viewed Knight's decision as an offense against Mexico's national dignity. Further, they intended to appeal the decision, even knowing that it would not be overturned, because they wanted to send the message that Mexico would not tolerate being treated in such a manner by the United States.

However, after talking with Welles, Castillo Nájera reported to his superiors:

> The American Government has been the first in being surprised at the unexpected and inopportune ruling of Judge Knight . . . , [and] laments this incident as much as we do. . . . It remains perfectly settled that the decision in Buffalo, influenced by the [California Joint Immigration Committee], does not answer to official instruction from Washington. . . . The good will of the Government in Washington, and in particular of the high officials with which we have discussed the subject . . . allow us to predict that Washington will do all that is possible in finding a satisfactory solution for Mexico.[16]

Then, in a very pragmatic move, Castillo Nájera suggested that Mexico reconsider the idea of appealing the decision, because it would not bring practical results. Just as Reed had told Quintanilla, Welles informed the ambassador that an appeal would likely be sustained, which would force the State Department to deny immigration visas to hopeful Mexican immigrants. However, if Mexico did not push the appeal, then perhaps the State Department could find a solution amenable to both nations.

The State Department's initial efforts to gain Mexico's cooperation helped prove to the ambassador that the State Department shared its agenda. However, Castillo Nájera remained skeptical that the State Department had a plan to counter the decision and continued to seek answers on his own terms. Although both the SRE and the Mexican Embassy in Washington agreed to cooperate fully with the State Department, and the ambassador did involve State Department officials in the planning stages of Mexico's efforts to counter Judge Knight's ruling, the Mexican government was not prepared to allow the State Department to act alone in the matter.

The Mexican Government's Efforts

Castillo Nájera and the State Department officials left those December 17 talks with a contingency plan. Along with Edward Reed and the State Department's legal advisers, the ambassador met with the attorney recommended by Leon Lancaster, Frederick T. Devlin of Buffalo. After discussing the case with Lancaster and doing some legal background research, Devlin traveled to Washington on his own to meet with Castillo Nájera. Devlin struck Castillo Nájera as a competent attorney who was very knowledgeable on the subject, and the ambassador believed that with the help of the State Department and the Roosevelt administration on one hand, and Devlin's expertise on the other, "a strong probability exists that this incident will be repaired, putting completely safe and sound the decency of our country."[17]

Castillo Nájera took advantage of Devlin's trip to arrange the meeting with State Department officials on December 17. At this time, the group discussed several options, most of which were rejected as ineffective. Finally, Devlin proposed a different approach to appealing the decision; not to a higher court, but to Judge Knight himself. Devlin sought to ask Knight to simply reconsider his ruling. In the end, Reed and the legal advisers agreed that Devlin's proposal was probably the only practical solution. The meeting ended with agreements that Devlin would follow up on his course of action, and that Reed would (through the Labor Department) discreetly order naturalization examiners to abstain from further objections in the cases of Mexican nationals seeking US citizenship. Ambassador Castillo Nájera agreed that Mexico would quietly cooperate in the matter to avoid causing "a true international scandal . . . , even though [Knight's ruling] was truly insulting to our country."[18]

Besides being a competent attorney, Devlin impressed Castillo Nájera for other important reasons. The ambassador wrote of Devlin:

> This lawyer is of some importance in the Magistrate of the State of New York . . . and has many friends in [Buffalo] who may be of exceptional value to this case and to Mexico. He is friends, for example, with Judge Knight, author of the decision that has caused this incident. He is also friends with the Mayor of the city, and with the local immigration authorities. He is, in sum, someone who has all the requirements needed in order to, with all probabilities of success, handle the delicate situation before us.[19]

Devlin's motives for working on behalf of the Mexican government are not entirely clear, but he certainly was not working for the money. The Mexican government, in fact, received a great deal of legal assistance for the price it paid. When Castillo Nájera and Devlin negotiated the fee, Devlin at first stated that money was of no importance to him, and that the Mexican government should decide how much he deserved for his efforts. Since, as the ambassador put it, Mexico wanted to avoid any confusion in the matter, he insisted that Devlin estimate his potential legal fees. Devlin suggested $4,000, based on his qualifications and the time he would spend both in New York and in Washington, DC. The ambassador agreed that that was a fair price (he had received estimates from the Washington Bar Association). However, Castillo Nájera informed Devlin that the Mexican treasury might not be able to afford such fees. He suggested that Mexico pay $1,000 in advance and $1,000 upon conclusion of the case. Devlin agreed.[20]

After the combined efforts of Devlin and the State Department convinced Knight to postpone his signature, the State Department, the Mexican Embassy, and Devlin planned their next moves. At the end of December, Devlin petitioned Judge Knight to reconsider his decision, and Knight granted the request. At that point, Devlin began working with Rafael de la Colina, the new consul general in New York, who replaced Enrique Elizondo. Before coming to New York, de la Colina had been consul general in Los Angeles, and thus he was very familiar with the exclusionist organizations that had developed the Knight precedent. He was surprised to find that Devlin was representing only Timoteo Andrade, and not Porfirio Bravo and Francisco Velez, but trusted that Devlin knew what he was doing. De la Colina stated, "he does not doubt that the other cases will be resolved in the same manner as that of Andrade."[21]

Andrade's Appeal to Judge Knight

Officially, the Immigration and Naturalization Bureau had to agree to allow Judge Knight to reconsider Andrade's petition. That, however, was not a problem. First, the bureau removed John Murff from the case and assigned naturalization examiner Ralph White. Then, on February 28, 1936, Acting District Director William Marshall and Devlin signed the agreement that allowed for the rehearing.

Devlin then went about building the grounds for the appeal. On March 11 and April 13, 1936, Devlin introduced further testimony on behalf of Andrade. First, he took sworn testimony from Bernard Malvern and Thomas Harding, the two salesmen who had witnessed Andrade's petition, as character references. Devlin asked both if Andrade had ever had any trouble with the law, what race they thought him to be (Malvern answered "Mexican," while Harding answered

"Spanish"), and whether either had any personal knowledge of his actual race (both answered no).[22]

Second, Devlin questioned Andrade before the court, addressing the issue of his racial heritage. Devlin began by reminding Andrade that he had stated on one affidavit that he was of about 75 percent Indian blood and 25 percent Spanish blood, and on another that he was of equal amounts of both. Devlin then asked why Andrade had made claims to such high percentages of Indian blood, which led to a conversation that, in part, helps explain how a common Mexican national understood the philosophy of *mestizaje*:

Andrade: It happened this way. In Mexico, even if we have full Spanish blood, we say that we have Indian blood, because in Mexico we are all Mexicans. There is no distinction, no matter in what part of the Country we are born, and I thought that it would put me in a better position.

Devlin: Is the having of Indian blood something that is to be boasted of? Is it something to be proud of?

Andrade: We are proud that we are Mexicans and we don't like to be told that we have Spanish or French blood.

. . .

Devlin: Do you know whether it was a common practice for Spaniards, who had no Indian blood, to boast of having Indian blood in their veins?

Andrade: Yes.

. . .

Devlin: Will you explain the circumstances under which you changed your statement concerning the percentage of Indian blood and the percentage of Spanish blood to fifty percent Indian?

Andrade: I was asked how much Indian blood I had in me. I said, "Maybe I have seventy-five percent; maybe fifty".

Devlin: To whom did you state that?

Andrade: To the Immigration Inspector in this office.

Devlin: I state for the record that the above was stated in answer to Examiner White's question.

White: I understood him to say that he thought it would be to his advantage to state he had fifty percent Indian blood. Is that correct?

Andrade: In Mexico, we hold (the Mexicans), even if we have not Indian blood, we are proud that we descended from Indians.
White: That was all right when you were in Mexico, but now you are up here you have no reason to feel that way.
Andrade: Since asking my mother, I think I have not two percent.[23]

Devlin and Examiner White then turned their questioning toward Andrade's mother, Maria Andrade (with Consul Leon Lancaster interpreting). In this conversation, Sra. Andrade stated that her parents and grandparents had all been white. With respect to Timoteo's paternal grandparents, she stated she never personally knew them, but she knew that the husband was French, while the wife was Spanish. Devlin then asked her and Timoteo if they had ever discussed their racial background. Both answered no, which prompted White to ask Timoteo why he had previously answered "Mexican" when asked about his race. Timoteo simply answered, "I don't know."

At this point, Devlin requestioned Andrade and apparently attempted to guide him toward acceptable answers:

Devlin: When you came . . . and made application for citizenship, did anyone here in this office say to you, in words or in substance, "You look like an Indian"? Did anybody make that comment to you?
Andrade: No.
Devlin: Would it refresh your recollection any if I told you that I think Mr. Marshall told me that he had made that observation when you first came in and before you had made any declaration as to what you were?
Andrade: I'll tell you what happened. I went to a dance and danced until four o'clock in the morning and I don't remember what I said or what I did.
Devlin: Are you acquainted with what might be called whatever Mexican colony there is in this district?
Andrade: Yes, I was formerly a secretary of one of their clubs.
Devlin: Are those people actually made up of Indian blood?
Andrade: There are one or two.

Devlin: Is it possible that you may have had in mind what the effect would be upon the good will of that Mexican colony if you indicated that you did not have Indian blood in you?
Andrade: I might have.

Finally, examiner White addressed Sra. Andrade again to establish why Timoteo was unfamiliar with his own ancestry, while she knew extensive details. She answered simply, "We never had any conversation about this. He worked and then when he came home, he went out and we had no time to talk about things like this."[24]

After reviewing the testimony, White filed his recommendation to Judge Knight. He stated that since the testimony showed that Andrade had made a mistake as to his racial background and that since the government's only objection had been on racial grounds, "the Government now withdraws its objection and your designated examiner recommends that the petition for citizenship be granted."[25] On June 1, 1936, Timoteo Andrade became a citizen of the United States of America. Not long after, he applied for a Social Security number, and on the application he checked "White."[26]

The State Department Legal Office

While Devlin, Lancaster, and de la Colina began working on Andrade's appeal, the State Department's legal advisers began their research into the legal precedents that Knight had relied upon and assessed the State Department's existing policies regarding its role in the implementation of US immigration policy. Legal adviser Richard Flournoy led the legal team's efforts. Simmons of the Visa Division informed Flournoy that it was the general practice of consuls in Mexico to assume that visa applicants who were apparently "half-breed" were principally of white descent. When Flournoy asked how they treated those who looked entirely Indian, Simmons answered that "the consul would probably assume that the Indian must have had a white grandfather or great-grandfather, and would issue a visa." In other words, "the consuls [were] simply evading the issue in these cases and granting the visas" to any prospective immigrant who was not otherwise denied under the literacy qualifications, the contract labor provision, or the "likely public charge" law.[27]

Simmons suggested to Flournoy that the best solution to the situation would be to amend the laws to allow naturalization of American Indians, but he acknowledged that from a practical standpoint, Californians like Senator Hiram Johnson and V. S. McClatchy would strongly oppose such legislation. Simmons's suggestion would later be given further and more serious consideration in the State Department, because even though Andrade had received his citizenship, the crisis was far from over.

Failure to Resolve the Issue

On June 11, 1936, the Mexican Embassy informed Edward Reed that Judge Knight had reversed his decision in the case, and Andrade had been admitted to citizenship. Because Devlin had pushed the angle that Andrade had made a misstatement on his petition, and he had been admitted to citizenship as a white person, Knight took the opportunity in his second ruling to state, "Other authorities quoted in [*Morrison v. California*] fully sustain the conclusion that where one is half Indian and half Spanish blood, he is not entitled to naturalization under the provisions of Section 359, Title 8, of the U.S. Code."[28] In other words, Judge Knight had reaffirmed the precedent that he had previously established, despite the fact that he had admitted Andrade to citizenship. Furthermore, since Andrade's petition had been granted, he became a nonissue, and all immediate routes of appeal were closed.

Because of the manner in which Judge Knight changed his decision, the Mexican Embassy and the State Department were left in the same position they had been in after Knight's original decision. Simply put, Devlin's strategy had backfired in terms of the overall agenda. Chargé d'affaires Quintanilla of the Mexican Embassy wrote of this situation:

> It is clear . . . that the repeal of the judgment (based on the mere pretext that the applicant Timoteo Andrade has Indian

> blood, but it is not predominant) does not satisfy our desires completely, because in order to do so, it would be necessary that Judge Knight contradict his first judgment totally, that is, declare that Andrade should be granted naturalization even if he were of pure Indian race, which is really what he had admitted to in the beginning.[29]

Also, even if Knight had totally reversed himself, McClatchy could have found other judges who would likely follow Knight's first decision because it was consistent with existing US legislation and case law. Quintanilla believed that Knight's second decision was likely to be the maximum concession that Mexico could expect from American judges deciding such cases. Finally, he concluded, "we should not lose sight of the eventuality of a repetition of a case similar to this case of Timoteo Andrade."[30]

At that time, the State Department legal advisers considered their options. On July 23, 1936, legal advisers Flournoy and Green H. Hackworth met with the commissioner of immigration and naturalization, Colonel MacCormack, his administrative assistant, Dr. Henry B. Hazard, and a Justice Department official to discuss alternatives.[31] Hazard informed Hackworth and Flournoy that Knight's decision had prompted a new crisis. In the Southern District of New York (New York City), Judge Alfred Coxe raised the question of the eligibility of several Mexicans, two Peruvians, and one Ecuadorian. In March 1936, Judge Coxe had agreed to postpone these petitions while Judge Knight reheard Andrade's petition. After Andrade's second hearing failed to resolve the issue, the Immigration and Naturalization Bureau sought to have these and all new cases further postponed, to keep the California Joint Immigration Committee's argument from reemerging.

Also at the July 23 meeting, MacCormack informed Hackworth and Flournoy that he had not yet issued formal instructions to the naturalization examiners in the field that would advise them not to raise the racial issue in these cases. However, most of the examiners, especially in the Southwest and California, had been informally notified that they were not to raise such objections.[32] Closing the meeting, Hackworth and Flournoy stressed the importance of not allowing even a single repeat of Knight's first decision, as even one case could do as much harm as several consistent rulings. Ironically, however, the Labor Department may have been too successful at keeping the cases postponed. Both the State and Labor Departments forgot about Andrade until March 1937, when Judge Coxe and the judge in the Eastern District (Brooklyn) became impatient and sought to force the issue.

After the July 23 meeting, Hackworth sent the Andrade file to the records desk for indexing, and the issue did not reemerge until March 1937.[33] Since State and Labor officials apparently neglected to follow through with their efforts, their agenda was set back by those eight months. However, that delay may have actually been beneficial. March 1937 is also the month of the infamous "switch in time" and the beginning of judicial acquiescence to the New Deal. This political change ended up contributing to one of the two ultimate resolutions of the problem.

8

Applying Administrative Law to the Andrade *Decision*

STATE DEPARTMENT LEGAL ADVISER GREEN HAYWOOD HACKWORTH was not as prolific as Flournoy in his writings, but if the writings of others are any indication, Hackworth was better known than Flournoy and at least as well respected for his knowledge of international law. Although Hackworth was a Democrat, President Coolidge appointed him to the position of State Department solicitor in 1925. In 1931, Congress changed the position to State Department legal adviser, which required a new presidential appointment. President Hoover appointed Hackworth to that position as well. In 1946, Hackworth became the first US judge on the International Court of Justice.[1] Like Flournoy, Hackworth was one of the US delegates to the First Conference for the Codification on International Law in The Hague in 1930.[2] And like Flournoy, Hackworth fit well as an adviser on the Andrade issue because of his expertise. Unlike Flournoy, however, Hackworth would appreciate the new direction that the State Department was about to take with respect to using the technocratic approach to solve their problem.

Between December 1935 and July 1936, State, Labor, and Justice Department officials, along with those from the Mexican Embassy, went to great lengths to postpone and even overturn Judge Knight's decision denying Timoteo Andrade US citizenship. Despite their obvious concern that Knight's precedent not be applied to further naturalization cases, the three administration departments mishandled the situation after July 1936. They allowed it to become a low-priority issue and, in fact, may have even forgotten about it totally until the federal judges began to force the issue in March 1937.

The McClatchy-Knight Precedent Reemerges

On Monday, March 15, 1937, representatives of the Labor Department went to the State Department's offices to discuss the situation with legal adviser Flournoy. They reminded him of both the Andrade situation and the fact that several naturalization petitions had been put on hold before the US District Courts for the Southern (New York City) and now the Eastern (Brooklyn) Districts of New York. Although the naturalization examiners in these cases had managed to postpone the hearings, the judges had grown impatient and wanted to continue. Far worse, these judges were likely to issue rulings consistent with Judge Knight's December 1935 decision.[3]

Hackworth and Flournoy brought this new information to the attention of Assistant Secretary of State R. Walton Moore and Edward Reed, chief of the Mexican Division, and reminded them of where the situation had been left in July 1936. Flournoy had to summarize the entire situation in detail to remind his superiors of the origins and importance of the current problems. Most important, Flournoy reviewed Knight's June 1936 ruling granting Andrade citizenship and stated that it was not likely that the pending cases could be resolved in the same manner. Other judges, he believed, would be obligated to deny the pending petitions based on Knight's first ruling, in the event that the cases could not be further postponed before the State Department could formulate a solution to the problem.

Flournoy had spoken with Henry Hazard of Immigration and Naturalization regarding the orders given to the naturalization examiners to avoid raising the issue of racial ineligibility. Flournoy asked whether these orders would be sufficient to prevent further decisions consistent with Knight's or if the judges would deny petitions even if the assigned examiners did not oppose them. Hazard replied, "the Judges would insist that the Naturalization Examiners submit with each case a brief setting forth their views and containing 'findings and recommendations' as to the eligibility of the applicants under the law, as provided in [the current US naturalization laws]. Thus it appears to be impossible to dodge the issue."[4]

Arguments over Potential Legislation

As the legal advisers briefed Moore and Reed, these State Department officials proposed only one potential solution, the same idea that they had already let fall by the wayside: to amend existing legislation to remove racial barriers to naturalization. While Flournoy did not bring up the issue in any of the State Department memoranda regarding Timoteo Andrade, he was in a perfect position not only to advocate such a change, but to make one happen. On April 25, 1933, President Roosevelt had issued an executive order that established a committee to "review the nationality laws of the United States, to recommend revisions, and to codify those laws into one comprehensive nationality law for submission to the Congress."[5] The State, Justice, and Labor Departments established a technical advisory committee made up of several experts, including Flournoy and several other officials who were involved in the Andrade case. That committee drafted the Nationality Act of 1940, which did end up removing the racial barriers, at least with respect to Latin Americans. In 1937, though, Flournoy advocated removing those barriers entirely. He believed that removing the racial exclusions and perhaps even replacing them with quota restrictions would be acceptable to Mexico and other Latin American countries, because the quotas did not represent negative racial characterizations of the inhabitants of those nations. Labor Department officials, however, did not believe that this solution would pass over the objections of certain political elements, especially those in California. The California Joint Immigration Committee, for one, would certainly oppose removing the racial bar to immigration, even though quotas for both Asian and Latin American nations would allow insignificant numbers of new immigrants. Edward Shaughnessy, deputy commissioner of immigration and naturalization, also reminded

Moore and the legal staff that it had been the State Department that had fought so hard to oppose a Western Hemisphere quota in the first place.

The main objection to the immigration of Mexican nationals, of course, rested on the idea that they competed with American labor. "There is no danger," wrote Flournoy, "that the citizenship of the United States will become seriously contaminated by Indian blood. The ground for limiting the immigration of Mexicans is primarily, if not solely, economic."[6] Flournoy made further suggestions for dealing with the objections that the California groups would obviously introduce if the State Department pushed to amend the law to remove the racial barriers. He suggested that the State Department could endorse Senate Bill S. 1803, introduced on March 8, 1937, which would restrict the "habitual commuting" of aliens from "foreign contiguous territory to engage in skilled or unskilled labor or employment."[7] Furthermore, since most Mexican nationals who did commute usually did so without crossing through border checkpoints (i.e., they crossed the border illegally), a solution to that problem would be to increase the number of Border Patrol personnel from the current average of one per eighty miles of border. This, of course, would have to be done discreetly, so that outside observers would not make the connection between the legislative changes aimed at Mexico and the increased presence of border guards.

Flournoy believed that ultimately the State Department and the Roosevelt administration would have to follow one of two paths: amend the laws to avoid offending Mexico or give in to the demands of the exclusionist organizations and live with the *Andrade* decision, "regardless of its lack of any real necessity or of the offense which such discrimination gives to foreign countries."[8] No one in the State Department had conceived of other options that would achieve their goals without having to face the objections of the California exclusionists.

Later, the legal advisers sought input to the policy conversation from John Simmons of the Visa Division. Looking only at the numbers involved, and not nativist philosophies, Simmons argued that the proposed amendments to the law would bring insignificant amounts of new immigration to the United States. Simmons did, however, recognize those philosophical leanings and stated that the nativists would grossly exaggerate the situation in congressional debates.[9] He believed that such exaggerations could be countered by showing Congress the numbers and labeling the proposed measure a simple "clarification" of the existing laws. Simmons reminded his superiors that the State Department had been, since 1929, successfully restricting Mexican immigration through administrative measures. He believed that reminding Congress of this fact would give the department credibility in its efforts to obtain the proposed legislation. Finally, Simmons argued that the State Department's best approach would be to handle the matter internally. He believed that if they pointed out to the Californians that the State Department's prior efforts had benefited their agenda, the California groups would see that these new efforts were not aimed at opening the doors to immigration.[10]

The White Standard Emerges

While various State and Labor Department officials persisted in exploring legislative alternatives, the Mexican Foreign Relations Ministry continued to watch racial issues related to Mexican nationals (and therefore, Mexican Americans) in the United States. As a part of that overall effort, the Mexican Diplomatic Corps kept a close eye on the issue of racial classification and referred many press articles to the ministry and to Ambassador Castillo Nájera. In March 1937, the Mexican ambassador issued a formal complaint regarding a racial classification incident, which sparked an idea among the State Department officials. In this new complaint, the ambassador pointed out that as of October 15, 1936, the US Census Bureau officially classified all Mexican nationals and Mexican Americans as racially white, despite the conventional wisdom regarding the racial status of those of Mexican descent. The Census Bureau standard, of course, emerged from the El Paso reclassification incident of October 1936.[11]

Clearly, the Foreign Relations Ministry had correlated the El Paso incident to the Andrade situation, since information regarding that event can be found in its Andrade file. Viewed only within the context of that file, the El Paso information almost appears to have been misfiled. However, when seen from a much broader perspective, taking into consideration all available information, Ambassador Castillo Nájera surely saw the Census Bureau's actions as a potential solution to the Andrade problem.

In the new complaint brought forward by the ambassador (one which was truly insignificant), the consul general in El Paso had informed the embassy that a Mexican citizen, Andrés Ortiz, had been listed as Mexican under the race category on his death certificate. The ambassador quoted the October 1936 Census Bureau circular in his letter to the secretary of state and further noted that many Mexican consuls in the United States had recently complained that US immigration authorities had been classifying Mexican nationals as Mexican rather than white. He requested assistance from the State Department in having Mexican citizens uniformly classified as white, in accordance with the Census Bureau standard.[12]

The ambassador's complaint was written in such a way that he obviously intended for the State Department officials to catch on to the idea and use it to solve the Andrade problem. "As this [policy] is in contradiction with said circular of the Director of the Census Bureau, I come to request Your Excellency that if there is no objection, you be so kind as to render me your aid in the sense of having the said discrepancy brought to the attention of the Department of Labor to the end that the corresponding instructions be issued to the officials dependent upon it."[13] Fortunately, the State Department officials who were working on the Andrade case understood Ambassador Castillo Nájera's intent and filed the El Paso complaint with their other Andrade materials—and then took action on the issue.

The State Department's Views

Apparently, the Census Bureau's policy came as a complete surprise to both the State and Labor Departments. When LULAC made the efforts that had resulted in the Census Bureau's policy on Mexican Americans, news of their achievements never reached the State or Labor Departments, which were then in the process of considering their options with regard to the *Andrade* decision. LULAC had apparently been satisfied with the outcome when the Census Bureau and the Social Security Board began to use the white classification for Mexican Americans. The subsequent lack of protests and publicity, combined with poor interdepartmental communication, helps to explain why the State and Labor Departments continued to view Mexicans as a problem under existing immigration and naturalization statutes, even after the Census Bureau's ruling. Officials from both departments believed that because of Judge Knight's decision they could no longer informally (unofficially, that is) assume a white standard and simply neglect to raise objections (thereby dodging the issue), because judges would require naturalization examiners to assess the eligibility of each applicant.[14] Despite their assumptions, however, these administration officials certainly did understand the subtle message that Ambassador Castillo Nájera had conveyed to them, and they began to explore the possibility that the Census Bureau's policy might be a precedent that would allow naturalization examiners to officially classify Mexican immigrants as white. Doing so might establish a system in which the judges presiding over naturalization petitions could not reject them on racial grounds.[15]

The State Department Explores Administrative Law

When Judge Knight rendered his initial decision in 1935, the courts and the administration had a tenuous relationship. The Supreme Court was still dominated by the same conservatives who had rendered decisions in *Ozawa*, *Thind*, and *Morrison* with respect to naturalization laws. More important, this was the same Supreme Court that had asserted in *Morrison* that a Mexican naturalization test case would result in Mexican exclusion. Even after Knight had reversed himself in June 1936, the political and legal frameworks were still the same.

However, in March 1937, when the State Department picked up where it had left off in July 1936, political conditions had changed considerably. The struggle between the FDR administration and the federal courts resulted in a shift in both federal policymaking and the balance of power between the FDR administration, the US Congress, and the federal judiciary. Roosevelt had been reelected in that eight-month period, and the administration had made some serious challenges to the judiciary, which it eventually won.

With Roosevelt's victory over the courts, progressive philosophies on policymaking became the rule of the day. So in 1937, with these new approaches guiding public policy, State Department officials began to examine their options and explored the Mexican ambassador's suggestion of "policy consistency" in the racial classification of Mexican nationals and therefore Mexican Americans.

Racial Classification: Policy Versus Law

After Ambassador Castillo Nájera sent his March 1937 complaint about Andrés Ortiz's death certificate, State, Labor, and Justice Department officials conferred to explore these policy options.[16] Labor Department officials had to inquire of the Commerce Department and Census Bureau to confirm that the Census Bureau's standard existed.[17] But once they had this confirmation, they were quick to explore its potential.

The main point of this policy discussion focused on whether it would be justifiable to classify all Mexican immigrants as white, as the ambassador had requested. Those involved suggested three reasons why the classification would work: first, such a policy would be consistent with the Census Bureau's existing policy; second, it would be consistent with *In re Rodriguez* (even though *Ozawa*, *Thind*, *Morrison*, and Knight's decision in *Andrade* might work against this); and third, because "it is practically impossible to ascertain the proportion of white and Indian blood in [the majority of] cases of Mexicans applying for naturalization."[18]

As he had done in the past, Hazard raised the issue of judges requiring naturalization examiners to file a brief of findings and recommendations for eligibility and suggested that the examiners would find it difficult to express an opinion that someone who was obviously an Indian was a member of the white race. Hazard, looking at the wider perspective of Latin America, raised this issue with respect to pending cases in which South Americans had listed themselves as Indian. He did agree, however, that with respect to

Mexicans, the pending cases could be disposed of in favor of the applicants in accordance with the three previously mentioned suggestions. Taking up Hazard's issue, officials from all three departments agreed that the courts likely would not rule consistently for South and Central Americans as they would for Mexicans. However, they believed that other governments were not as likely to protest as was the Mexican government, and therefore they agreed that, for the time being, they would focus their efforts on the pending cases of Mexican nationals.

Finally, they revisited the issue of the proposed legislation that would remove racial barriers from the naturalization laws. The representatives from the three departments believed that with the proposed administrative solution, they could defer the legislation at least until the outcome of the pending Mexican cases, at which time they would reevaluate their administrative efforts and the need for advocating the proposed legislation. During this discussion, then, they decided that the situation with the Mexican petitions could be "handled through administrative action . . . rather than by proposed legislation."[19]

Internal Debates

Upon reading memoranda from Carr, Flournoy, and Hazard detailing their discussions, Sumner Welles took issue with the speculation that South and Central American nations would not object to decisions against the naturalization of their citizens in the United States. He also did not like the idea of attempting to handle the Mexican cases in the manner suggested during that meeting, as he believed that the State Department should handle all of the pending petitions consistently. His own suggestion to Secretary Hull was to continue to advocate the proposed legislation to remove racial barriers for Western Hemisphere natives. Welles believed that the costs of obtaining such legislation would pale in comparison to the costs of press attacks and damage to the Good Neighbor Policy if courts upheld the *Andrade* standard with other Latin American nationals.[20] Welles's propensity to object to other officials' suggestions and find his own path is well documented.[21] He often opposed the new technocratic approach being refined across the FDR administration and preferred to follow the traditional legislative approach. His memoranda regarding the *Andrade* case clearly show his desire to pursue legislation.

Assistant Secretary Carr fired back a memorandum to Welles pointing out that promoting the planned legislation could backfire. If the debates in the Congress were not confined to legislators only, the measure would likely be defeated and could, in fact, be used by the California lobbyists as a vehicle to gain further undesirable legislation, which would only put the State Department in an even worse position than it already was.[22] Carr then informed Secretary Hull that Assistant Attorney General Brien McMahon held the opinion that the only way to favorably dispose of the pending cases would be for the State and Labor Departments to issue an order formally classifying Mexican immigrants as white, consistent with the Census Bureau's policy. McMahon further suggested that this be done as quickly as possible, because the Justice Department "was speedily reaching the 'end of its rope'" in trying to hold off the pending cases, and new postponements were being added daily. The federal judges in New York were ready to rule against the petitioners.[23]

Secretary of State Hull and Secretary of Labor Frances Perkins ultimately agreed with Carr's assessment. At this point, either Secretary Hull shut Welles out of the issue, or Welles removed himself from the discussion, possibly because of his pending promotion to under secretary of state.[24] On April 30, Labor Secretary Perkins approved the plan for the Immigration and Naturalization Service to order naturalization examiners to withdraw all appeals based on race, as well as to order that in all future cases, immigrants be classified as white. Initially, this order was to apply to both Mexican petitioners and other Latin American nationals. Immigration officials, however, noting that the Census Bureau policy applied only to Mexicans, believed that such an order could not be applied to applicants from other Latin American nations. So while the order was issued on behalf of the Mexican petitioners, Labor and State Department officials agreed to defer the issue with respect to other Latin Americans until they could carry out further legal research.[25]

Implementation

On May 18, 1937, Edward Shaughnessy, acting commissioner of immigration and naturalization, issued the following order to all naturalization examiners:

> The Census Bureau of the Department of Commerce classifies Mexicans as white and in the interest of uniformity it has been determined to continue that practice in naturalization cases.
>
> In the future, therefore, an applicant for naturalization who is of Mexican decent [*sic*] is to be regarded as a person of a race eligible to citizenship. Objections in such cases should not be made on the ground of inadmissibility by reason of the provisions of Section 2169 of the Revised Statutes. If any case arises where you are in doubt as to the course to pursue, the particulars should be reported to the Central Office before action is taken.[26]

Following Shaughnessy's order, Labor Department officials brought up the issue of policy consistency throughout the US government. No one had yet considered the matter, and apparently they had assumed that the problem would end with the Immigration and Naturalization Service order. However, Labor Department officials suggested to Carr that since State Department consular officials also dealt directly with immigrants, they should also issue such an order. Carr reported to Hull, "This would strengthen our position before the Courts in the event that the eligibility to naturalization of a person of predominately Mexican descent would be questioned."[27] In addition to the departments and agencies that had already adopted the white policy, Assistant Secretary Carr contacted the Works Progress Administration (WPA) because of a complaint made by the Mexican Embassy regarding the use of "Mexican" on some of the WPA's forms. The WPA, too, agreed to classify Mexicans and Mexican Americans as white, and changed the questioned forms.[28]

In October 1937, US consular officers from throughout Mexico met in Mexico City in a general conference to discuss numerous issues. Of course, one of these issues was the State Department's orders to classify Mexicans applying for visas as white. The consular officers willingly followed these orders, and further agreed that "the use of all means available to the Department should be continued with the view to maintaining the interpretation already adopted by various United States Government Departments that Mexicans be treated as members of the 'white race' . . . with reference to eligibility to immigrate and become naturalized as American citizens."[29]

Interestingly, the following month, Ambassador Castillo Nájera and his US-based diplomatic corps held a similar meeting in San Antonio, Texas. Their meeting, however, focused entirely on Mexican emigration to the United States. The ambassador extended an invitation to State and Labor Department officials, many of whom did attend. Among issues such as deportation by US immigration authorities, immigrants' rights, the treatment of Mexican women migrants by US Immigration authorities, and others, the Mexican consuls discussed the adoption by US authorities of the white standard and "agreed to invoke in all cases the disposition of the authorities of the United States so that Mexicans might be considered as of the white race."[30] With both US and Mexican official documents stating that an immigrant was white, those who opposed Mexican immigration on racial grounds could do little to prevent immigrants from entering the country.

Conclusion

We can see how these issues played themselves outwithin the framework of larger internal State Department struggles. There was an obvious disagreement placing Welles and Flournoy on one side, against Hull, Moore, and Carr on the other. The well-known split between Sumner Welles and Cordell Hull is reflected in the *Andrade* case. Those who supported Hull also supported the technocratic efforts to circumvent Judge Knight's decision. Welles and his supporters, on the other hand, continued to push for a legislative solution even after they saw that the administrative solution had begun to work. Welles was ultimately isolated from the decision making in this situation, just as he would eventually be discredited and forced to resign from the State Department.

Richard Flournoy, on the other hand, continued to push for the legislative option through his position on President Roosevelt's committee to review and revise the nationality laws of the United States. As is shown in the following pages, he was quite successful, with Section 303 of the Nationality Act of 1940.

9

The Racial Classification Policy: Problems and Successes

ONCE THE FDR ADMINISTRATION BEGAN TO IMPLEMENT THE UNIform racial classification policy, it began to see great success. Further, the policy was also successful in the long term, although it did have to overcome several obstacles, including objections from within the administration itself.

Success in the Short Run

As soon as Edward Shaughnessy issued the May 18 order to the naturalization examiners, the Labor and Justice Departments allowed the pending cases to go before the judges in the Eastern and Southern Districts of New York. Henry Hazard of the Immigration and Naturalization Service reported that the judge in the Eastern District had approved all petitions. In the Southern District, however, the judge had denied one petition, that of a Mexican national named Godoy. Hazard believed, however, that this would be a single case, and he assured legal adviser Flournoy that "no opinion giving the grounds for denial of naturalization would be published."[1]

Flournoy, however, was not so optimistic. Like Sumner Welles, he believed that the only solution to the naturalization problem lay in following the traditional approach and amending the existing laws to allow for the naturalization of Western Hemisphere natives. Flournoy viewed the situation entirely in constitutional and legal terms, and argued, "Indians of the Western Hemisphere, including Mexican Indians, are not 'white persons'. This is a simple fact which any school boy knows. It is a matter of common knowledge that from the beginning, Indians have been spoken of as 'red men', to distinguish them from persons of white European extraction."[2] Flournoy reasserted the legal precedents of *Thind* and *Camille* and maintained that there was no reason to believe that the courts would go against these rulings with respect to Latin American nationals of more than 50 percent Indian blood. Finally, Flournoy argued that "the problem of the naturalization of natives of these countries . . . can never be satisfactorily settled unless (1) the racial discrimination is removed entirely from the naturalization law, or (2) the law is amended by express provision to the effect that persons born in the Western Hemisphere and descended from the aboriginal inhabitants thereof shall be eligible to naturalization."[3]

Flournoy, however, assumed too much. After the State and Labor Departments issued their formal orders, Godoy's petition was the only one rejected on the grounds that the petitioner was racially ineligible for naturalization. Judicial acquiescence, it seems, had played its role in this area of administrative law. The success of administrative law, however, did not stop Flournoy from drafting Section 303 (permitting the naturalization of Western Hemisphere natives) of the bill, which became the Nationality Act of 1940.

Long-Term Success: The End of Exclusionism

In addition to the "switch in time" in the Supreme Court and further judicial acquiescence in the lower federal courts, another important aspect of the State Department's success was the changing political mood in the United States during the New Deal era. Those who had the political power and the desire to crusade against classifying Mexicans as white, the California exclusionists, were losing power after 1938. That year was a turning point for the California Joint Immigration Committee, in a negative sense. On May 15, Valentine Stuart McClatchy, the committee's executive secretary, died at the age of eighty. In the same year, California Attorney General Ulysses S. Webb retired after serving for thirty-six years. Webb was succeeded by Republican Earl Warren—the same Earl Warren who, as chief justice of the US Supreme Court, presided over some of America's most important civil rights rulings, such as *Brown v. Board of Education* and *Hernandez v. Texas*, and some of the most important cases of the rights of the criminally accused, such as *Gideon v. Wainwright*, *Escobedo v. Illinois*, and *Miranda v. Arizona*. Because of Warren's progressive attitudes, President Eisenhower said that his appointment was "the biggest damned-fool mistake I ever made."[4]

Without the leadership of McClatchy, the legal presence of the state attorney general's Office, and the political clout of both, the committee weakened after 1938. The committee received little attention until the United States entered World War II, and the new executive secretary, H. J. McClatchy (son of the late V. S.), used the war to publicly argue against the concept of dual citizenship. He cited Tokyo Rose, who, as a US citizen, "obtained her education from kindergarten to university degree" in the United States.[5] McClatchy pointed out that the three nations that most insisted upon the concept of dual citizenship were Germany, Italy, and Japan, which helped create fifth columnists for the Axis powers within the United States.[6] After World War II, McClatchy used the war as an obvious reason to continue to fight for total exclusion and against efforts to apply quotas to Japan.[7]

But because the committee had no real power to continue the legal battle that would reinforce Knight's precedent, and because the federal judiciary would not likely have sustained any appeals after 1937, the administration's Good Neighbor and civil rights agendas were safe from strong political opposition. In addition to the decline of the California Joint Immigration Committee, nativism as a whole had become so weakened by the mid-1930s that for all intents and purposes, it was dead.[8]

The Legislative Solution: Still an Option?

The success of the administrative policy was not the only factor that led some in the State Department to abandon their efforts to change the law. Although Sumner Welles and Richard Flournoy both believed that the only viable solution was to amend the law, a new situation emerged that interfered and temporarily forced them to be less open with an agenda of revising the naturalization requirements. In the summer of 1937, Senator Richard B. Russell (D-GA), chair of the Senate Immigration Committee, informed the State Department of pending legislation (S. 2784) that would allow for the naturalization of East Indians, who had been excluded under *Thind*. Senator Russell wrote to the State Department seeking its views on the proposed legislation.

Senator Royal S. Copeland (D-NY), the author of this bill, and Senator Russell supported the bill because it related directly to a commercial treaty with Great Britain that dealt with East Indian products and East Indian business representatives who would be required to travel abroad to engage in trade. In 1917, Congress prohibited immigration from Asia and India by creating a "barred zone." These senators interpreted the barred zone to prohibit even temporary visitors from entering the United States, and believed that one of the requirements for removing India from that zone would be to allow the naturalization of East Indians.[9]

News of this bill left State Department officials in a quandary. Certainly, amending the law to allow East Indian naturalization would raise the issue of Asian exclusion in China and Japan. And since State Department officials were in the process of proposing legislation that would allow for the naturalization of North and South American Indians, they might possibly find themselves in the embarrassing position of proposing one change while opposing the other.

In a draft reply to Senator Russell that the State Department never sent, the secretary of state suggested that Senator Russell should take up the issue with the secretary of labor because the secretary of state "desire[d] to make no comment upon the Bill," as naturalization laws were administered by the Labor Department.[10]

But Richard Flournoy seized upon S. 2748 to further argue in favor of the legislative approach over the administrative approach. He insisted that the letter not be sent and argued, in fact, that racial barriers should be removed completely and that all nations should be placed on the quota system. Although his agenda was to obtain consistency in US naturalization law, his demeanor proved that it was not oriented toward humanitarian or civil rights in any way. "It is an absurdity," he wrote, "to leave the doors wide open to the admission of negroes, one of the most backward races in the world, while keeping them closed to prevent the admission of a few Chinese and Japanese who might enter under the quotas."[11]

Flournoy further argued that legal consistency could solve their entire problem, because placing exempted countries on the quota system, which he called "the most far reaching and beneficial law adopted by this country in recent years," would allow only an insignificant number of Asians to enter the United States. However, under the pressure of "certain organizations," the insertion of Section 13(c) (barring the immigration of those ineligible for naturalization), produced the troublesome inconsistencies in naturalization and immigration law that led to the State Department's problems in the first place. Flournoy recognized, however, that State Department senior officials did not share his opinions. While he supported further quota legislation, he pointed out to them that the best course of action for their agenda would be to oppose S. 2784.[12]

However, he did not give up his disagreement in regard to Latin American immigration. He argued that the State Department should not give up efforts to pass legislation that would allow for American Indian naturalization even if it opposed the other Senate bill. He argued that the State Department could legitimately take such a stand because

> there are special reasons for favoring American Indians. In the first place, they are natives of this hemisphere and inhabitants of neighboring American republics, and in the second place, they belong to races closely connected with the races to which the original inhabitants of the United States belonged. On the other hand, a change . . . to make East Indians eligible . . . would certainly have the effect of opening up again the whole

> question of Oriental exclusion [because] the Ozawa and Thind cases show that the questions of the eligibility of the Japanese and the question of the eligibility of East Indians . . . are practically the same, and present a single problem.[13]

Of course, he casually pointed out that even the Asian issue could be dealt with if the racial bar was removed altogether and the Asian nations put on the quota system.

Although the State Department never sent that draft letter, the secretary of state did reply to Senator Russell. He delayed the issue by stating that he wanted to give the bill careful consideration before formulating an answer.[14] The real reason for the delay was that State Department officials wanted to discuss the issue with the senator personally, to inform him, if S. 2784 were passed, that it would "bring about a revival of the agitation in Japan over the question of the discriminatory character of our immigration and naturalization laws; that even a public discussion of the bill would be prejudicial to our relations with Japan; that a similar reaction might be expected in China; and that it is therefore hoped that the Committee will take no action on the bill."[15] Further, the State Department suggested that the Senate could still ratify such a commercial treaty with Great Britain if Congress amended the barred zone provisions of the Immigration Act of 1917 to allow ineligible aliens to enter the United States for commercial purposes only.[16] But opposing S. 2784 still left open the question as to whether the State Department could legitimately oppose that bill while supporting the efforts to obtain the Western Hemisphere legislation, as Flournoy continued to suggest.

In the same manner that Assistant Secretary Carr was attempting to circumvent Sumner Welles's efforts to obtain the proposed legislation,[17] State Department legal adviser Green H. Hackworth shut his colleague Flournoy out and reported to State Department senior officials that while the State Department should continue working to prevent committee hearings on S. 2784, it also "should not stir up any other questions either of immigration or naturalization at this time. Such questions are certain to bring about difficulties of which we now have a sufficient number."[18] While Flournoy had continued to give sound legal advice, which the State Department kept following, he also interjected his opinions with respect to the legislation that he and Sumner Welles had so strongly advocated.

In terms of policy approach, the record shows that Sumner Welles and R. W. Flournoy continued to follow the traditional approach to policymaking and pushed for the legislation that would have removed racial restrictions on Western Hemisphere natives. However, other senior State Department officials saw that the political and judicial changes that had occurred since December 1935 had created an environment that would allow an administrative racial classification policy to solve the problems associated with the ineligibility of American Indians (i.e., Latinos/as) to be naturalized in the United States.

Ironically, Welles and Flournoy would also ultimately have their way. In 1940, Congress passed the Nationality Act, Section 303 of which formally allowed for the naturalization of Western Hemisphere natives. That law had its origins in the executive order of April 25, 1933, in which President Franklin D. Roosevelt ordered the State, Labor, and Justice Departments to establish a committee to "review the nationality laws of the United States, to recommend revisions, and to codify those laws into one comprehensive nationality law for submission to the Congress."[19] The three departments established a technical advisory committee made up of six experts from the State Department, six from the Labor Department, and one from the Justice Department. These thirteen officials worked until 1938 drafting the legislation. After they completed their draft, Representative Samuel Dickstein, chair of the Immigration Committee, submitted the bill to Congress on June 13, 1938.[20] The bill did not pass during the Seventy-Fifth Congress, so Representative Dickstein reintroduced it in the Seventy-Sixth, on May 3, 1939.

This recodification of US nationality and naturalization law was a massive undertaking that changed several aspects of those laws. However, there was only one major change in the existing racial qualifications for naturalization eligibility: adding Western Hemisphere natives to the list that up until 1940 included only whites and those "of African nativity or African descent." That clause is almost hidden in the legislation.

Among the experts who were on the committee that drafted the bill were Assistant Secretary of State Wilbur J. Carr (committee chair), State Department legal advisers Richard W. Flournoy and Green H. Hackworth, and the Immigration Commission's Henry B. Hazard and Edward J. Shaughnessy. All of these officials were simultaneously active in crafting the administration's racial classification policy in response to Judge Knight's ruling regarding Timoteo Andrade. As mentioned before, Flournoy and Hackworth were obvious choices for the State Department to assign to both the Andrade issue and the committee. Henry Hazard, assistant to the commissioner of immigration, also fit that criterion, having published a few articles on US citizenship. As an executive in the Immigration Bureau, he was certainly acknowledged as an expert on the issue. One of Hazard's published articles was, in fact, a companion piece to one of Flournoy's.[21]

Flournoy appears to have been the key author of the Nationality Act of 1940, and a careful examination of his writings shows that he long had an agenda with respect to American and international nationality laws. A comparison of these writings and the Nationality Act reveals Flournoy's influence. Interestingly, one major issue missing from his published writings is Western Hemisphere naturalization. However, the extent to which he discussed the possibility of legislative change in connection with the Andrade case shows that it was very likely the Andrade issue that led to that major change.

In all of his published writings that dealt directly with the legislation, Flournoy never mentioned the issue. And when Flournoy and Henry Hazard testified together before the House Immigration Committee, Hazard answered instead of Flournoy when Representative Edward Rees (R-KS) asked them for clarification on Section 303. Hazard called it "a fundamental change, an enlargement."[22]

> This present act adds . . . descendants of races indigenous to the Western Hemisphere, and that was brought about through the desirability that was felt of not prohibiting from being naturalized natives of those races in the Western Hemisphere, countries which were so closely tied to the United States by

> bonds of friendship. The number who might be naturalized was felt to be very small, and it was felt that the good to be accomplished by such a provision far outweighed the possibility that a few persons who would other wise not be racially eligible might become naturalized.[23]

It seems odd that a representative of the State Department would remain silent on a matter of foreign affairs, letting a representative from the Immigration Bureau answer Representative Rees's question. Perhaps Flournoy allowed Hazard to answer the questions because of the earlier issues that had pitted him and Sumner Welles against Hackworth and Cordell Hull.

Three of Flournoy's published articles directly prefaced the Nationality Act of 1940, and one was a report on that act.[24] The first, "The Need for Amending Existing Citizenship Laws," appeared in the *Federal Bar Association Journal* (March 1932). In this article, Flournoy wrote briefly about the existing racial qualifications in naturalization law and the problems in defining "white person." He cited the *Thind* decision and its relevance to that definition. But this was his only mention of the racial prerequisite to naturalization. Flournoy focused on some of his favorite issues, such as dual nationality, the right of expatriation, what it meant to be a "natural-born citizen" (both in general, and with respect to the presidency of the United States),[25] the independent nationality of married women, and international consistency in law (referring to the 1930 convention at The Hague). His main point, however was that US nationality law was scattered over thirty-two separate statutes, and that a comprehensive piece of legislation was needed to clarify the issues.[26]

This first article was written near the end of Herbert Hoover's term in the White House and was, perhaps, an effort to get President Hoover to consider the issues. His second article, "Proposed Codification of Our Chaotic Nationality Laws," appeared in the *American Bar Association Journal* (December 1934), more than a year and a half after President Roosevelt formed the committee that drafted the legislation. This article was largely a rewriting of the March 1932 article, from a point of view that justified the formation of the committee. Flournoy wrote, "There is ample justification for the Order of the President of April 25, 1933 . . . to 'review the nationality laws of the United States, to recommend revisions . . . and to codify those laws into one comprehensive nationality law for submission to the Congress.'"[27] But he made no mention of Western Hemisphere naturalization.

Flournoy's third article, written shortly before the final testimony on the bill, was "Revision of Nationality Laws of the United States," which appeared in the January 1940 issue of the *American Journal of International Law*. In this article, he wrote about "the outstanding provisions" of the bill, none of which included Western Hemisphere naturalization eligibility. Most important, he wrote that the bill did not address the issue of dual nationality, which Flournoy had been advocating should be terminated.[28] Dual nationality originates in the fact that virtually every nation recognizes both those born within their boundaries and those born to their citizens as "native born," meaning that citizenship is granted to children born outside the boundaries of their parents' country. Perhaps Flournoy was trying to influence those who coauthored the legislation with him or the legislators who would soon debate the bill through outside publications. In his criticism of the bill, he advocated that those with dual nationality should elect one nation over the other once they reach the age of majority.[29]

Writing about the Nationality Act of 1940 after its passage, he commented that it was authored "due to the conviction on the part of officials of the Departments of State, Justice and Labor that the old nationality laws of the United States, which were scattered among about fifty statutes, were inadeqate [*sic*]."[30] This article dealt in detail with much of the legislation. But Flournoy's review of chapter III, which contained the naturalization change, simply summarized the entire chapter as follows: "Chapter III of the Act embodies various changes in the laws governing naturalization. The most important changes related to procedure and in general serve to give administrative officials a more important part in the examination of petitions for naturalization."[31]

After the passage of the 1940 act, other scholars were quick to catch the change and report it in legal and scholarly journals of the time. An anonymous article in the *Harvard Law Review* reported on the change and speculated whether or not the definition of

"Western Hemisphere Native" might be extended to include "the Tongans, the Maoris, the Marquesans, and other Melanesians and Micronesians." In the strict geographical definition of "Western Hemisphere," these groups would certainly qualify, although the author pointed out that Congress intended to mean Latin Americans and nonwhite Canadians. One criticism of the new legislation was that it made, the author said, "no effort to clarify the term 'white persons' which has been the basis of endless seemingly futile litigation."[32] It was, perhaps, that endless litigation that caused him to question the meaning of "Western Hemisphere" in the legislation. In the *American Journal of International Law*, Charles Cheney Hyde, a well-known former State Department legal adviser, also reported on the addition of Western Hemisphere natives, although he did so without editorial comment.[33]

Objections to the Policy Within the FDR Administration

At the same time that the State Department legal advisers and the Division of Near Eastern Affairs pondered the issue of Senate Bill 2784, they also had to deal with opposition to their efforts from an unexpected quarter. One division of the very agency that first began using the white classification in an official capacity, the Census Bureau, objected to the use of "white" with respect to Latin Americans.

Assistant Secretary Carr, in his efforts to apply the policy uniformly to all Latin American immigrants, raised the issue with Halbert L. Dunn, MD, chief statistician of the Division of Vital Statistics (Census Bureau). This department, it is important to remember, took the blame for the Census Bureau's role in the El Paso reclassification of Mexicans from white to colored.[34] Dunn, it turned out, was not at all happy with this new policy and had no intention of helping Carr to further apply the standard to other Latin American nations. Dunn informed Carr, "carrying into effect the decision with respect to Mexicans means the virtual destruction of the census of vital statistics insofar as concerns their scientific use in determining certain facts in regard to health, length of life, birth rate and other important matters."[35]

Dunn protested the policy on the grounds that all statistical data gathered under the classification Mexican would be rendered useless when compared to data gathered after Mexicans and Mexican Americans were to be classified as white. He presented several reasons why separate classifications should be maintained, many of which Carr had not even considered until his conversation with Dunn. Dunn cited "fundamental biological differences between the average American and the average Mexican in the way in which they react to diseases" and in their birth rates.[36] He also pointed out that the Census Bureau was not alone in needing a separate classification. The "Central Statistical Bureau, the WPA, the Social Security Board, the Public Health Service, the Census and the Bureau of Labor Statistics" all had valid reasons for distinguishing between Mexican and white data.[37] For example, life insurance companies had long distinguished between the races, and the new Social Security Board would soon be adopting the practices used by these corporations. Before advising Carr on any aspect of this policy, Dunn decided that he must consult with his counterparts in Public Health, Central Statistics, and Labor Statistics. Carr, however, was not willing to give up his agenda of applying the policy uniformly to all Latin American immigrants. He suggested that the State Department pursue a dual agenda of finding a way of applying the classification while still separating Latin Americans from white Americans for statistical purposes.[38]

John F. Simmons and Raleigh Gibson of the State Department consulted with Dunn and suggested that additional categories might be used, such as "'origin', 'lineage', or 'descent', in order to secure the information that [Dunn] felt was essential for vital statistics."[39] With these suggestions in mind, Dunn was more agreeable to the classification and suggested that the best approach to fulfill the needs of both the State Department and the Census Bureau would be a "racial distribution . . . as follows:

White – unspecified
White – Mexico
White – Central, South America, and Caribbean area,
Negro
Other Races – Japan, China, Philippine Island, Hawaii, Indians."[40]

Finally, Dunn, Simmons, and Gibson suggested that the State Department obtain input from Mexican Ambassador Castillo Nájera regarding this system, to ascertain whether the government of Mexico would find such a classification offensive.

Ultimately, or so it would seem, everyone involved was happy with the implementation of this revised racial classification policy. The State Department had its uniform classification that would allow immigration and naturalization of Latin American natives, and the whole FDR administration, as well as the Mexican government, was using this classification on all paperwork. This reinforced the standard and made any judicial objections practically impossible. In addition, the subcategories suggested by Dunn allowed for continued statistical separation of Mexicans, Mexican Americans, and other Latin Americans from Anglo-Americans.

The 1940 Census of Population and Housing

Ironically, despite the State Department's earlier efforts, and despite the agreement between the Census Bureau and the State Department, the issue of classifying Mexicans and Mexican American emerged one more time. In August 1939, when Census Bureau Director William Lane Austin had to prepare the final instructions to enumerators, he again raised Dunn's objections to classifying Mexicans as white.

History of Racial Classification in the US Census

In the first through tenth censuses (1790–1880), the only racial classifications listed in the instructions were white, mulatto, and black.[41] The eleventh through fourteenth censuses (1890–1920) included Chinese, Japanese, and Indian. The 1890 Census also instructed the enumerators to subdivide the racial intermixture between whites and blacks. They were to use "mulatto" for those who were half African, "quadroon" for those of one-quarter African blood, and "octoroon" for those of one-eighth African blood (prior censuses had mentioned quadroon and octoroon but instructed that they be classed together with mulatto). These additions characterize the changing face of the American population in the era, with the geographic growth of the United States, the closing of the American frontier, the subjugation of the American Indian, and increasing Asian immigration. The Census Bureau added these classifications because enumerators were now very likely to be counting Indians and Asians as well as whites and blacks. Changes in the 1910 and 1920 censuses were the work of chief statistician Joseph A. Hill, who "added new questions . . . in the hope of elucidating differences in race and nationality in increasing detail. He was particularly interested in creating indices to gauge assimilation, and he presented data in tables that made racial comparisons convenient."[42]

The next major change in racial classification, the one most important to the Census Bureau and the State Department with regard to developing a policy to counter *Andrade*, came in the fifteenth census in 1930. "In order to obtain separate figures for Mexicans," states a Census Bureau publication about its own history, "it was decided that all persons born in Mexico, or having parents born in Mexico, who were not definitely White, Negro, Indian, Chinese, or Japanese, would be returned as Mexicans (Mex)."[43] This, of course, reflected the growing Latin American population in the United States, as well as the fact that white America did not recognize Latinos/as as a part of their culture and society.

For those who know how to analyze census data, however, as the statisticians were trained to do, the census questions (especially Hill's) already made it quite possible to separate out the data for the Latin American populations. Censuses generally asked for the place of birth of the respondent, as well as whether or not the mother and father were foreign born. Beginning with the tenth census (1880), which took place while Mexican immigration was still relatively minor, the questionnaire stopped asking the yes/no question of whether the parents were foreign born, and asked specifically where the parents had been born. The statistical separation became even easier in 1890, when the Census Bureau added the question of citizenship and naturalization, and again in 1910, when the census asked for the "mother tongue" or native language of the respondent.

By analyzing the answers to these questions, statisticians and other researchers can easily separate Mexican and other Latin American immigrant data from Anglo-American and other statistics. Most Mexican Americans can also be separated through this filtering process, although those whose families were longtime US residents and who spoke predominantly English fell entirely into the white category, regardless of their racial heritage. The addition of the Mexican classification in 1930 only made this separation easier. It did not create a large quantity of new statistics that would simply disappear if the policy were not followed in the 1940 Census. This, in fact, proved itself true. Mexicans and Mexican Americans were indeed classified as white in the 1940 Census, but in the data evaluation stage the coding staff managed to separate out their data "on the basis of a combination of entries for the person in columns 10 [Color or race], C [Place of Birth], 36 [Place of Birth—Father], and 37 [Place of Birth—Mother]."[44] Of course, column 38, Mother Tongue, also helped in that determination. So, even being classified as white, Mexican immigrants and most Mexican Americans appeared in the final tabulation as "White—Mexican," just as Dr. Dunn had suggested in 1937.

Census Director Austin's efforts to maintain *Mexican* as a racial classification in 1939 indicate that he and the Census Bureau may have been following one of two potential thought patterns. First, perhaps the bureau did not want to have to use the filtering process and preferred to have the separate classification immediately at its disposal. Second, and more likely, it may be that bureau officials lacked an institutional memory (historical knowledge of how their own agency had functioned in the past), took the Mexican classification for granted as something that had always existed and would always continue.

With the 1940 Census being in the final preparation stages, Austin raised the issue of the racial classification policy with George Wythe of the Commerce Department. He wanted help in arguing with the State Department to revert to the 1930 Census classifications, and under the time constraints urgently requested input into the situation. He told Wythe:

> Two years ago, the State Department expressed its interest in this matter because certain representatives of the Mexican population groups in the southern states found it distasteful to

> be termed Mexicans or classified as other races rather than white. At that time I issued an order that all Mexican statistics were to be classified as white and so published. Because of the ramifications of this decision, it seems necessary to reconsider before applying the ruling to the 16th decennial census.[45]

Austin then cited many of the same reasons Dunn had argued two years previously: different birth and death rates, differences in social and cultural patterns, and, of course, the simple need for statistical separation of Caucasians and Latinos/as. Supporting his argument, Austin even predicted, "It is quite likely that the State Department itself will be seriously embarrassed at a later date by not having this knowledge in its relations with Mexico. The Chief of the Statistical Commission from Mexico . . . indicated . . . that leaders in the Mexican Government would, in his opinion, be handicapped if such facts were not available for their use."[46] Finally, Austin cited the costs that the Census Bureau would incur if it had to recompute past census data to be consistent. Here again, Austin overlooked the fact that censuses prior to 1930 already classified Mexicans as white.

While Austin acknowledged that the Census Bureau was committed to following the State Department's lead, he made perfectly clear that he would prefer to "collect data on Mexicans and tabulate it in accordance with 1930 census procedures."[47] On the State Department's side, by 1939, the sense of urgency regarding the racial classification of Mexican immigrants as white had waned. There appeared to be a strong possibility that Austin would manage to convince State Department officials of the necessity to classify Mexicans and Mexican Americans separately from the Anglo-American population.

The Mexican Perspective

In the midst of this 1939 debate, the State Department asked US Ambassador Josephus Daniels in Mexico City to inform the Secretaria de Relaciones Exteriores (SRE) of the potential return to the 1930 policy. Daniels informed the SRE, "[The] Census Bureau of the Department of Commerce is now of the opinion that the 1936 decision was hasty and unfortunate and that the decision should be reconsidered," due to the need for separate vital statistics.[48] Daniels's letter, although almost casual in its manner, was very succinct. It simply stated the facts as Austin had presented them to the State Department and asked the SRE for its opinion in the matter.

The SRE referred the matter to Mexico's own census bureau, the Departamento Demografico. As had Ambassador Daniels, the chief of this department, Dr. Manuel Gamio, responded without the urgency that the classification issue had possessed from 1935 to 1937:

> Concerning the classification "Mexican," which was recommended by the registrars as a possible classification in the 1940 census for the mixed race individuals, it is preferable, for obvious reasons, to the previously used "colored," even though it lacks the ethnic/cultural significance which is what, in fact, it tried to express.
>
> In view of this, [the Secretaria de Gobernacion] made the following suggestion . . . : Mexicans could be categorized in two groups: first, individuals "of European origin," a classification which generally suggests ethnic characteristics corresponding to that of the "white race," but also a higher standard of living and cultural index. Second, individuals "of Indo-European origin," which generally indicates ethnic characteristics of mixed origin and a lower standard of living, compared to the first group.[49]

The SRE also sought input from Mexico's director general of statistics, Dr. E. Alanís Patiño. Patiño apparently shared Dunn's scientifically minded drive to statistically separate the Mexican and white American populations. He also agreed to the need for a distinctive classification: "I am of the opinion that we should accept the Census Bureau's classification of Mexicans residing in the United States, with the exception that they don't classify the racially mixed as 'Mexican,' as they are known as Spanish Americans, and that such be stated in the instructions that will be given to the census takers of the 1940 Census."[50]

It appears that Mexican officials viewed the racial situation far more realistically than did American officials in Washington. US Census officials still wanted to use the classification "Mexican," which even the restrictionists had recognized as inappropriate for Mexicans who were racially Indian or mestizo.

At the same time, however, the US Census Bureau was not the only group that lacked an institutional memory. The relevance of the Andrade situation, which had occurred within the previous four years, had already receded from the institutional memory of the SRE.[51] Ambassador Castillo Nájera's earlier efforts to obtain the classification "white" seemed to be forgotten by those who formulated a response to Ambassador Daniels's memorandum.

Not only did the SRE lack institutional memory, but it appears that SRE officials had never before discussed the topic with other departments of the Mexican government that would have valuable input in such a situation. When the SRE involved Mexico's Census Department, for example, that department had no idea what problems might arise from the separate classification of Mexican expatriates seeking naturalization in the United States. So when the Mexican government finally wrote a formal response to Ambassador Daniels, the SRE simply transcribed and quoted Dr. Gamio's letter as the Secretaria de Gobernacion's official position.[52] In other words, the Mexican government officially had no objection to the separate classification of Mexican nationals, as long as the term "Mexican" was used only to represent nationality and not race.

Final Implementation

Ultimately, however, those who did retain an institutional memory (the State Department and Ambassador Castillo Nájera) prevailed in the final decision regarding the classification of Mexicans and Mexican Americans in the 1940 US Census. The State Department had been the only obstacle to Austin's proposed return to the 1930 policy, and when Austin requested permission to do so, State Department officials refused.[53] These officials had, in fact, grown impatient with the Mexican government for taking too much time in considering its position. Ambassador Daniels reported to the Mexican Foreign Office that the "State Department . . . is very anxious to hear from this matter, as the questionnaires must now be printed for the 1940 census."[54]

The State Department officials did not wait for the Mexican response (which they likely would not have appreciated anyway). While the Mexican Census Department's Central Statistical Office was still pondering the issue, State Department officials conferred with Ambassador Castillo Nájera and informed him that the decision had already been made to remain consistent with the policy established after the Andrade situation. On November 22, 1939, Ambassador Castillo Nájera telegraphed Secretary Eduardo Hay that the State Department had already made the decision that Mexicans would still "be globally classified within the white race."[55] He also mentioned that the State Department had already instructed Ambassador Daniels to inform the Mexican government of that decision. Ambassador Daniels's memorandum arrived the following week.[56]

This, however, was the only major change in racial classification in the 1940 Census.[57] Like all prior censuses, this one asked all of the questions (respondent's place of birth, nationality, native language, and place of birth of both parents) that were used to separate Mexicans and most Mexican Americans statistically from the Anglo-American population. Therefore, the statistical data from the prior census would still be consistent with the 1940 data. So, although Mexicans were indeed classified as white, the supplementary questions still covered the issue of the respondent's ethnic or national origin. As one would hope for any major government program, the Census Bureau had a system of checks and safeguards to ensure that proper standards were maintained in the counting process. With respect to the classification of Mexicans as white, there were additional procedures beyond the instructions to the enumerators to use that classification. If an enumerator had entered "Mexican" or "Mex" under the race column, the processing staff who coded the data in Washington, DC, were required to enter that particular tabulation as a code 1, which was synonymous with white, on their coding sheets.[58]

10

Consequences, Unintended Consequences, and Failures

ONE OF THE MOST IMPORTANT ASPECTS OF POLICYMAKING AND implementation is policy analysis; that is, reviewing any given policy to determine successes, failures, and possible unintended consequences. The "Andrade policy" is no exception. Until the passage of the Nationality Act of 1940, which added Western Hemisphere natives to the list of those racially eligible for naturalization, the Andrade policy did exactly as it was intended with respect to Mexican immigration. In terms of foreign affairs, it helped to keep US-Mexican relations at a friendly level, at least until Mexico's oil expropriation of March 1938. But it failed in one respect, although not from the perspective of the policy makers. Civil rights activists had been fighting for this official recognition for several years, in the hopes that it would support their agenda. But being officially classified as white did not cause Latinos/as to be suddenly accepted by Anglo-Americans as white. It also had unintended consequences when it was applied to Latinos/as in a negative aspect: putting Latinos/as on trial with an all-white jury of their "peers."

The Course of Mexican Immigration After Knight's Ruling

An analysis of official Census Bureau statistics on Mexican immigration shows that the implementation of the policy to classify Mexicans as white did effectively neutralize Judge Knight's application of the *Ozawa*, *Thind*, and *Morrison* decisions to Mexican immigrants, at least until the implementation of the Nationality Act of 1940. Had the nativists been successful in having Knight's judgment affirmed, the numbers would have substantially decreased afterward. Instead, for each year after the *Andrade* decision, the numbers of immigrants continued to increase at a steady rate, consistent with the kind of immigration that would result from the continually improving economy (table 10.1).

A look at the numbers illustrates that immigration increased steadily, so that within ten years of the *Andrade* decision, the number of immigrants had more than quadrupled. These numbers remained high throughout the 1940s.

One major reason for the increase in this period is that as the United States geared up for war, Mexican labor again became desirable. The Roosevelt administration implemented temporary labor programs such as the Emergency Farm Labor Program (1942) and

TABLE 10.1. Mexican Immigrants to the United States, 1935–1950

Year	*N Immigrants*	*Year*	*N Immigrants*
1935	1,560	1943	4,172
1936	1,716	1944	6,598
1937	2,347	1945	6,702
1938	2,502	1946	7,146
1939	2,640	1947	7,558
1940	2,313	1948	8,384
1941	2,824*	1949	8,083
1942	2,378	1950	6,744

*From 1937 to 1940, Mexican immigration was allowed under the *Andrade* policy. After January 1941, it was allowed under Section 303 of the Nationality Act of 1940, which was also a direct result of the *Andrade* decision.

SOURCE: Adapted from US Department of Commerce, Bureau of the Census, *Historical Statistics of the United States, Colonial Times to 1970* (Washington, DC: US Department of Commerce, Bureau of the Census, 1975), Series C 89-119, Immigrants by Country: 1820–1970.

other *bracero* (helping arms) programs that allowed Mexican laborers to enter the United States. These programs continued in the postwar period and were finally terminated at the end of 1964.

US-Mexican Relations During and After *Andrade*

Just before both governments learned of Knight's first decision regarding Timoteo Andrade's naturalization petition, Ambassador Castillo Nájera had told Sumner Welles that "relations between Mexico and the United States had never seemed so promising as at this moment."[1] Obviously, the State Department went to great lengths to keep relations moving in that direction.

From south of the border, Ambassador Josephus Daniels reported the same sentiment directly to President Franklin Roosevelt. In two personal letters, Daniels marveled at the fact that "the Mexican Government and the Mexican people . . . opened their hearts to representatives of the Navy of our country" despite memories of the Tampico incident.[2] Daniels and Roosevelt had both been senior Navy Department officials at the time of the 1914 Vera Cruz intervention where President Woodrow Wilson ordered the US Navy and Marines to occupy the city of Vera Cruz in response to the arrest of several US sailors in Tampico, and to prevent German weapons from being delivered to the armies of General Victoriano Huerta. Daniels viewed the openness as an indication that the Good Neighbor Policy had "won the hearts of the people and officials."[3]

Immigration restriction has a prominent place in the historical record of the Good Neighbor agenda. In May 1937, the Latin American press reported that US Secretary of State Cordell Hull had taken up the issue with the US Senate. Although the restrictionists had no success getting bills out of committee in either house after 1930, several members of both houses annually proposed the same legislation. In 1937, there appeared to be a chance that such a bill would again pass the Senate Immigration Committee.

In response, both Secretary Hull and Secretary of Labor Perkins wrote to the committee suggesting that such a bill would violate the terms of the Good Neighbor Policy. Hull also reminded the committee that the administration had already taken administrative steps to curtail immigration from Mexico (taking credit for the initiatives that had begun under President Hoover in 1929).[4]

Some of the issues that mattered most to the FDR administration can, in part, be identified based upon materials found in the senior administration officials' personal collections at the FDR Presidential Library. Sumner Welles, for example, kept records that dealt with the overall effort that he and other State Department officials put into the development of the Good Neighbor Policy. He kept few documents relating to specific issues, and the particular matters for which he did keep personal records dealt with the larger issues that affected relations, such as land expropriations and the oil issue. Communiqués between Assistant Secretary Welles and Ambassador Josephus Daniels in the months immediately following Knight's decision dealt almost exclusively with matters of direct communication between Presidents Roosevelt and Cárdenas.[5] Other official documents in Welles's private papers, specifically correspondence with Edward L. Reed, chief of the Division of Mexican Affairs, deal specifically with issues such as the expropriation of properties belonging to US citizens or to the pan-American conference that was held in Buenos Aires in 1936.[6]

During that period, one of the main issues for the Roosevelt administration was the revolutionary ideology of the Lázaro Cárdenas administration. Cárdenas took office in 1934. For the first year of his term, he, like his three predecessors, was thought simply to be a puppet of *El Jefe Máximo*, Plutarco Elías Calles. President Calles had taken the revolutionary ideology to the right (he was, in fact, reading Hitler's *Mein Kampf* when he was arrested and sent into exile in Los Angeles), and Cárdenas moved relatively far to the left, again embracing the original ideology that had emerged from the revolution. Cárdenas had made campaign promises to redistribute land to the *campesinos* (the Mexican peasant class) through expropriation of large estates.

Many of these large estates belonged to American corporations or citizens, and the owners of these properties demanded protection from the State Department. When these demands reached the White House in early 1937, Roosevelt agreed that Mexico had the right to expropriation but insisted that Cárdenas provide fair compensation to the former owners of the lands. US Ambassador Josephus Daniels realized that Mexico could not afford to pay the full amounts for the lands in question. He sought compromise and pushed for full payment only for the smaller landholders, who likely had not undervalued their property for tax purposes, as had the large corporations operating in Mexico.[7]

Sumner Welles also sought compromise in the situation, but reminded Ambassador Castillo Nájera that the American public would support the Good Neighbor Policy only if the Latin American nations responded with policies that were not one sided. Latin Americans, on the other hand, were also not willing to accept the Good Neighbor Policy unconditionally. Mexico in particular expected not only that the Roosevelt administration should exercise the policy, but that US investors and businesses operating in Mexico should also. This applied especially to American oil interests.[8]

Thus, the biggest test of the Good Neighbor Policy toward Mexico, which came after the Andrade situation had been settled, was the Mexican oil expropriation of March 18, 1938. While the British, whose citizens owned 70 percent of the Mexican oil industry, broke off relations with Mexico, the United States followed the lead of Ambassador Daniels, who did not want to break the "bilateral bonds" that had greatly improved since 1933. Therefore, the United States recognized the legitimacy of the expropriation so long as US nationals received appropriate compensation. Although there were dissenters within the State Department, in the end, the department supported Mexico's position. This crisis "indicated that Latin Americans were demanding two things from the United States: greater authority in their own economic decision-making, and a greater share of the wealth produced from their own resources."[9] Certainly, with the Good Neighbor and New Deal policies of the Roosevelt administration, FDR could not protest a nation's right to expropriation. Sometime after the expropriations, Ambassador Castillo Nájera was asked if Mexico had feared US intervention. He answered that Mexico had "confidently relied upon . . . the good faith of President Roosevelt" to live up to the commitments made in the Good Neighbor Policy.[10]

Did the Policy Benefit Mexicans and Mexican Americans?

Despite being officially classified as white (and therefore being officially exempted from the consequences of *Plessy v. Ferguson*), both Mexicans and Mexican Americans continued to suffer discrimination and segregation: "Yet none of this segregation was formally encoded in law. For legal purposes, Mexican Americans were white. They were counted as white in the census and, unlike non-whites (other than those from Africa), were able to naturalize. However, law clashed with perceptions of racial 'reality,' creating a citizenship status for Mexican Americans that many considered to be a legal fiction."[11]

To many white Americans, both Mexicans and Mexican Americans were still considered nonwhite and therefore non-American. Official documents accepted only "white" (which included Latinos/as), "colored," and "other" as racial classifications. But people in Texas and much of the southwest still viewed "Mexican" as a legitimate classification during and after World War II. In addition, white Americans continued to treat Mexican Americans as second-class citizens. For example, Sergeant Macario García, a *tejano* who had been awarded the Congressional Medal of Honor, was chased out of a restaurant by a man with a baseball bat because he was in a whites-only establishment.[12]

During the same period in California,

> segregation statutes permitted school boards to establish separate schools for "Indian children . . . and for children of Chinese, Japanese, or Mongolian parentage." Despite the absence of Mexican Americans from the statutory list, the parties "admitted that segregation per se is practiced in the above-mentioned school districts as the Spanish-speaking children enter school life and as they advance through the grades in the respective school districts." One commentator found it ironic that "the Code did not mention the group that was most commonly segregated by 1945: children of Mexican descent."[13]

Of course, like Mexican Americans, Mexican immigrants also suffered discrimination from Anglo-Americans during and after World

War II. However, the face of Mexican immigration changed substantially during the war due to labor shortages. The United States and Mexico entered into agreements to import *braceros.* Growers would have preferred that the US government simply open the border and allow unrestricted immigration, which would substantially lower the wages paid to day laborers. The Mexican government, however, favored regulating the crossings to protect Mexican migrant workers from losing the minimum wage protections afforded by the *bracero* program.[14]

The racial classification issue and the transnational effort ultimately emerged in this issue also. Texas growers initially refused to hire *braceros* because of the government regulations, but sought to do so after 1943. Because of the far-reaching racism against Mexicans in Texas, the Mexican government refused to permit *bracero* workers to enter Texas from 1943 to 1947. As it did for the *Andrade* decision, the government of Mexico became active in the Caucasian rights efforts of Mexican Americans to protect the rights of Mexican nationals in America. Before being banned from receiving *bracero* labor, in an effort to appease Mexico, Texas Governor Coke Stevens convinced the state legislature to pass the "Caucasian Race Resolution" in 1943. This resolution, based on the fact that Mexicans were classified as white, "affirmed the rights of all Caucasians to equal treatment within Texas."[15] Unfortunately, it created no change in attitude among white American racists, as they certainly did not consider Mexican immigrants or Mexican Americans to be Caucasian.

The resolution was actually a limited response to failed efforts in the Texas Legislature to pass a racial equality bill beginning in 1941 and 1943. Because it was a resolution, and not a bill, it angered civil rights activists, who wondered if it had any real meaning. And by 1944, a Texas appeals court issued a ruling that did, in fact, show that the resolution had no teeth.[16] More important, it did not end prejudice. During the war, Mexicans and Mexican Americans seeking skilled positions or advancement in their current positions suffered a great deal of job discrimination. One Mexican antidiscrimination publication, *Fraternidad*, editorialized against these practices. This journal cited several instances of discrimination, including one laborer who had claimed French-Italian heritage but had been demoted when his Mexican ancestry was discovered, and another man who had received a promotion but not the accompanying pay raise.[17]

Almost as soon as the 1943 bill failed, the government of Mexico and LULAC began to prepare for the next session of the Texas Legislature. Often, the primary focus of a civil rights movement is to change a restrictive or repressive policy. Once policy changes have been made, then cultural changes can follow. LULAC's leadership understood this, as can be seen in the case of Texas's Caucasian Race Resolution; while Latinos/as were agitating for civil rights legislation, their opponents argued that they should begin with education and change the culture first. Then legislation could be considered. But LULAC knew that the legislation needed to come first and the cultural changes would come second.

At a December 1943 conference on inter-American relations, attended by Texas Governor Stevenson and Mexican Ambassador Rafael de la Colina, Mexican government officials stressed the need for the passage of such a civil rights law. However, those who opposed such legislation also mobilized. One of their primary arguments was that education and "gradualism" were preferred to legislation that forced an end to discrimination.[18]

Early in 1945, Texas State Senator J. Franklin Spears sponsored legislation that would make racial discrimination a misdemeanor criminal offense. The bill, SB 1, was "designed to halt racial discriminatory acts against our people by reason of their race."[19] Mexican newspapers gave the bill positive coverage, and the Texas LULAC leadership urged its local councils to write to the senators on the State Affairs Committee as well as their local representatives in support of the bill. Of course the Mexican antidiscrimination publication *Fraternidad* supported Spears's efforts as well. The February 1945 issue presented the bill to its readers, while the April issue editorialized on the value of such a law to good relations between the United States and Latin America.

The editors of *Fraternidad* supported two simultaneous efforts to eliminate racial discrimination in Texas. First, they agreed with their opponents on the value of using education to slowly persuade Texans against discrimination, "that is to say the lifting of the cultural level of the inhabitants of Texas."[20] More important, the editors supported combining education with legal sanctions against those who practiced discrimination, as the Spears bill would have done if it had passed. Their support of the Spears bill motivated them to ask such questions as the following:

> If the acts of discrimination are being practiced only by an insignificant minority—as everyone has recognized—and the same cause deep injury to a large percentage of the Texas population, why not sanction the few in defense of the majority?
>
> How would the average North American man feel if he were to enter a café in Mexico and be refused service? What reaction would their countrymen have with respect to our country?
>
> What would the North American people think if the Chairman of the United States Senate Foreign Relations Committee—Senator Thomas Connally, an illustrious Texan—were to be refused service in a restaurant in a Mexican town?[21]

The last question referred to the fact that two Mexican federal congressmen (one was the president of that body) and the former mayor of Ciudad Juárez had recently been refused service at the Lone Star Café in Pecos, Texas. They had been referred instead to a nearby restaurant for "colored" people. Opponents of the Spears bill argued that the three had deliberately set out to be refused service as a publicity stunt to garner support for the bill.[22]

Although the bill passed the Texas State Senate, it unfortunately did not pass the House of Representatives. The news had negative repercussions in Mexico. In Puebla, for example, student protesters prevented a group of Texas students, who were in Mexico for the summer, from attending classes.[23] While *Fraternidad* editors spoke out against such reprisals, because "Mexicans should not lower themselves to the same level as our ignoramus discriminators," they also lamented the failure of the bill. Commenting on the efforts to educate Texans, they asked, "how much time will be needed in order to re-educate the discriminators? And will the victims have to wait, patiently suffering molestation, while the bad Texans are educated?" More important, the editors asked, "Why do the legislators . . . who say to look for the reaffirmation of the friendship between the American countries, and who reject the principles of Nazism (which supports the existence of 'superior and inferior races,') now reject a law that has those democratic ideals of reaffirmation and the banishment of the vestiges of Fascist Nazism?"[24]

Conditions worsened for the Mexican groups after World War II. American veterans returned to their jobs, and wartime labor agencies were dissolved, ending what little protection the Mexican groups had against job discrimination. Some Texas politicians attempted to reverse this trend. State Senator Spears made several postwar attempts to pass the legislation that had been defeated early in 1945, only to see every attempt defeated.[25]

Not surprisingly, Mexican American attitudes about immigrants also did not change much as a result of the official classification or during World War II. The Mexican American generation continued to support immigration restriction for reasons similar to those they had given in the 1930s.[26] However, with respect to their own civil rights, the Mexican American generation did lay the foundations for its children, those that historian Mario García labels the "Chicano generation," to obtain better jobs, more education, and social mobility. However, there was no quantum leap in the achievement of civil rights as suggested by the "rhetoric and symbols of the Chicano Movement."[27]

An Unintended Consequence: *Hernandez v. Texas*

The US Census Bureau continued to classify Mexican Americans and Mexican immigrants as white until the 1980 Census of Population and Housing (when the bureau began to use the term "Hispanic"). However, in Texas at the very least, the white classification policy began to backfire when Anglo racists found a way to use it against Latinos/as. Although Mexican Americans were legally white, de facto discrimination kept them off juries in east Texas. By law, a white jury was considered a jury of their peers, and thus Mexican Americans suffered from "whiteness without benefits" and were "damned as too white to be covered by the Equal Protection Clause of the Fourteenth Amendment to the U.S. Constitution."[28] As a result, "being judged by a jury composed solely of those who rarely understood them and often discriminated against them was tantamount to having the legal system against them."[29]

One of the most overlooked landmark civil rights cases decided by the US Supreme Court, *Hernandez v. Texas* (347 U.S. 475), corrected this issue. Pete Hernández had been convicted of murdering Joe Espinosa in Jackson County, Texas. During his trial, his attorneys moved to quash both the indictment and the jury panel, on the grounds that "persons of Mexican descent were systematically excluded from service as jury commissioners, grand jurors and petit jurors, although there were such persons fully qualified to serve residing in Jackson County."[30] These attorneys argued that since his class of citizen had been excluded from jury duty, Hernández's rights to equal protection had been violated. Hernández's trial judge denied the motions on the grounds that Mexican Americans were officially white persons and that therefore Hernández's class of people were indeed represented on the jury. When Hernández appealed on the same grounds, the Texas Court of Criminal Appeals sided with the trial judge on the issue.

In assessing this particular form of discrimination, civil rights activists discovered a dilemma, and a way to deal with that predicament:

> To accept that they were white was to accept that there was no discrimination. To accept that they were colored, was to add an extra burden to their plight. So they chose to deal within the concept of not who they were but how they were "treated." In this way, they could be both white in the way they wanted to be treated and brown in order to fit into the law. It is important at this juncture, to remember that not everybody wanted to be white and there were also many who did not want to be brown.[31]

In fact, years after arguing for Hernández before the Supreme Court, retired judge Juan Carlos Cadena reported having a conversation with a colleague who did not appreciate having his status as white taken away by the *Hernandez* decision:

> Cadena commented that Mexicans are Mongoloid, according to anthropologists, and that they came across the Bering Straits. His friend indignantly replied, "'you're going to make a Chinaman out of me.' And I said, 'Well, would you rather be a Chinaman with full rights . . . or a white person with no rights?'" The judge's friend replied that he would rather be subjected to discrimination than give up his claim to whiteness.[32]

Prior to the Supreme Court's *Hernandez* decision, since segregation was unofficial or based on "language difficulties," Mexican American reformers were hampered by Texas segregation because they had to prove intent.[33] At first, their approach had been to prove that they were "good Americans," by learning English and emphasizing "civic duty" and education. But this approach led to "implicit differences" between those who sought to be loyal Americans and those who "still looked toward Mexico or simply found it hard to integrate into what continued to be a hostile environment."[34] After World War II, those seeking to be known as loyal Americans began to practice the "politics of similarity," trying to show that they were very much like mainstream Americans. This approach provided even more reason to fight against jury exclusion.[35]

Another issue for south Texas Mexican Americans was that publicly and on the surface, white Texans made efforts to treat Mexican Americans as "whites with all the rights and privileges of citizenship." But in reality, racial differences were discussed "in private conversations, in backroom politics [and in] labor disputes."[36]

To fight this discrimination within the confines of the dilemma of their racial definition, they had to develop a strategy:

> Whiteness, with all its inherit advantages, was always the preferred status, but because there were many Mexican Americans who did not want to consider themselves Anglo and many Anglos who also did not want to consider them as such, the strategy of race could not be ignored. Mexican American lawyers claimed that their constituencies were treated as a dif-

ferent race and thus deserved protection under the Fourteenth Amendment.[37]

To gain those protections, civil rights lawyers decided to appeal Hernández's criminal trial on jury discrimination grounds.The US Supreme Court overturned the Texas court's decision, ruling that Mexican Americans were indeed a distinct class of citizen. The Supreme Court ruled that "race and color did not set Mexicans apart, but 'other differences from community norm' perhaps did so."[38] This was entirely contrary to the accepted standard established by the US government in the wake of the *Andrade* ruling. One of the Supreme Court's main arguments was that most white citizens clearly distinguished between whites and Mexican Americans, and that the participation of Mexican Americans in local economies and communities was "slight." In fact, in many cases Mexican Americans were being forced into the same segregated schools and other facilities that blacks of the era were forced to use.[39] Thus, the policy of classifying Mexicans and Mexican Americans as white, which had been started by the Mexican American generation and the FDR administration, became a nonpolicy as the following generation "abandon[ed] the white ethnic identity" that their predecessors had fought so hard to establish.[40]

One of the potential negative aspects of the *Hernandez* decision, because it did declare Mexican Americans a distinct class of citizen, was that it would have applied *Plessy v. Ferguson* to the Latino/a community. However, the main reason that it has only recently received attention from scholars, journalists, and even civil rights activists is that the very next case decided by the US Supreme Court was *Brown v. Board of Education* (347 U.S. 483), the landmark case that overturned *Plessy v. Ferguson* and ruled that "separate but equal" segregation is unconstitutional.[41] Also, despite the potential of a double triumph for Mexican American civil rights of *Hernandez* and *Brown*, many Mexican American civil rights activists continued to assert their whiteness in their civil rights battles until the late 1960s along the same lines as they had before 1954.[42] To them, the ultimate outcome of the *Andrade* ruling was the triumph, and *Hernandez* was a slap in the face.

Notes

Notes to Chapter 1

1. Citizenship Petition of Timoteo Andrade, including opinion of Judge Knight, December 11, 1935.

2. Ngai, "The Architecture of Race in American Immigration Law," 70.

3. Quote from ibid., 91. Thomas Guglielmo coined the term *Caucasian rights* in "Fighting for Caucasian Rights."

4. Alvarez, *Familia: Migration and Adaptation in Baja and Alta California*, 153–154.

5. Rosales, "Shifting Self Perceptions and Ethnic Consciousness Among Mexicans in Houston," 83.

6. Rodriguez, *Mongrels, Bastards, Orphans and Vagabonds*; Calderón-Zaks, "Constructing the 'Mexican Race.'"

7. Ngai, *Impossible Subjects*, 53.

8. James J. Davis (Secretary of Labor) to Albert Johnson (Chair, House Immigration Committee), February 5, 1929, Decimal File 811.111 QUOTA 12/152, *Records of the Department of State Relating to the Internal Affairs of the United States of America, 1914–1940* (hereafter cited as Decimal File 811).

9. See García, "Mexican Americans and the Politics of Citizenship."

10. The terms *traditional model* and *technocratic model* are borrowed from Pops, "Administrative Law as Public Policy."

11. This did not include "persons of African nativity or descent," who were allowed naturalization under an 1870 amendment to the naturalization laws.

12. Sheridan, "A Genealogy of Citizenship," 5.

13. Ibid., 152.

14. García, *White but Not Equal*, 14.

15. Perea, "The Black/White Binary Paradigm of Race," 1219.

16. Ibid., 1214.

17. Ibid., 1219.

18. Ibid., 1222–1223.

19. García, *White but Not Equal*, 15.

20. Ibid., 82.

21. Ibid., 87–88.

22. Ibid., 88.

23. Noel, "'The Swinging Door,'" 4–5.

24. García, "Mexican Americans and the Politics of Citizenship," 187–204.

25. William Lane Austin to George Wythe (Liaison Officer, Department of Commerce), August 29, 1939, Decimal File 811.4016/236.

26. Guglielmo, "Fighting for Caucasian Rights," 1212–1237.

27. Ibid., 1215.

28. In an e-mail to me, Thomas Guglielmo commented, "So whereas I wanted to push the Cold War Civil Rights folks to pay attention to the WWII years, you're saying we've got to go back even further. This is great."

29. Gellman, *Good Neighbor Diplomacy*; Gellman, *Secret Affairs*; Welles, *Sumner Welles.*

Notes to Chapter 2

1. "The Battling Bees," *Los Angeles Times*, September 7, 1923, II4.

2. "Charles Kenney McClatchy, 1858–1936," *McClatchy: The Employee Magazine of the McClatchy Company*, Spring 2007, 19–22. http://www.mcclatchy.com/129/.

3. "Valiant Val: McClatchy of the Bee Pummels a Deposed City Clerk," *Los Angeles Times*, January 23, 1896.

4. "Charles Kenney McClatchy," 22.

5. "Anti-Japan Land Law Discussed," *Los Angeles Times*, November 13, 1920, I2.

6. "M'Clatchy Split is Seen," *Los Angeles Times*, August 18, 1923, I1.

7. "Papers in Two Cities are Sold," *Los Angeles Times*, September 2, 1923, I5; "Buy Two Newspapers," *New York Times*, September 5, 1923, 26.

8. "Charles Kenney McClatchy," 22.

9. Divine, *American Immigration Policy*, 2; Van Vleck, *The Administrative Control of Aliens*, 3–6.

10. Van Vleck, *The Administrative Control of Aliens*, 6.

11. Curran, *Xenophobia and Immigration*, 18; Franklin, *The Legislative History of Naturalization in the United States*, 48.

12. Francisco Castillo Nájera (Mexican ambassador, Washington, DC) to Secretaría de Relaciones Exteriores (Mexico City), December 24, 1935, Secretaria de Relaciones Exteriores, *Timoteo Andrade File, 1935–37*, Serie III, legajo 2335, expediente 2 (hereafter cited as SRE File III-2335-2). All translations, and any errors therein, are by this author unless otherwise noted.

13. US House of Representatives, Committee on Immigration and Naturalization, *To Revise and Codify the Nationality Laws of the U.S. into a Comprehensive Nationality Code,* 76th Cong., 3rd Sess., 66.

14. Flournoy, "Naturalization and Expatriation (Part I)," 707.

15. Haney López, *White by Law*, 2.

16. Ibid., 7.

17. Ibid., 11.

18. Higham, *Strangers in the Land*, 4.

19. Ibid.

20. Curran, *Xenophobia and Immigration*, 47, 75.

21. Higham, *Strangers in the Land*, 45.

22. Divine, *American Immigration Policy*, 4; Higham, *Strangers in the Land*, 96.

23. Divine, *American Immigration Policy*, 4. See also Curran, *Xenophobia and Immigration*, 122.

24. Divine, *American Immigration Policy*, 4–5.

25. Gutiérrez, *Walls and Mirrors*, 47.

26. Reisler, *By the Sweat of Their Brow*, 24.

27. Divine, *American Immigration Policy*, 19.

28. President Rutherford B. Hayes vetoed the first bill in 1879 on the grounds that it violated the Burlingame Treaty of 1868, which allowed for reciprocal free entry for citizens of either country to the other. This treaty was renegotiated to allow immigration regulation, but not permanent exclusion. Making the act permanent in 1904 violated the treaty rights of the Chinese. Ibid., 20. See also Curran, *Xenophobia and Immigration*, 89–90.

29. Higham, *Strangers in the Land*, 166.

30. Gutiérrez, *Walls and Mirrors*, 43.

31. "Naturalization of Orientals Urged," *Los Angeles Times*, June 13, 1919, 19; "Sees Japanese Back of Dillingham Bill," *New York Times*, August 18, 1919, 4; "Phelan Calls Gulick Simply Agent of Japan," *Atlanta Constitution*, August 18, 1919, 2.

32. "Naturalization of Orientals Urged," *Los Angeles Times*, June 13, 1919, 19.

33. "Sees Japanese Back of Dillingham Bill," *New York Times*, August 18, 1919, 4; "Phelan Calls Gulick Simply Agent of Japan," *Atlanta Constitution*, August 18, 1919, 2.

34. Arthur Sears Henning, "Washington News in Brief," *Chicago Daily Tribune*, September 26, 1919, 3; "Passport Fake, 'Picture Brides,' Arousing West," *Chicago Daily Tribune*, September 26, 1919, 17; "Jap Exclusion Urged in House," *Los Angeles Times*, September 26, 1919, 13. See also "Congress Asked to Exclude the Japanese Accused of Breaking Immigration Barrier," *New York Times*, September 26, 1919, 13; "Charge Japanese Violate Agreement," *Boston Daily Globe*, September 26, 1919, 2.

35. Robert B. Armstrong, "Would Bar Japanese," *Los Angeles Times*, October 11, 1919, I1.

36. "Anti Japan Law Discussed," *Los Angeles Times*, November 13, 1920, I2.

37. "McClatchy in Star Chamber," *Los Angeles Times*, December 23, 1920, II1; "Stephens Confers on Jap Situation," *Los Angeles Times*, December 29, 1920, I6.

38. McClatchy, *Japanese Immigration and Colonization*.

39. "Congress Asked for Exclusion of All Japanese," *Chicago Daily Tribune*, April 19, 1921, 6.

40. Divine, *American Immigration Policy*, 22, 68.

41. Graham, "Introduction," in *The Idea of Race in Latin America*, 2.

42. Ibid., 2.

43. Divine, *American Immigration Policy*, 12. See also Higham, *Strangers in the Land*, 155; Thatcher, *Immigrants and the 1930s*, 26.

44. Higham, *Strangers in the Land*, 9.

45. Ibid., 151.

46. Divine, *American Immigration Policy*, 12; Higham, *Strangers in the Land*, 272.

47. Divine, *American Immigration Policy*, 22, 68.

48. Ngai, "The Architecture of Race," 70.

49. Tichenor, *Dividing Lines*, 170.

50. Divine, *American Immigration Policy*, 53.

51. James J. Davis (Secretary of Labor) to Albert Johnson (Chair, House Immigration Committee), February 5, 1929, *Records of the Department of State Relating to the Internal Affairs of the United States of America, 1914–1940*, Decimal File 811.111 QUOTA 12/152; Divine, *American Immigration Policy*, 52; Gutiérrez, *Walls and Mirrors*, 44; Reisler, *Sweat of Their Brow*, 58.

52. Gutiérrez, *Walls and Mirrors*, 39–40.

53. *Christian Science Monitor*, April 8, 1933, 14.

Notes to Chapter 3

1. "Four Bodies Act to Keep Ban Intact," *Los Angeles Times*, August 4, 1924, 2. Although the Los Angeles Times lists C. S. McClatchy as secretary, this is likely a typographical error, and the intended name is probably C. K. McClatchy.

2. Arthur Sears Henning, "New U.S. Alien Law Effective, Reed Says," *Washington Post*, March 15, 1925, F3.

3. "Most of Immigrants Now From New World," *Washington Post*, April 13, 1925, 9.

4. Divine, *American Immigration Policy*, 53.

5. Ibid.; Hoffman, *Unwanted Mexican Americans*, 13–14.

6. Divine, *American Immigration Policy*, 54.

7. *Congressional Record* (February 9, 1928), 2817–2818.

8. "Box Bill Plank Might Shaky," *Los Angeles Times*, July 31, 1930, 8.

9. James J. Davis (Secretary of Labor) to Albert Johnson (Chair, House Immigration Committee), February 5, 1929, Decimal File 811.111 QUOTA 12/152, *Records of the Department of State Relating to the Internal Affairs of the United States of America, 1914–1940* (hereafter cited as Decimal File 811). See

also Acuña, *Occupied America*, 185–186; Curran, *Xenophobia and Immigration*, 145; Hoffman, *Unwanted Mexican Americans*, 26.

10. Divine, *American Immigration Policy*, 56.

11. Gamio, *Mexican Immigration to the United States*, 31.

12. Acuña, *Corridors of Migration*, 90.

13. Ibid., 280–281.

14. "U. S. Labor Will Meet Mexicans in Capital," *Washington Post*, January 20, 1927, 5; see also "Labor Would Limit Mexican Immigration," *New York Times*, January 20, 1927, 48; "Labor Will Discuss Immigration Quota," *Atlanta Constitution*, January 20, 1927, 4.

15. "Will Urge Mexico to Curb Emigration," *New York Times*, October 9, 1927, 24.

16. "Labor Chiefs Hear Immigration Laws Praised by Davis," *Washington Post*, October 5, 1927, 3.

17. "Labor Men Clash on Mexican Influx," *New York Times*, October 12, 1927, 14.

18. "Labor Council Asks Union Drive in South," *New York Times*, October 7, 1929, 23.

19. "Pershing is Hailed as 1928 Candidate at Farm Gathering," *Washington Post*, December 8, 1927, 4.

20. C. M. Goethe, "For Immigration Restriction" letter to the editor, *Los Angeles Times*, August 8, 1930, A4.

21. "New Alien Ban Bill Presented," *Los Angeles Times*, January 21, 1931, 3.

22. "Seek to Tighten Immigration Laws," *Hartford Courant*, May 23, 1925, 5; "Registering Aliens is Plan to Tighten Immigration Law," *Washington Post*, August 16, 1925, AT7.

23. "Negro Population Found Decreasing," *New York Times*, March 20, 1927, 17.

24. Divine, *American Immigration Policy*, 56; See also Lipshultz, "American Attitudes Toward Mexican Immigration," 7; Reisler, *Sweat of Their Brow*, 160–163.

25. "Immigration From Mexico," *Washington Post*, May 15, 1926, 6.

26. Gutiérrez, *Walls and Mirrors*, 60.

27. Davis to Johnson, February 5, 1929, Decimal File 811.111 QUOTA 12/152.

28. Foerster, *The Racial Problems Involved in Immigration.*

29. Divine, *American Immigration Policy*, 57.

30. "Wants Limit Placed on All Immigration," *New York Times*, May 13, 1926, 8.

31. "Wants Quota Laws to Cover All Lands," *New York Times*, June 13, 1926, 24.

32. Mildred Adams, "Once More the Immigration Issue Rises," *New York Times*, January 16, 1927, XX1.

33. "Wants Quota Law Applied to Mexico," *New York Times*, May 19, 1927, 7.

34. "Curb Asked on Aliens: Move for Mexico Barrier Gains," *Los Angeles Times*, May 29, 1927, 6.

35. "Limitation on Mexican Immigration Discussed," *Washington Post*, August 1, 1927, 13; "Expects Move in House to Limit Entry of Mexicans: Chairman Johnson Says More Than 65,000 Came in During Year," *Hartford Courant*, August 1, 1927, 9.

36. Davis to Johnson, February 5, 1929, Decimal File 811.111 QUOTA 12/152.

37. Divine, *American Immigration Policy*, 58. See also Gutiérrez, *Walls and Mirrors*, 46–48; Hoffman, *Unwanted Mexican Americans*, 27; Reisler, *Sweat of Their Brow*, 174–175.

38. "Danger Seen in Mexican Quota," *Los Angeles Times*, January 12, 1926, 7.

39. "Fruit Growers Discuss Labor," *Los Angeles Times*, November 18, 1927, 7.

40. "Vitally Important Labor Supply Menaced by Impending Bill," *Los Angeles Times*, January 8, 1928, J4.

41. "It Must Not Pass!" editorial, *Los Angeles Times*, January 22, 1928, J4.

42. "Texan Defends Mexican Labor," *Los Angeles Times*, February 24, 1928, 7.

43. Hoffman, *Unwanted Mexican Americans*, 14–15.

44. Gutiérrez, *Walls and Mirrors*, 56.

45. Sheridan, "A Genealogy of Citizenship," 166.

46. Balderrama and Rodríguez, *Decade of Betrayal*, 19. See also Acuña, *Corridors of Migration*.

47. Lipshultz, "American Attitudes Toward Mexican Immigration," 5.

48. Divine, *American Immigration Policy*, 59. For these quotes, Divine cites "Immigration from Western Hemisphere," House *Hearings* (1928), 426; "Seasonal Agricultural Laborers," House *Hearings* (1926), 190; and "Restriction of Western Hemisphere Immigration," Senate *Hearings* (1928), 30, without specifying which quotes came from which hearings. See also Acuña, *Occupied America*, 187, who attributes the last quote to Texas Representative John N. Garner; and Reisler, *Sweat of Their Brow*, 179.

49. "Immigration Problems" editorial, *Washington Post*, May 17, 1927, 6.

50. "Our Mexican Residents" editorial, *Los Angeles Times*, May 25, 1927, A4.

51. Chapin Hall, "What the Country is Thinking About" editorial, *New York Times*, June 26, 1927, E1.

52. "Immigration Responsibilities" editorial, *Los Angeles Times*, September 26, 1927, A4.

53. Acuña, *Occupied America*, 188.

54. "Mexicans Watching Quota Move Here," *New York Times*, March 5, 1928, 8.

55. *Los Angeles Times*, March 6, 1928, 2.

56. State Department Memorandum from J. F. Simmons (Visa Division), April 29, 1929, Decimal File 811.111 QUOTA 12/152.

57. "Oppose Quota for Mexico," *Los Angeles Times*, April 22, 1925, 1.

58. "Kellogg Opposes David Quota Plan," *New York Times*, March 6, 1928, 13.

59. "Kellogg Pleas Kill Box Bill," *Los Angeles Times*, March 11, 1928, 9.

60. "Box Quota Bill Lost," *Los Angeles Times*, March 6, 1928, 1.

61. "Opposes Quota on Mexicans Now," *New York Times*, July 3, 1929, 8.

62. "Bar Sought on Canada," *Los Angeles Times*, July 16, 1929, 1.

63. Divine, *American Immigration Policy*, 61.

64. "Mexican Immigration" editorial, *Washington Post*, August 10, 1930, S1.

65. "Free Opposes Quota Scheme," *Los Angeles Times*, August 20, 1930, 3.

66. State Department Memorandum from Simmons, April 29, 1929, Decimal File 811.111 QUOTA 12/152; Thatcher, *Immigrants and the 1930s*, 103.

67. Hoffman, *Unwanted Mexican Americans*, 30.

68. See documents located in Decimal File 811.111 QUOTA 12/152.

69. Wilbur J. Carr (Assistant Secretary of State) to Henry L. Stimson (Secretary of State), May 1, 1929, Decimal File 811.111 QUOTA 12/152.

70. James J. Davis (Secretary of Labor) to Albert Johnson (Chair, House Immigration Committee), February 5, 1929, Decimal File 811.111 QUOTA 12/152.

71. Wilbur J. Carr (Assistant Secretary of State) to Henry L. Stimson (Secretary of State), July 12, 1929, Decimal File 811.111 QUOTA 12/152.

72. State Department Memorandum from J. F. Simmons (Visa Division), April 29, 1929, Decimal File 811.111 QUOTA 12/152.

73. Reisler, *Sweat of Their Brow*, 231; Thatcher, *Immigrants and the 1930s*, 105.

74. Divine, *American Immigration Policy*, 68.

75. Arthur Sears Henning, "New U.S. Alien Law Effective, Reed Says," *Washington Post*, March 15, 1925, F3.

76. "Quota Battle Starts Next Week," *Los Angeles Times*, January 28, 1928, 1.

77. "Battles Brew on Quota Issue," *Los Angeles Times*, February 20, 1928, 5.

78. "Quota for Canada Meets Opposition," *New York Times*, February 22, 1928, 38.

79. "Hearing on Box Measure Opens," *Los Angeles Times*, February 22, 1928, 8.

80. "Box Shifts Emphasis," *Los Angeles Times*, March 3, 1928, 2.

81. "Mexican Quota Fight Renewed," *Los Angeles Times*, March 29, 1928, 7.

82. "Final Hearing Given Box Bill," *Los Angeles Times*, April 6, 1928, 9.

83. "Alien Curb for Border Passed Up," *Los Angeles Times*, May 22, 1928, 4.

84. "Mexican Quota Fight to go on," *Los Angeles Times*, October 2, 1928, 5.

85. "Mexican Quota Plans Mapped," *Los Angeles Times*, November 6, 1928, 8.

86. "Mexican Quota Hearing Balked," *Los Angeles Times*, November 22, 1928, 2.

87. "Pleas for Peon Ban Held Rising," *Los Angeles Times*, November 23, 1928, 4.

88. "Influx Cut at Border," *Los Angeles Times*, January 11, 1929, 1.

89. "Immigrant Bill Sent to Senate," *Los Angeles Times*, December 15, 1928, 1.

90. "Kellogg Seeks Cut on Mexican Entry," *New York Times*, January 16, 1929, 9.

91. "Bar Sought on Canada," *Los Angeles Times*, July 16, 1929, 1.

92. "Mexican Quota Bobs Up Again," *Los Angeles Times*, September 7, 1929, 3.

93. "Plans Limit on Entry from the Americas," *New York Times*, December 1, 1929, 27.

94. "Restriction Idea Hit," *Los Angeles Times*, December 10, 1929, 1.

95. "Would Cut Influx of Western Aliens," *New York Times*, January 14, 1930, 11.

96. Laurence M. Benedict, "Bills Banning Mexicans Attacked at Hearing," *Los Angeles Times*, January 21, 1930, 7.

97. "Day in Congress," *Washington Post*, February 18, 1930, 2; Laurence M. Benedict, "Harris Bill Reported," *Los Angeles Times*, February 18, 1930, 1.

98. "For Quota of 76,064 from the Americas," *New York Times*, February 27, 1930, 14.

99. Laurence M. Benedict, "Immigration Bill Reported," *Los Angeles Times*, February 28, 1930, 4.

100. "A Dangerous Proposal," *Hartford Courant*, March 1, 1930, 14.

101. "Free to Protest Against Mexican Quota Measure," *Los Angeles Times*, March 13, 1930, 1; "Mexican Quota Bill Attacked," *Los Angeles Times*, March 19, 1930, 3.

102. "Move Made for Bill on Mexicans," *Los Angeles Times*, March 22, 1930, 1.

103. "Immigration Law Praised by Cotton," *Washington Post*, April 6, 1930, 15; see also "Exclusion Bill Stirs New Foes," *Los Angeles Times*, April 6, 1930, 7.

104. "7,000,000 Need Jobs in U.S. says Harris," *Washington Post*, April 11, 1930, 2.

105. "Pass Bill to Apply Quota to Mexicans," *New York Times*, May 14, 1930, 56; "Senate Passes Bill to Limit Mexicans," *Washington Post*, May 14, 1930, 7.

106. Laurence M. Benedict, "Bill Barring Mexicans Goes Through Senate," *Los Angeles Times*, May 14, 1930, 1.

107. Laurence M. Benedict, "Bill Barring Mexicans Goes Through Senate," *Los Angeles Times*, May 14, 1930, 1.

108. "Mexican Quota Fight Thickens," *Los Angeles Times*, May 15, 1930, 12.

109. "Seeks Drastic Curb on Entry of Aliens," *New York Times*, May 18, 1930, 16.

110. Laurence M. Benedict, "Quota Fight Finis [*sic*] Near," *Los Angeles Times*, May 22, 1930, 1.

111. Laurence M. Benedict, "Quota Bill Advanced," *Los Angeles Times*, May 23, 1930, 1.

112. Laurence M. Benedict, "Harris Bill Hard Hit," *Los Angeles Times*, May 29, 1930, 1.

113. "Labor Inquiry move Favored," *Los Angeles Times*, June 12, 1930, 3.

114. "Farm Labor Survey Bill Smothered," *Los Angeles Times*, June 20, 1930, 1.

115. "Immigration Slash of One-Half Asked," *Washington Post*, June 24, 1930, 2; "Immigration Cut Of 50 P. C. Proposed To Aid Unemployment," *Hartford Courant*, June 24, 1930, 2.

116. Laurence M. Benedict, "Mexican Flood Ebbs to Dribble," *Los Angeles Times*, September 25, 1930, 13.

117. "Box Bill Plank Might Shaky," *Los Angeles Times*, July 31, 1930, 8.

118. Biographical Directory of the United States Congress, 1774–Present, http://bioguide.congress.gov.

119. A. H. Ulm, "Most of World Now Curbs Immigration," *New York Times*, December 14, 1930, XX5.

120. "New Alien Ban Bill Presented," *Los Angeles Times*, January 21, 1931, 3.

121. "Bill to Restrict Aliens Approved," *Washington Post*, January 23, 1931, 2; "Would Cut Immigration," *New York Times*, January 28, 1931, 15; "Bill to Curb Alien Entry is Reported," *Washington Post*, January 28, 1931, 3.

122. Divine, *American Immigration Policy*, 66.

123. "Aliens Barred Out," *Washington Post*, March 30, 1931, 6.

124. Laurence M. Benedict, "Mexico Facing Quota System," *Los Angeles Times*, December 13, 1931, 18.

125. "Senate Bill Reported to Fix Mexican Quota," *New York Times*, January 17, 1932, 2.

126. "Mexican Quota Bill Deferred," *Los Angeles Times*, January 26, 1932, 6.

127. "State Against Mexican Bars," *Los Angeles Times*, February 24, 1932, 5.

128. Tucker et al., *Immigration and U.S. Foreign Policy*, 50.

Notes to Chapter 4

1. Green, *The Containment of Latin America*, vii.
2. Wood, *The Making of the Good Neighbor Policy*, 7.
3. Gellman, *Good Neighbor Diplomacy*, 1.

4. Schoultz, *Beneath the United States*, 295.

5. Gellman, *Good Neighbor Diplomacy*, 11–12.

6. Ibid., 14; Welles, *Sumner Welles*, 2.

7. Memorandum from Sumner Welles, December 12, 1935, Decimal File 812.404/1829A, *Records of the Department of State Relating to the Internal Affairs of Mexico, 1930–1939*.

8. Conkin, *The New Deal*, 21.

9. Leuchtenberg, *Franklin D. Roosevelt*, 63.

10. Conkin, *The New Deal*, 51.

11. Pops, "Administrative Law as Public Policy," 98–117.

12. Shapiro, "Judicial Activism," 110. Shapiro argues, however, that this model "is just as universally wrong as it is universally held."

13. Pops, "Administrative Law as Public Policy," 101.

14. Schwartz, *An Introduction to American Administrative Law*, 35. See also Shapiro, "On Predicting," 19.

15. Woll, *Administrative Law*, 7–8. See also Shapiro, "Administrative Discretion," 1496; Shapiro, "On Predicting," 19.

16. Shapiro, "Administrative Discretion," 1496; Shapiro, "On Predicting," 19.

17. Shapiro, "Judicial Activism," 113.

18. Badger, *The New Deal*, 80.

19. Nonet, *Administrative Justice*, 3.

20. Pops, "Administrative Law as Public Policy," 102.

21. Conkin, *The New Deal*, 90.

22. Ibid., 58; Badger, *The New Deal*, 74; Leuchtenberg, *Franklin D. Roosevelt*, 96.

23. Shapiro, "On Predicting," 19; Shapiro, *Who Guards the Guardians?*, 36–38.

24. Cooper, *Public Law and Public Administration*, 80.

25. Nonet, *Administrative Justice*, 5.

26. Rosenbloom, *Public Administration and Law*, 53, referring to the title of chapter 4 in Jackson, *The Struggle for Judicial Supremacy*.

27. Rosenbloom, *Public Administration and Law*, 54. Emphasis in original.

28. Jackson, *The Struggle for Judicial Supremacy*, 115.

29. Leuchtenberg, *Franklin D. Roosevelt*, 144.

30. Jackson, *The Struggle for Judicial Supremacy*, chapter 4.

31. *A. L. A. Schechter Poultry Corp. et al. v. United States*, 295 U.S. 495 (1935), 529.

32. Rosenbloom and O'Leary, *Public Administration and Law*, 37.

33. Conkin, *The New Deal*, 92.

34. See the *American Historical Review* Forum, a series of four articles by Alan Brinkley, Laura Kalman, William Leuchtenburg, and G. Edward White, published in the October 2005 issue. Quote from Brinkley, "AHR Forum: Introduction," par. 7.

35. Conkin, *The New Deal*, 93; Cooper, *Public Law and Public Administration*, 78; Rosenbloom and O'Leary, *Public Administration and Law*, 37.

36. Rosenbloom and O'Leary, *Public Administration and Law*, 38. See also Shapiro, "Judicial Activism," 113.

37. Shapiro, "Judicial Activism," 123. See also Shapiro, *Who Guards the Guardians?*, 62.

Notes to Chapter 5

1. Graham, "Introduction," 1.

2. Morner, *Race Mixture*, 4.

3. Perea, "The Black/White Binary Paradigm of Race," 1235.

4. Stepan, *"The Hour of Eugenics,"* 136.

5. Graham, "Introduction," 1.

6. Grace E. Benjamin, University of Texas, Austin, to Cordell Hull, Secretary of State, September 21, 1935, Decimal File 812.401/8, *Records of the Department of State Relating to the Internal Affairs of Mexico, 1930–1939* (hereafter cited as Decimal File 812).

7. R. Walton Moore to Grace Benjamin, September 26, 1935, Decimal File 812.401/8.

8. Chief, Bureau of American Ethnology, Smithsonian Institution to Grace Benjamin, September 30, 1935, Decimal File 812.401/9.

9. University of Texas, *Texas' Children*.

10. Meyer et al., *The Course of Mexican History*, 550.

11. Ruiz, *Triumphs and Tragedy*, 375.

12. Acuña, *Corridors of Migration*, 21–22.

13. While blacks and Indians were near the bottom of the caste system, those who were a product of their racial intermixture were believed to have inherited the worst of both races. Unlike a social class system, where societal position is based on economic standing, in a caste system, individuals are born to their position in life based on race. There is little opportunity for those at the bottom of a caste system to move up the social ladder.

14. González Navarro, "*Mestizaje* in Mexico," , 146; Knight, "Racism, Revolution, and *Indigenismo*," 72–73.

15. Morner, *Race Mixture*, 6.

16. Justo Sierra, quoted in Knight, "Racism, Revolution, and *Indigenismo*," 78.

17. Stepan, *"The Hour of Eugenics,"* 135.

18. Graham, "Introduction," 2–3.

19. Stepan, *"The Hour of Eugenics,"* 137.

20. Knight, "Racism, Revolution, and *Indigenismo*," 80.

21. Graham, "Introduction," 3. See also Knight, "Racism, Revolution, and *Indigenismo*," 82; Stepan, *"The Hour of Eugenics,"* 146.

22. Stepan, *"The Hour of Eugenics,"* 146.

23. Knight, "Racism, Revolution, and *Indigenismo*," 83.

24. Ibid., 85.

25. Stepan, *"The Hour of Eugenics,"* 147.

26. Knight, "Racism, Revolution, and *Indigenismo*," 87.

27. Stepan, *"The Hour of Eugenics,"* 148.

28. Ibid., 149.

29. Knight, "Racism, Revolution, and *Indigenismo*," 86–87.

30. Stepan, *"The Hour of Eugenics,"* 153.

31. Editorial, *El Día*, December 13, 1935, attached to R. Henry Norweb (Chargé d'Affairs, US Embassy, Mexico City) to Secretary of State (Washington, DC), December 20, 1935, Decimal File 132.1/34, *Records of the Department of State Relating to Citizenship of the United States* (hereafter cited as Decimal File 132). Translated by US Embassy, Mexico City.

32. Graham, "Introduction," 4.

33. Knight, "Racism, Revolution, and *Indigenismo*," 74.

34. González Navarro, "*Mestizaje* in Mexico," 152.

35. Biography of Alonso Perales, Handbook of Texas Online, http://www.tshaonline.org/handbook/online/articles/PP/fpe56.html.

36. Márquez, *LULAC*, 25.

37. Biography of J. T. Canales, Handbook of Texas Online, http://www.tshaonline.org/handbook/online/articles/CC/fcaag.html.

38. Biography of Ben Garza, Handbook of Texas Online, http://www.tshaonline.org/handbook/online/articles/GG/fga85.html.

39. Rosales, *Chicano*, 70.

40. Alvarez, *Familia*, 153–154.

41. Pike, *FDR's Good Neighbor Policy*, 106–107.

42. Gómez, *Manifest Destinies*, Kindle Edition Locations 1855–1875.

43. Ibid., Kindle Edition Locations 1007–1033.

44. McCoyer, "Darkness of a Different Color," 136–137.

45. Ibid., 168.

46. Montejano, *Anglos and Mexicans in the Making of Texas*, 50–51; 113–115 (quote from 115).

47. Acuña, *Corridors of Migration*, 220–221.

48. Ibid., 88.

49. Ibid., 90.

50. Ibid.

51. Ibid., 222. Also see 204.

52. Noel, "'The Swinging Door,'" 110–111.

53. Editorial, *El Mensajero* (Phoenix, Arizona), December 15, 1935, quoted in *El Tucsonense* (Tucson, Arizona), December 17, 1935, 1.

54. Editorial, *El Tucsonense* (Tucson, Arizona), October 30, 1936.

55. Pike, *FDR's Good Neighbor Policy*, 102–103.

56. Montejano, *Anglos and Mexicans in the Making of Texas*, 181.
57. Sheridan, "'Another White Race,'", 112 (citing Montejano).
58. Ngai, "The Architecture of Race," 91.
59. Gamio, *Mexican Immigration to the United States*, 53.
60. Pike, *FDR's Good Neighbor Policy*, 104–105.
61. Gómez-Quiñones, *Roots of Chicano Politics*, 360–361.
62. Gutiérrez, *Walls and Mirrors*, 70.
63. García, *Mexican Americans*, 32.
64. James J. Davis (Secretary of Labor) to Albert Johnson (Chair, House Immigration Committee), February 5, 1929, Decimal File 811.111 QUOTA 12/152, *Records of the Department of State Relating to the Internal Affairs of the United States of America, 1914–1940* (hereafter cited as Decimal File 811).
65. Gutiérrez, *Walls and Mirrors*, 85–86.
66. García, *Mexican Americans*, 6–7.
67. Guglielmo, "Fighting for Caucasian Rights," 1213.
68. Haney López, *White by Law*, 153.
69. Haney López, *Racism on Trial*, 77.
70. Perales, *En Defensa de mi Raza*, Primero tomo, 29.
71. Gutiérrez, *Walls and Mirrors*, 75.
72. US Congress, House Immigration Committee, *Western Hemisphere Immigration*. 71st Cong., 2nd Sess., January 29, 1930, testimony of J. T. Canales, 172–173, 178–179.
73. Ibid., testimony of Alonso S. Perales, 181.
74. Ibid. In his statement, Perales cited Floyd H. Allport, professor of social and political psychology, Syracuse University.
75. Ibid., January 30, 1930, 191.
76. Ibid., January 29, 1930, testimony of J. T. Canales, 171.
77. Ibid., testimony of Alonso S. Perales, 183.
78. Gómez-Quiñones, *Roots of Chicano Politics*, 308.
79. Perales, *En Defensa de mi Raza*, Primero tomo, 29.
80. García, *Mexican Americans*, 43.
81. Ibid., n.p.
82. Ibid., 17–20.
83. Gutiérrez, *Walls and Mirrors*, 72.
84. Balderrama and Rodríguez, *Decade of Betrayal*, 2–3.
85. Gómez-Quiñones, *Roots of Chicano Politics*, 374.
86. Hoffman, *Unwanted Mexican Americans*, 126.
87. Aguila, "Protecting 'México de Afuera,'" 211.
88. Balderrama and Rodríguez, *Decade of Betrayal*, 122.
89. Gutiérrez, *Walls and Mirrors*, 77–78.
90. Montejano, *Anglos and Mexicans in the Making of Texas*, 225.
91. García, "The Case of El Paso," 188; *Eagle Pass Daily Guide* (section in Spanish), October 15, 1936, attached to J. Gorostiza (Head of the Press and

Publications Section) to Head of the Diplomatic Department, October 21, 1936, Secretaria de Relaciones Exteriores, *Timoteo Andrade File, 1935–37*, (hereafter cited as SRE File III-2335-2).

92. García, "The Case of El Paso," 188.

93. *Eagle Pass Daily Guide*, October 15, 1936, SRE File III-2335-2.

94. "Los Mexicanos Como Negros en El Paso, Texas," *El Tucsonense* (Tucson, Arizona), October 27, 1936.

95. *El Continental* (El Paso, Texas), October 7, 1936.

96. García, "The Case of El Paso," 191.

97. See, e.g., *El Continental* (El Paso, Texas) from October 6 to November 22, 1936.

98. *El Paso Herald-Post*, October 8, 1936, cited in García, "The Case of El Paso," 192.

99. Frank J. Galván to all LULAC Councils, October 8, 1936, reproduced in Perales, *En Defensa de mi Raza*, Segundo tomo, 32–33.

100. García, "The Case of El Paso," 198–199; Perales, *En Defensa de mi Raza*, Segundo tomo, 27–28.

101. Maury Maverick (Representative of the Twentieth District of Texas) to William Austin (Director, US Census Bureau), October 15, 1936, reproduced in Perales, *En Defensa de mi Raza*, Segundo tomo, 35.

102. García, "The Case of El Paso," 199; Perales, *En Defensa de mi Raza*, Segundo tomo, 35.

103. *La Prensa* (San Antonio), October 20, 1936, reproduced in Perales, *En Defensa de mi Raza*, Segundo tomo, 39.

104. Francisco Castillo Nájera (Mexican Ambassador, Washington, DC) to Cordell Hull (Secretary of State, Washington, DC), March 19, 1937, Decimal File 132.1/83; William Lane Austin (Director, Census Bureau) to Edward J. Shaughnessy (Acting Commissioner, INS), March 31, 1937, Decimal File 132.1/83. Emphasis in original.

105. García, "The Case of El Paso," 199. See also William Lane Austin to Maury Maverick, October 15, 1936, reproduced in Perales, *En Defensa de mi Raza*, Segundo tomo, 35.

106. William Lane Austin to George Wythe (Liaison Officer, Department of Commerce), August 29, 1939, Decimal File 811.4016/236.

107. García, "The Case of El Paso," 199; Perales, *En Defensa de mi Raza*, Segundo tomo, 53; Rosales, "Shifting Self Perceptions," 80.

108. Rosales, "Shifting Self Perceptions," 81; Joe Eagle (Texas Representative) to Frank Bane (Executive Director, Social Security Board), November 25, 1936, from Kreneck Private Papers (in the possession of Professor F. Arturo Rosales, Department of History, Arizona State University).

109. *La Prensa* (San Antonio), November 24 and 26, 1936, reproduced in Perales, *En Defensa de mi Raza*, Segundo tomo, 52–55, 55–59.

110. *La Prensa* (San Antonio), November 26, 1936; Perales, *En Defensa de mi Raza*, Segundo tomo, 59–60.

Notes to Chapter 6

1. Andrade's citizenship petition lists January 24, 1898, as his date of birth, but both his draft registration and his Social Security application list January 24, 1897. Timoteo's draft registration from El Paso Local Board No. 2 can be found through a search on http://www.ancestry.com. Social Security application (Form SS-5) of Timoteo Andrade, 070-07-6041, provided by SSA through Freedom of Information request (Form SSA-711). See http://www.ssa.gov/foia/html/foia_guide.htm.Citizenship Petition of Timoteo Andrade.

2. Andrade appears in the 1920 Census in Tucson, Arizona, with a ten-month-old daughter named Maria, born in Texas. The Andrade family's 1920 Census listing was found through a search on http://www.ancestry.com.

3. Andrade appears in the 1930 Census in Buffalo, New York, with a nine-year-old daughter whose name is illegible, born in Texas, an eight-year-old son named Michael, born in Illinois, a six-year-old daughter named Maria (obviously not the same Maria born in 1919), and a three-year-old son named Timoteo Jr., both born in Buffalo. Timoteo and Sara must have lost two daughters, as his Declaration of Intention, dated 1929, and his naturalization petition, dated 1935, list only Michael, Maria, and Timoteo Jr. Citizenship Petition of Timoteo Andrade. The Andrade family's 1930 Census record was found through a search on http://www.ancestry.com.

4. Biography of John Knight, Biographical Directory of Federal Judges, http://www.fjc.gov/servlet/nGetInfo?jid-1296&cid-999&ctype-na&instate-na; "Knight is Slated for Federal Bench," *New York Times*, February 22, 1931, 5:3.

5. Biography of John Knight, http://www.fjc.gov/servlet/nGetInfo?jid-1296&cid-999&ctype-na&instate-na.

6. "Judgeship for Knight Causes Erie Revolt," *New York Times*, February 25, 1931, 15:6; and "Erie Man for Judge Urged Upon President," February 26, 4:3.

7. "For Knight's Nomination," *New York Times*, January 5, 1932, 17:2.

8. Divine, *American Immigration Policy*, 22, 68.

9. California Joint Immigration Committee, "Mexican Indians Denied Naturalization," Press Release, December 30, 1935, Folder 9, Item 6; California Joint Immigration Committee Collection.

10. "Mexico Indians in Barred List," *Los Angeles Times*, October 8, 1929, 10.

11. V. S. McClatchy (Executive Secretary, California Joint Immigration Committee, San Francisco, CA) to W. N. Doak (Secretary of Labor, Washington, DC), December 11, 1931, Folder 4, Item 5, California Joint Immigration Committee Collection. McClatchy quoted Doak back to himself when he took over the correspondence begun by Regan.

12. James J. Davis (Secretary of Labor) to Albert Johnson (Chair, House Immigration Committee), February 5, 1929, Decimal File 811.111 QUOTA 12/152, *Records of the Department of State Relating to the Internal Affairs of the United States of America, 1914–1940*.

13. McCoyer, "Darkness of a Different Color," 178.

14. *In re Rodriguez*, 81 Fed. 337 (May 3, 1897), 337.
15. de Leon, *The Tejano Community*, 25, 33.
16. *In re Rodriguez*, 348.
17. Ibid., 338.
18. Ibid., 339–340.
19. Ibid., 342–343.
20. Ibid., 344, 346.
21. Ibid., 338.
22. Ibid., 349.
23. *In re Camille*, 6 Fed. 256 (1880), 257.
24. Ibid., 258.
25. *In re Rodriguez*, 349.
26. Ibid., 352.
27. Ibid., 353.
28. Gold, "The Racial Prerequisite," 499.
29. Gómez, *Manifest Destinies*, Kindle Edition Locations 3096–3125. Emphasis in original.
30. R. W. Flournoy (Legal Adviser) to R. Walton Moore (Assistant Secretary of State), July 26, 1937, Decimal File 132.1/96, *Records of the Department of State Relating to Citizenship of the United States* (hereafter cited as Decimal File 132).
31. McClatchy to Doak, December 11, 1931; California Joint Immigration Committee Collection, Folder 4, Item 5.
32. Gold, "The Racial Prerequisite," 500–501.
33. McClatchy to Doak, December 11, 1931, California Joint Immigration Committee Collection, Folder 4, Item 5.
34. Gold, "The Racial Prerequisite," 463–464.
35. "Mexico Indians in Barred List," *Los Angeles Times*, October 8, 1929, 10; *Takao Ozawa v. United States*, 260 U.S. 178 (1922); *United States v. Bhagat Singh Thind*, 261 U.S. 204 (1923).
36. McClatchy to Doak, December 11, 1931, California Joint Immigration Committee Collection, Folder 4, Item 5.
37. *Ozawa v. United States*, 182.
38. Ibid., 188. Interestingly, although it was not included in the record, it is noted that Ulysses S. Webb, attorney general for the state of California and member of the CJIC, also filed a brief in this case as amicus curiae. This case set the precedent that Japanese were ineligible for naturalization. Then, in 1924, the Johnson-Reed Act prohibited the immigration of those ineligible for naturalization.
39. Ibid., 195. Emphasis in original.
40. The cases cited in both *Rodriguez* and *Ozawa* are *In re Ah Yup* (1 Fed. 223), *In re Camille* (6 Fed. 256), *In re Kanaka Nian* (21 Pac. 993), and *In re Saito* (62 Fed. 256).
41. *Ozawa v. United States*, 198.
42. *United States v. Thind*, 205.

43. Ibid., 214–215.

44. Flournoy, "The Need of Amending Existing Citizenship Laws," 49.

45. McClatchy to Doak, December 11, 1931, California Joint Immigration Committee Collection, Folder 4, Item 5.

46. California Joint Immigration Committee, "Mexican Indians Denied Naturalization," December 30, 1935, Folder 9, Item 6.

47. *Morrison et al. v. People of the State of California*, 291 U.S. 82 (1934).

48. McGovney, "Naturalization of the Mixed-Blood," 377.

49. *Morrison v. California*, 86.

50. Ibid., 95 footnote 5.

51. Henry Hazard of the Labor Department subsequently called Murff's recommendation a "mistake" that was not in line with the Labor Department's policy toward the naturalization of Mexican nationals. See J. F. Simmons (State Department Visa Division) to Sumner Welles (Assistant Secretary of State), December 17, 1935, Decimal File 132.1/31.

52. Francisco Castillo Nájera (Mexican Ambassador, Washington, DC) to Secretaria de Relaciones Exteriores (Mexico City), December 18, 1935, Secretaria de Relaciones Exteriores, *Timoteo Andrade File, 1935–37*, (hereafter cited as SRE File III-2335-2).

53. Ibid.

54. Opinion of Judge Knight, December 11, 1935, Citizenship Petition of Timoteo Andrade.

55. *In re Camille*, 257–258.

56. Opinion of Judge Knight, December 11, 1935, Citizenship Petition of Timoteo Andrade.

57. California Joint Immigration Committee, "Mexican Indians Denied Naturalization."

58. Ibid.

59. R. W. Flournoy (State Department Legal Adviser) to Cordell Hull (Secretary of State), March 16, 1937, Decimal File 132.1/221.

60. Ibid.

61. Walter E. Barry (Attorney at Law, Los Angeles) to Julian Velarde (President, Latin American Chamber of Commerce, Los Angeles), February 5, 1936, SRE File III-2335-2.

62. Velarde to Eduardo Hay (Secretario de Relaciones Exteriores, Mexico City), February 7, 1936, SRE File III-2335-2.

63. Francisco Castillo Nájera (Mexican Ambassador to the United States, Washington, DC) to Secretaria de Relaciones Exteriores, March 12, 1936, SRE File III-2335-2.

Notes to Chapter 7

1. Flournoy published several legal essays on US and international nationality laws, as well as delivering an address on the topic before the Federal Bar

Association. Also, historian Mary Anne Thatcher made several references to Flournoy's role in advising the State Department on immigration and naturalization. See Thatcher, *Immigrants and the 1930s*, 120, 259. Much of Flournoy's work is also currently being reproduced as a part of Kessinger Publishing's Legacy Reprint Series.

2. Borchard, "Three Hague Conventions on Nationality," 127; Flournoy, "The Nationality Act of 1940," 1.

3. "Indian Blood Bars Mexicans as Citizens: Judge Knight at Buffalo Denies Petitions of Three for Naturalization," *New York Times*, December 12, 1935, 4:4; *Buffalo Courier-Express*, December 12, 1935. See also "Mexicans Barred?," *Dallas Journal*, date unknown, attached to A. Teja Zabre (Head of the Department of Publicity, Mexico City) to Head of the Diplomatic Department (Mexico City), December 21, 1935, Secretaria de Relaciones Exteriores, *Timoteo Andrade File* (hereafter cited as SRE File III-2335-2).

4. Alexander K. Sloan (American Consul, Mexico City) to Secretary of State (Washington, DC), December 12, 1935, Decimal File 132.1/32 1/2, *Records of the Department of State Relating to Citizenship of the United States* (hereafter cited as Decimal File 132).

5. Memorandum from J. F. Simmons (State Department Visa Division), December 13, 1935, Decimal File 132.1/32.

6. Enrique Elizondo (Mexican Consul General, New York, NY) to Mexican Ambassador (Washington, DC), December 13, 1935, SRE File III-2335-2.

7. Elizondo to Secretario de Relaciones Exteriores (Mexico City), December 12, 1935, SRE File III-2335-2.

8. Mexican Embassy Press Release, December 13, 1935, SRE File III-2335-2.

9. Francisco Castillo Nájera (Mexican Ambassador, Washington, DC) to SRE, December 13, 1935, SRE File III-2335-2.

10. Memorandum from Sumner Welles, December 12, 1935, Decimal File 812.404/1829A, *Records of the Department of State Relating to the Internal Affairs of Mexico, 1930–1939*.

11. "Mexico Protests Ruling," *New York Times*, December 14, 1935, 3:5; *El Nacional* article summarized in Norweb to Secretary of State, December 20, 1935, Decimal File 132.1/34.

12. Memorandum from Edward L. Reed (State Department Division of Mexican Affairs), December 14, 1935, Decimal File 132.1/30.

13. J. F. Simmons to Sumner Welles (Assistant Secretary of State), December 17, 1935, Decimal File 132.1/31.

14. Elizondo to SRE, December 14, 1935, SRE File III-2335-2.

15. Castillo Nájera to SRE, December 18, 1935, SRE File III-2335-2.

16. Ibid.

17. Ibid.

18. Castillo Nájera to SRE, December 24, 1935, SRE File III-2335-2.

19. Ibid.

20. Ibid.

21. Rafael de la Colina (Consul General, New York, NY) to SRE, February 17, 1936, SRE File III-2335-2. While no explanation of the decisions is provided on their naturalization petitions, Bravo became a US citizen, while Velez did not. Citizenship Petition of Porfirio Bravo, Box 24, Petition #24022; Citizenship Petition of Francisco Velez, Box 25, Petition #24272.

22. Record of Testimony, Citizenship Petition of Timoteo Andrade.

23. Ibid.

24. Ibid.

25. Examiner White's notes, Citizenship Petition of Timoteo Andrade.

26. Social Security application (Form SS-5) of Timoteo Andrade, 070-07-6041, provided by SSA through Freedom of Information request (Form SSA-711). See http://www.ssa.gov/foia/html/foia_guide.htm

27. R. W. Flournoy (Legal Adviser) to Sumner Welles, May 18, 1936, Decimal File 132.1/28.

28. Opinion of Judge Knight, June 1, 1936, Citizenship Petition of Timoteo Andrade.

29. Luis Quintanilla (Chargé d'Affaires, Mexican Embassy, Washington, DC) to Eduardo Hay (Secretario de Relaciones Exteriores, Mexico City), June 17, 1936, SRE File III-2335-2.

30. Ibid.

31. Like Flournoy, Henry Hazard was a federal attorney who was experienced in naturalization and immigration law. In fact, Hazard had written a companion piece to Flournoy's Federal Bar Association article. See Hazard, "Safeguarding American Citizenship," 19–21.

32. Green H. Hackworth (Legal Adviser) to Wilbur J. Carr (Assistant Secretary of State) and Cordell Hull (Secretary of State), July 23, 1936, Decimal File 132.1/51. The Hackworth memorandum mentions only "Judge Cox" and "Southern District of New York." The only "Judge Cox" in that district in July 1936 was federal judge Alfred Conkling Coxe Jr. See the records of the Federal Judicial Center (http://www.fjc.gov/history/home.nsf) for biographical sketches of all federal judges since 1789.

33. See handwritten note attached to Hackworth to Carr and Hull, July 23, 1936, Decimal File 132.1/51.

Notes to Chapter 8

1. Whiteman, "Green Haywood Hackworth," 91–94.

2. Ibid., 92.

3. The State Department records in Decimal File 132 contain no documents relating to this situation for the period of July 1936 to March 1937. When the issue resurfaced in 1937, Flournoy's memo stated, "see memoranda in this office, the Mexican Division, and the Visa Division in December 1935–July 1936, including the memorandum of this office of July 23, 1936, concerning a previ-

ous discussion of these cases." R. W. Flournoy (Legal Adviser) to Cordell Hull (Secretary of State), March 16, 1937, Decimal File 132.1/221, *Records of the Department of State Relating to Citizenship of the United States* (hereafter cited as Decimal File 132).

4. Ibid.

5. US Congress, Senate, *Revision and Codification of the Nationality Laws of the United States*, 76th Cong., 3rd Sess., September 23, 1940, 2.

6. Flournoy to Hull, March 16, 1937, Decimal File 132.1/221.

7. Ibid.

8. Ibid.

9. J. F. Simmons (Visa Division) to Wilbur J. Carr (Assistant Secretary of State) and Cordell Hull (Secretary of State), March 31, 1937, Decimal File 132.1/77.

10. Ibid.

11. García, "The Case of El Paso," 187–204.

12. Mexican Ambassador Francisco Castillo Nájera to Secretary of State Hull, March 19, 1937, Decimal File 132.1/83.

13. Excerpt from Castillo Nájera's letter to Hull, transcribed in memorandum from J. F. Simmons (Visa Division) and R. W. Flournoy (Legal Adviser), April 6, 1937, Decimal File 132.1/83. Translated by State Department.

14. Flournoy to Hull, March 16, 1937, Decimal File 132.1/221.

15. Joint Memorandum from Simmons and Flournoy, April 6, 1937, Decimal File 132.1/83.

16. Ibid. Those involved in these discussions were Carr, Hackworth, Flournoy, and Simmons of the State Department, Shaughnessy, Hazard, and Hiss of the Labor Department, and Butler and Fischer of the Justice Department.

17. W. L. Austin (Director, Census Bureau) to Edward Shaughnessy (Acting Commissioner, INS), March 31, 1937, Decimal File 132.1/83; Leon Truesdell (Chief Statistician for Population, Census Bureau) to Henry Hazard (Assistant to the Commissioner, INS), March 31, 1937, Decimal File 132.1/83; Wilbur J. Carr (Assistant Secretary of State) to Cordell Hull (Secretary of State), April 12, 1937, Decimal File 132.1/83.

18. Joint Memorandum from Simmons and Flournoy, April 6, 1937, Decimal File 132.1/83; Wilbur J. Carr (Assistant Secretary of State) to Cordell Hull (Secretary of State), April 12, 1937, Decimal File 132.1/83.

19. Joint Memorandum from Simmons and Flournoy, April 6, 1937, Decimal File 132.1/83; Joint Memorandum from Henry B. Hazard (Administrative Assistant to Commissioner of Immigration and Naturalization) and Edward J. Shaughnessy (Deputy Commissioner of Immigration and Naturalization), April 7, 1937, Decimal File 132.1/83; Wilbur J. Carr (Assistant Secretary of State) to Cordell Hull (Secretary of State), April 12, 1937, Decimal File 132.1/83.

20. Sumner Welles (Assistant Secretary of State) to Cordell Hull (Secretary of State), April 20, 1937, Decimal File 132.1/85.

21. Gellman, *Secret Affairs*; Welles, *Sumner Welles.*

22. Wilbur J. Carr to Sumner Welles, April 21, 1937, Decimal File 132.1/85.

23. Wilbur J. Carr to Cordell Hull, April 29, 1937, Decimal File 132.1/87; Brien McMahon (Assistant Attorney General) to Wilbur J. Carr, April 29, 1937, Decimal File 132.1/88.

24. Carr's April 21 note to Welles is the last record in the State Department's Andrade file bearing any indication of Welles's participation in the matter, although he was a recipient of one final memorandum on May 12. Welles became under secretary of state on May 20, 1937. Wilbur J. Carr to Sumner Welles, April 21, 1937, Decimal File 132.1/85.

25. Wilbur J. Carr to Cordell Hull and Sumner Welles, May 4, 1937, Decimal File 132.1/90.

26. Edward J. Shaughnessy to All Districts, Immigration and Naturalization Service, May 18, 1937, Decimal File 132.1/91A.

27. Wilbur J. Carr to Cordell Hull and Sumner Welles, May 12, 1937, Decimal File 132.1/91.

28. Wilbur J. Carr to Laurence Duggan (State Department Division of Latin American Affairs), June 1, 1937, Decimal File 132.1/93. As of that time, the Census Bureau, the Social Security Board, the State Department, and the Labor Department had uniformly adopted the policy of classifying Mexicans and Mexican Americans as white.

29. James B. Stewart (Consul General, Mexico City) to Secretary of State (Washington, DC), November 17, 1937, Decimal File 811.111 MEXICO/1263, *Records of the Department of State Relating to the Internal Affairs of the United States of America.*

30. Ambassador Francisco Castillo Nájera to Cordell Hull, November 22, 1937, Decimal File 812.5611/57, *Records of the Department of State Relating to the Internal Affairs of Mexico.* Translated by State Department.

Notes to Chapter 9

1. R. W. Flournoy (Legal Adviser) to Green H. Hackworth (Legal Adviser) and R. Walton Moore (Assistant Secretary of State), August 26, 1937, Decimal File 132.1/100, *Records of the Department of State Relating to Citizenship of the United States* (hereafter cited as Decimal File 132).

2. Ibid.

3. Ibid.

4. Alden Whitman, "For 16 Years, Warren Saw the Constitution as Protector of Rights and Equality," *New York Times*, July 10, 1974, 24.

5. H. J. McClatchy, "Dual Citizenship" letter to the editor, *Washington Post*, November 22, 1945, 6.

6. H. J. McClatchy, "Race Consciousness" letter to the editor, *Washington Post*, November 3, 1942, 6; H. J. McClatchy, "Japanese-American Dual Citi-

zenship" letter to the editor, *New York Times*, April 24, 1944, 18; H. J. McClatchy, "Intellectual Slavery" letter to the editor, *Washington Post*, November 21, 1944, 8; H. J. McClatchy, "The Enemy Within" letter to the editor, *Hartford Courant*, June 18, 1945, 6.

7. H. J. McClatchy, "Stratton Bill" letter to the editor, *Washington Post*, September 16, 1947, 10.

8. Knobel, *America for the Americans*, 277.

9. Memorandum from Flournoy, December 16, 1937, Decimal File 132.1/96.

10. Letter from Cordell Hull (Secretary of State) to Senator Richard B. Russell (Chair, Senate Immigration Committee), July 20, 1937, Decimal File 132.1/96. Both the original and a carbon copy of this letter remained in State Department files, with the text crossed out on both copies.

11. Memorandum from Flournoy, July 22, 1937, Decimal File 132.1/96.

12. Ibid.

13. Memorandum from Flournoy, July 24, 1937, Decimal File 132.1/96.

14. Letter from Hull to Senator Russell, July 26, 1937, Decimal File 132.1/96.

15. Memorandum from Division of Far Eastern Affairs, July 24, 1937, Decimal File 132.1/96.

16. Memorandum from Flournoy, December 16, 1937, Decimal File 132.1/96.

17. Wilbur J. Carr to Sumner Welles, April 21, 1937, Decimal File 132.1/85; Wilbur J. Carr to Cordell Hull, April 29, 1937, Decimal File 132.1/87; and Brien McMahon (Assistant Attorney General) to Wilbur J. Carr, April 29, 1937, Decimal File 132.1/88.

18. Green H. Hackworth (Legal Adviser) to Wallace Murray (Division Chief, Near Eastern Affairs), December 17, 1937, Decimal File 132.1/96. Just as Welles's involvement disappeared from the records in April 1937, Flournoy's participation ceased in December 1937.

19. US Senate, *Revision and Codification*, September 23, 1940, 2.

20. Ibid.

21. Hazard, "Safeguarding American Citizenship," 19–21; Flournoy, "The Need of Amending Existing Citizenship Laws," 48–56.

22. US House of Representatives, Committee on Immigration and Naturalization, *To Revise and Codify the Nationality Laws of the U.S.*, 65.

23. Ibid., 66.

24. Flournoy, "The Need of Amending Existing Citizenship Laws," 18, 48–56; "Proposed Codification of Our Chaotic Nationality Laws," 780–783; "Revision of Nationality Laws of the United States," 36–46; "The Nationality Act of 1940."

25. Flournoy's perspectives on presidential eligibility emerged during the 2008 presidential campaign, when scholars cited his research to argue that Senator John McCain, who was born in Panama in 1936, was ineligible to run for

the office. See Solum, "Originalism and the Natural Born Citizen Clause," 22–31.

26. Flournoy, "The Need of Amending Existing Citizenship Laws," 18, 48–56.

27. Flournoy, "Proposed Codification of Our Chaotic Nationality Laws," 782–783.

28. See Flournoy, "Dual Nationality and Election (Part 1)," 545–564; "Dual Nationality and Election (Part 2)," 693–709.

29. Flournoy, "Revision of Nationality Laws," 43.

30. Flournoy, "The Nationality Act of 1940," 4–5.

31. Ibid., 7.

32. Harvard Law Review, "The Nationality Act of 1940," 864–865.

33. Hyde, "The Nationality Act of 1940," 316.

34. García, "The Case of El Paso," 199.

35. Wilbur J. Carr to J. F. Simmons and Laurence Duggan, June 26, 1937, Decimal File 132.1/111; see also Raleigh A. Gibson (Division of the American Republics, formerly the Division of Latin American Affairs) to Laurence Duggan, July 28, 1937, Decimal File 811.4016/236, *Records of the Department of State Relating to the Internal Affairs of the United States of America* (hereafter cited as Decimal File 811). The first two pages of Gibson's memorandum are almost a verbatim duplication of Carr's.

36. Carr to Simmons and Duggan, June 26, 1937, Decimal File 132.1/111.

37. Ibid.

38. Ibid.

39. Gibson to Duggan, July 28, 1937, Decimal File 811.4016/236.

40. Halbert L. Dunn (Chief Statistician for Vital Statistics) to Mr. Austin, July 23, 1937, Decimal File 132.1/113; see also Gibson to Duggan, July 28, 1937, Decimal File 811.4016/236.

41. See Bohme, *200 Years of U.S. Census Taking*. Bohme reproduces the "Instructions to Enumerators" throughout, and also discusses changes from year to year in these instructions. He also reproduces the actual census forms, which allows the reader to see how the questions changed over time. See also Anderson, *The American Census*, which puts census politics, procedures, and data in a social history context.

42. Ngai, "The Architecture of Race," 77.

43. Bohme, *200 Years of U.S. Census Taking*, 60.

44. Jenkins, *Procedural History of the 1940 Census*, 44, 74–75.

45. William Lane Austin (Director, Census Bureau) to George Wythe (Liaison Officer, Department of Commerce), August 29, 1939, Decimal File 811.4016/236.

46. Ibid.

47. Ibid.

48. Memorandum from US Embassy (Mexico City) to Secretaria de Relaciones Exteriores (Mexico City), October 3, 1939, Secretaria de Relaciones Ex-

teriores, *Race Classification in the 1940 U.S. Census* (hereafter cited as SRE File III-411-35).

49. Dr. Manuel Gamio (Chief of the Demographic Department) to Secretario de Relaciones Exteriores, October 24, 1939, SRE File III-411-35.

50. E. Alanís Patiño (Director General of Statistics) to Ernesto Hidalgo (Senior Official of the SRE), undated (ca. November 22, 1939), SRE File III-411-35.

51. The SRE has separate files on the census issue and the Andrade case. The two files are not cross-referenced to each other.

52. Secretario de Relaciones Exteriores to Ambassador Daniels, undated (ca. November 22, 1939), SRE File III-411-35.

53. While no documents explicitly show that the State Department overrode Austin's efforts, Austin clearly stated in his letter of August 29, 1939 (Decimal File 811.4016/236), that he would not act against the wishes of the State Department in his final policy decision, and that the State Department was the only obstacle to the separate classification of Mexicans and Anglo-Americans. It is, therefore, implicit that the State Department informed Austin that the Census Bureau should continue classifying Mexicans and Mexican Americans as white.

54. Memorandum from US Embassy to Secretaria de Relaciones Exteriores, November 2, 1939, SRE File III-411-35.

55. Francisco Castillo Nájera (Mexican Ambassador to the United States) to Eduardo Hay (Secretario de Relaciones Exteriores), November 22, 1939, SRE File III-411-35.

56. Josephus Daniels (US Ambassador to Mexico) to Secretaria de Relaciones Exteriores, November 29, 1939, SRE File III-411-35.

57. Bohme, *200 Years of U.S. Census Taking*, 69.

58. Jenkins, *Procedural History of the 1940 Census*, 42, 82.

Notes to Chapter 10

1. Memorandum from Sumner Welles, December 12, 1935, Decimal File 812.404/1829A, *Records of the Department of State Relating to the Internal Affairs of Mexico*.

2. Josephus Daniels (US Ambassador to Mexico) to Franklin D. Roosevelt, August 31, 1936, Roosevelt, *Papers as President*, Box 43.

3. Ibid. Three months later, on November 17, 1936, Daniels sent a personal letter to FDR reminiscing about the events that occurred in 1914. He even quoted his April 21, 1914, order to seize the Vera Cruz customs house just to remind Roosevelt of how much the "world moves and conditions change." Roosevelt, *Papers as President*, Box 43.

4. *El Nacional* (Mexico City), May 1, 1937, 8, Archivos Económicos, Biblioteca Miguel Lerdo de Tejada, Mexico City.

5. See correspondence between Welles and Daniels dated February 21–July 7, 1936: Welles, *Sumner Welles Papers,* Box 28, Folders 6–8.

6. See correspondence between Welles, Reed, Daniels, and Cordell Hull (Secretary of State), June 20–November 3, 1936, Welles, *Sumner Welles Papers,* Box 178, Folders 9–10.

7. Gellman, *Good Neighbor Diplomacy,* 50–51. Landowners self-assessed their property values in Mexico at the time.

8. Wood, *The Making of the Good Neighbor Policy,* 162.

9. Green, *The Containment of Latin America,* 35.

10. Wood, *The Making of the Good Neighbor Policy,* 121.

11. Sheridan, "'Another White Race,'" 112.

12. Acuña, *Occupied America,* 254.

13. Perea, "The Black/White Binary Paradigm," 1243.

14. Acuña, *Occupied America,* 262.

15. Ibid., 263.

16. Guglielmo, "Fighting for Caucasian Rights," 1220–1223, 1225.

17. "The Facts About Job Discrimination," *Fraternidad* (Mexico City), September 1, 1945, 14, in Carey McWilliams, Papers.

18. Guglielmo, "Fighting for Caucasian Rights," 1226–1227.

19. Texas LULAC Office of the Governor to LULAC Councils in Texas, February 21, 1945, from Kreneck, Private Papers. For an example, see LULAC Council 60 (Houston) to Senator Weaver Moore, March 5, 1945, from Kreneck, Private Papers.

20. "What Happened to the Spears Law?" *Fraternidad* (Mexico City), April 1, 1945, 5, McWilliams, Papers.

21. Ibid.

22. Guglielmo, "Fighting for Caucasian Rights," 1228–1229.

23. "The Rejection of the Spears Law," *Fraternidad* (Mexico City), July 1, 1945, 10, McWilliams, Papers.

24. Ibid.

25. Montejano, *Anglos and Mexicans in the Making of Texas,* 270.

26. García, *Mexican Americans,* 242, 270.

27. Ibid., 299.

28. García, *White but Not Equal,* 7.

29. Ibid., 2.

30. *Hernandez v. Texas,* 347 U.S. 475 (1954), 476–477.

31. García, *White but Not Equal,* 81.

32. Rosales, *Chicano!,* 107.

33. García, *White but Not Equal,* 49, 56.

34. Ibid., 58.

35. Ibid.

36. Ibid., 39.

37. Ibid., 8.

38. Haney López, *Racism on Trial,* 42.

39. *Hernandez v. Texas*, 479.

40. Rosales, *Chicano!*, 108.

41. For examples of other works that discuss the *Hernandez* case, see Sheridan, "'Another White Race,'" 109–144; San Miguel, *"Let All of Them Take Heed."* The *Hernandez* decision also received press coverage on its fiftieth anniversary. The May 14, 2004, *New York Times* presented a summary of the decision titled "A Quiet Victory for Civil Rights," from which the title of this work was borrowed.

42. See Wilson, "Brown over Other White," 145–194.

Bibliography

Archival and Manuscript Sources

Archivos Económicos (Newspaper Archives). Biblioteca Miguel Lerdo de Tejada, Mexico City.

California Joint Immigration Committee. *California Joint Immigration Committee Collection, 1924–1936.* MSS 88/202 c. The Bancroft Library, University of California, Berkeley.

Cárdenas, Lázaro. *Presidential Papers of Lázaro Cárdenas.* Numerical File 571.1/9. Archivo General de la Nación, Mexico City.

Citizenship Petition of Timoteo Andrade. Box 24, Petition #24049, Petitions for Naturalization. US District Court for the Western District of New York. Records of the US District Courts of the United States, Record Group 21. National Archives and Records Administration, Northeast Region, New York, NY. Attached to this petition are two opinions of District Judge John Knight (filed December 11, 1935, and June 1, 1936), and depositions of witnesses during a preliminary hearing (filed on June 2, 1936).

Citizenship Petition of Porfirio Bravo. Box 24, Petition #24022, Petitions for Naturalization. US District Court for the Western District of New York. Records of the US District Courts of the United States, Record Group 21. National Archives and Records Administration, Northeast Region, New York, NY.

Citizenship Petition of Eudaldo Godoy. Box 257, Petition #248646, Petitions for Naturalization. US District Court for the Southern District of New York. Records of the US District Courts of the United States, Record Group 21. National Archives and Records Administration, Northeast Region, New York, NY.

Citizenship Petition of Francisco Velez. Box 25, Petition #24272, Petitions for Naturalization. US District Court for the Western District of New York. Records of the US District Courts of the United States, Record Group 21. National Archives and Records Administration, Northeast Region, New York, NY.

Japanese-American Evacuation and Resettlement Records, 1930–1974. MSS 67/14 c. The Bancroft Library, University of California, Berkeley. These records contain some files of the California Joint Immigration Committee.

Kreneck, Tom. Private Papers, items in the possession of Professor F. Arturo Rosales, Department of History, Arizona State University.

McWilliams, Carey. Papers, ca. 1905–1980 (Collection 1319), Department of Special Collections, University Research Library, University of California, Los Angeles.

Records of the Department of State Relating to Citizenship of the United States. Decimal File 132. General Records of the Department of State, Passport Office, 1910–1949, Record Group 59. National Archives, Washington, DC.

Records of the Department of State Relating to Political Relations Between the United States and Mexico, 1930–1939. Decimal File 711.12 (National Archives Microfilm Publication S3159). General Records of the Department of State, Record Group 59. National Archives, Washington, DC.

Records of the Department of State Relating to the Internal Affairs of Mexico, 1930–1939. Decimal File 812 (National Archives Microfilm Publication M1370). General Records of the Department of State, Record Group 59. National Archives, Washington, DC.

Records of the Department of State Relating to the Internal Affairs of the United States of America, 1914–1940. Decimal File 811. General Records of the Department of State, Record Group 59. National Archives, Washington, DC.

Roosevelt, Franklin D. *Papers as President, President's Secretary's File, 1933–45.* Franklin D. Roosevelt Presidential Library, Hyde Park, NY.

Rosales, F. Arturo. "The Lynching of Antonio Rodríguez in 1910: An Historical Reassessment." Unpublished manuscript [photocopy]. Author's collection.

Secretaria de Relaciones Exteriores. *Race Classification in the 1940 U.S. Census.* Serie III, legajo 411, expediente 35. Archivo Histórico de la Secretaria de Relaciones Exteriores, Mexico City.

———. *Timoteo Andrade File, 1935–37.* Serie III, legajo 2335, expediente 2. Archivo Histórico de la Secretaria de Relaciones Exteriores, Mexico City.

———. *U.S. Senator Shortridge File.* Serie 37, legajo 18, expediente 74. Archivo Histórico de la Secretaria de Relaciones Exteriores, Mexico City.

Welles, Sumner. *Sumner Welles Papers.* MS. 96-1. Franklin D. Roosevelt Presidential Library, Hyde Park, NY.

Legal Citations

A. L. A. Schechter Poultry Corp. et al. v. United States, 295 U.S. 495 (1935).

Hernandez v. Texas, 347 U.S. 475 (1954).

In re Camille, 6 Fed. 256 (1880).

In re Rodriguez, 81 Fed. 337 (1897).

Morrison et al. v. People of the State of California, 291 U.S. 82 (1934).
Panama Refining Co. et al. v. Ryan et al., 293 U.S. 388 (1935).
Takao Ozawa v. United States, 260 U.S. 178 (1922).
United States v. Bhagat Singh Thind, 261 U.S. 204 (1923).

Published and Unpublished Sources

Acuña, Rodolfo F. *Corridors of Migration: The Odyssey of Mexican Laborers, 1600–1933*. Tucson: University of Arizona Press, 2007.

———. *Occupied America: A History of Chicanos*. 3rd ed. New York: Harper and Row, 1988.

Aguila, Jaime R. "Protecting 'México de Afuera': Mexican Emigration Policy, 1876–1928." PhD diss., Arizona State University, 2000.

Alterman, Hyman. *Counting People: The Census in History*. New York: Harcourt, Brace & World, 1969.

Alvarez, Robert R., Jr. *Familia: Migration and Adaptation in Baja and Alta California, 1800–1975*. Berkeley: University of California Press, 1987.

Anderson, Margo J. *The American Census: A Social History*. New Haven: Yale University Press, 1988.

Badger, Anthony J. *The New Deal: The Depression Years, 1933–1940*. New York: Hill and Wang, 1989.

Balderrama, Francisco E., and Raymond Rodríguez. *Decade of Betrayal: Mexican Repatriation in the 1930s*. Albuquerque: University of New Mexico Press, 1995.

Beelen, George D. *Harding and Mexico: Diplomacy by Economic Persuasion, 1920–1923*. New York: Garland, 1987.

Bernard, William Spencer, ed. *American Immigration Policy: A Reappraisal*. Port Washington, NY: Kennikat Press, 1969.

Blachly, Frederick Frank. *Administrative Legislation and Adjudication*. Washington, DC: Brookings Institution, 1934.

Bodayla, Stephen D. *Financial Diplomacy: The United States and Mexico, 1919–1933*. New York: Garland, 1987.

Bohme, Frederick G. *200 Years of U.S. Census Taking: Population and Housing Questions, 1790–1990*. Washington, DC: US Department of Commerce, Bureau of the Census, 1989.

Borchard, Edwin. "Three Hague Conventions on Nationality." *American Journal of International Law* 32:1 (January 1938): 126–128.

Brinkley, Alan. "AHR Forum: Introduction." *American Historical Review* 110:4 (October 2005): 1046–1051.

Buell, Raymond L. "Changes in Our Latin American Policy." *Annals of the American Academy of Political and Social Science: Elements of an American Foreign Policy* 156 (July 1931): 126–132.

Calderón-Zaks, Michael Aaron. "Constructing the 'Mexican Race': Racial Formation and Empire Building, 1884–1940." PhD diss., State University of New York, 2008.

Callahan, James M. *American Foreign Policy in Mexican Relations.* New York: Macmillan, 1932.

Cárdenas, Gilberto. "United States Immigration Policy Toward Mexico: An Historical Perspective." In *Law, Crime, Justice: Naturalization and Citizenship*, ed. George E. Pozzetta, 2–27. American Ethnicity and Immigration Series. New York: Garland, 1991.

Cardoso, Lawrence A. *Mexican Emigration to the United States, 1897–1931: Socio-Economic Patterns.* Tucson: University of Arizona Press, 1980.

Chiswick, Barry R., ed. *The Gateway: U.S. Immigration Issues and Policies.* Washington, DC: American Enterprise Institute for Public Policy Research, 1982.

Collings, Harry T. "Importance of Our Relations with Latin America." *Annals of the American Academy of Political and Social Science: Elements of an American Foreign Policy* 156 (July 1931): 133–135.

Conkin, Paul K. *The New Deal.* 3rd ed. Arlington Heights, IL: Harlan Davidson, 1992.

Cooper, Phillip J. *Public Law and Public Administration.* Englewood Cliffs, NJ: Prentice Hall, 1988.

Copp, Nelson Gage. *"Wetbacks" and Braceros: Mexican Migrant Laborers and American Immigration Policy, 1930–1960.* San Francisco: R and E Research Associates, 1971.

Cornelius, Wayne A. *Mexican Migration to the United States: Causes, Consequences, and U.S. Responses.* Cambridge: Migration and Development Study Group, Center for International Studies, Massachusetts Institute of Technology, 1978.

Curran, Thomas J. *Xenophobia and Immigration, 1820–1930.* Boston: Twayne, 1975.

Daniels, Roger. *Coming to America: A History of Immigration and Ethnicity in American Life.* New York: HarperCollins, 1990.

———. *Guarding the Golden Door: American Immigration Policy and Immigrants since 1882.* New York: Hill and Wang, 2004.

DeConde, Alexander. *Herbert Hoover's Latin-American Policy.* Stanford, CA: Stanford University Press, 1951.

de Leon, Arnoldo. *The Tejano Community, 1836–1900.* Albuquerque: University of New Mexico Press, 1982.

Delgado, Richard, and Jean Stefancic. *Critical Race Theory: An Introduction.* New York: New York University Press, 2001.

Delpar, Helen. *The Enormous Vogue of Things Mexican: Cultural Relations Between the United States and Mexico, 1920–1935.* Tuscaloosa: University of Alabama Press, 1992.

Divine, Robert A. *American Immigration Policy, 1924–1952.* New Haven: Yale University Press, 1957.

Estados Unidos Mexicanos. Departamento de la Estadística Nacional. *Memoria de los Censos de 1930.* Mexico City: Departamento de la Estadística Nacional, 1932.

———. Secretaria de la Economía Nacional. Dirección General de Estadística. *Catalogo de Estadísticas.* Mexico City: Secretaria de la Economía Nacional, 1937.

———. Secretaria de la Economía Nacional. Dirección General de Estadística. *Memoria de los Censos de 1935.* Mexico City: Secretaria de la Economía Nacional, 1936.

Flournoy, Richard Wilson, Jr. "Dual Nationality and Election (Part 1)." *Yale Law Journal* 30:6 (April 1921): 545–564.

———. "Dual Nationality and Election (Part 2)." *Yale Law Journal* 30:7 (May 1921): 693–709.

———. "The Nationality Act of 1940." *Contemporary Law Pamphlets*, Ser. 5, No. 4. New York: New York University School of Law, 1941.

———. "Nationality Convention, Protocols and Recommendations Adopted by the First Conference on the Codification of International Law." *American Journal of International Law* 24:3 (July 1930): 467–485.

———. "Naturalization and Expatriation (Part 1)." *Yale Law Journal* 31:7 (May 1922): 702–719.

———. "Naturalization and Expatriation (Part 2)." *Yale Law Journal* 31:8 (June 1922): 848–868.

———. "The Need of Amending Existing Citizenship Laws." *Federal Bar Association Journal* 1:2 (March 1932): 18, 48–56.

———. "Proposed Codification of Our Chaotic Nationality Laws." *American Bar Association Journal* 20:12 (December 1934): 780–783.

———. "Revision of Nationality Laws of the United States." *American Journal of International Law* 34:1 (January 1940): 36–46.

———. "Suggestions Concerning an International Code on the Law of Nationality." *Yale Law Journal* 35:8 (June 1926): 939–955.

Foerster, Robert F. *The Racial Problems Involved in Immigration from Latin America and the West Indies to the United States: A Report Submitted to the Secretary of Labor.* Washington, DC: GPO, 1925; reprint, San Francisco: R and E Research Associates, 1971.

Foley, Neil. *The White Scourge: Mexicans, Blacks, and Poor Whites in Texas Cotton Culture.* Berkeley: University of California Press, 1997.

Fox, Cybelle. "The Boundaries of Social Citizenship: Race, Immigration and the American Welfare State, 1900–1950." PhD diss., Harvard University, 2007.

Franklin, Frank G. *The Legislative History of Naturalization in the United States.* New York: Arno Press, 1969.

Gamio, Manuel. *Mexican Immigration to the United States: A Study of Human Migration and Adjustment.* Chicago: University of Chicago Press, 1930; reprint, New York: Dover, 1971.

García, Ignacio M. *White but Not Equal: Mexican Americans, Jury Discrimination, and the Supreme Court.* Tucson: University of Arizona Press, 2009.

García, Mario T. "Mexican Americans and the Politics of Citizenship: The Case of El Paso, 1936." *New Mexico Historical Review* 59 (Spring, 1984): 187–204.

———. *Mexican Americans: Leadership, Ideology, and Identity, 1930–1960.* New Haven: Yale University Press, 1989.

Garis, Roy L. *Immigration Restriction: A Study of the Opposition to and Regulation of Immigration into the United States.* New York: Macmillan, 1927.

Gellman, Irwin F. *Good Neighbor Diplomacy: United States Policies in Latin America, 1933–1945.* Baltimore: Johns Hopkins University Press, 1979.

———. *Secret Affairs: Franklin Roosevelt, Cordell Hull, and Sumner Welles.* Baltimore: Johns Hopkins University Press, 1995.

Gold, George W. "The Racial Prerequisite in the Naturalization Law." *Boston University Law Review* 15 (1935): 462–506.

Gómez, Laura E. *Manifest Destinies: The Making of the Mexican American Race.* New York: New York University Press, 2007.

Gómez-Quiñones, Juan. *Chicano Politics: Reality and Promise, 1940–1990.* Albuquerque: University of New Mexico Press, 1990.

———. *Roots of Chicano Politics, 1600–1940.* Albuquerque: University of New Mexico Press, 1994.

González Navarro, Moisés. "*Mestizaje* in Mexico During the National Period." In *Race and Class in Latin America*, ed. Magnus Morner, 145–169. New York: Columbia University Press, 1970.

Graham, Richard. "Introduction." In *The Idea of Race in Latin America, 1870–1940*, ed. Richard Graham, 1–5. Austin: University of Texas Press, 1990.

Green, David. *The Containment of Latin America: A History of the Myths and Realities of the Good Neighbor Policy.* Chicago: Quadrangle Books, 1971.

Guerin-Gonzales, Camille. *Mexican Workers and American Dreams: Immigration, Repatriation, and California Farm Labor, 1900–1939.* New Brunswick, NJ: Rutgers University Press, 1994.

Guglielmo, Thomas A. "Fighting for Caucasian Rights: Mexicans, Mexican Americans, and the Transnational Struggle for Civil Rights in World War II Texas." *Journal of American History* 92:4 (March 2006): 1212–1237.

———. *White on Arrival: Italians, Race, Color, and Power in Chicago, 1890–1945.* New York: Oxford University Press, 2003.

Gutiérrez, David G. "Sin Fronteras? Chicanos, Mexican Americans and the Emergence of the Contemporary Mexican Immigration Debate, 1968–1978." *Journal of American Ethnic History* 10:4 (Summer 1991): 5–37.

———. *Walls and Mirrors: Mexican Americans, Mexican Immigrants, and the Politics of Ethnicity.* Berkeley: University of California Press, 1995.

Halacy, Dan. *Census: 190 Years of Counting America*. New York: Elsevier/Nelson, 1980.

Haney López, Ian. *Racism on Trial: The Chicano Fight for Justice*. Cambridge: Belknap/Harvard University Press, 2003.

———. *White by Law: The Legal Construction of Race*. 10th anniv. ed. New York: New York University Press, 2006.

Harris, Marvin. *Patterns of Race in the Americas*. New York: Walker Press, 1964.

Harvard Law Review. "The Nationality Act of 1940." *Harvard Law Review* 54:5 (March 1941): 860–870.

Hazard, Henry B. "New Naturalization and Citizenship Legislation by the Congress." *American Journal of International Law* 23:2 (April 1929): 399–401.

———. "The Right of Appeal in Naturalization Cases in the Federal Courts." *American Journal of International Law* 21:1 (January 1927): 40–52.

———. "Safeguarding American Citizenship." *Federal Bar Association Journal* 1:2 (March 1932): 19–21.

Higham, John. *Strangers in the Land: Patterns of American Nativism, 1860–1925*. 2nd ed. New York: Atheneum Press, 1975.

Hing, Bill Ong. *Making and Remaking Asian America Through Immigration Policy, 1850–1990*. Stanford: Stanford University Press, 1993.

Hoffman, Abraham. *Unwanted Mexican Americans in the Great Depression: Repatriation Pressures, 1929–1939*. Tucson: University of Arizona Press, 1974.

Hutchinson, Edward Prince. *Legislative History of American Immigration Policy, 1798–1965*. Philadelphia: Published for Balch Institute for Ethnic Studies, University of Pennsylvania Press, 1981.

Hyde, Charles Cheney. "The Nationality Act of 1940." *American Journal of International Law* 35:2 (April 1941): 314–319.

Jackson, Robert H. *The Struggle for Judicial Supremacy: A Study of a Crisis in American Power Politics*. New York: A. A. Knopf, 1941.

Jacobson, Matthew Frye. *Whiteness of a Different Color: European Immigrants and the Alchemy of Race*. Cambridge: Harvard University Press, 1998.

Jenkins, Robert M. *Procedural History of the 1940 Census of Population and Housing*. Madison: University of Wisconsin Press, 1985.

Kalman, Laura. "AHR Forum: The Constitution, the Supreme Court, and the New Deal," *American Historical Review* 110:4 (October 2005): 1052–1080.

Kansas, Sidney. *U.S. Immigration Exclusion and Deportation and Citizenship of the United States of America*. 3rd ed. New York: Matthew Bender, 1948.

Kaplowitz, Craig A. *LULAC, Mexican Americans and National Policy*. College Station: Texas A&M University Press, 2005.

Knight, Alan. "Racism, Revolution, and *Indigenismo*: Mexico, 1910–1940." In *The Idea of Race in Latin America, 1870–1940*, ed. Richard Graham, 71–113. Austin: University of Texas Press, 1990.

———. *U.S.-Mexican Relations, 1910–1940: An Interpretation*. La Jolla: Center for US-Mexican Studies, University of California, San Diego, 1987.

Knobel, Dale T. *America for the Americans: The Nativist Movement in the United States*. New York: Twayne, 1996.

L., F. V., Jr. "The Nationality Act of 1940." *Virginia Law Review* 27:4 (February 1941): 531–543.

Langley, Lester D. *Mexico and the United States: The Fragile Relationship*. Boston: Twayne, 1991.

Leff, Mark H. *The Limits of Symbolic Reform: The New Deal and Taxation, 1933–1939*. New York: Cambridge University Press, 1984.

LePore, Herbert Patrick. "Exclusion by Prejudice: Anti-Japanese Discrimination in California and the Immigration Act of 1924." MA thesis, Brigham Young University, 1973.

Leuchtenberg, William E. "AHR Forum: Comment on Laura Kalman's Article." *American Historical Review* 110:4 (October 2005): 1081–1093.

———. *The FDR Years: On Roosevelt and His Legacy*. New York: Columbia University Press, 1995.

———. *Franklin D. Roosevelt and the New Deal: 1932–1940*. New York: Harper and Row, 1963.

Lipshultz, Robert J. "American Attitudes Toward Mexican Immigration, 1924–1952." PhD diss., University of Chicago, 1962.

Lorey, David E., ed. *United States-Mexico Border Statistics Since 1900*. Los Angeles: UCLA Latin American Center Publications, 1990.

Ludmerer, Kenneth M. "Genetics, Eugenics, and the Immigration Restriction Act of 1924." In *Nativism, Discrimination, and Images of Immigrants*, ed. George E. Pozzetta, 367–389. American Ethnicity and Immigration Series. New York: Garland, 1991.

Luna, Brandon Salvador. "Race, Immigration Law, and the U.S.-Mexico Border: A History of the Border Patrol and the Mexican-Origin Population in the Southwest." MA thesis, University of California, San Diego, 2008.

Macias, Leonardo. "Mexican Immigration and Repatriation During the Great Depression." MA thesis, Arizona State University, 1992.

Márquez, Benjamin. *LULAC: The Evolution of a Mexican American Political Organization*. Austin: University of Texas Press, 1993.

Masanz, Sharon D. *History of the Immigration and Naturalization Service*. Washington, DC: US Government Printing Office, 1980.

McClatchy, V. S. *Japanese Immigration and Colonization: Brief Prepared for Consideration of the State Department*. San Francisco: Japanese Exclusion League, 1921; reprint, San Francisco: R and E Research Associates, 1970.

McCoyer, Michael. "Darkness of a Different Color: Mexicans and Racial Formation in Greater Chicago, 1916–1960." PhD diss., Northwestern University, 2007.

McGovney, Dudley O. "Naturalization of the Mixed-Blood: A Dictum." *California Law Review* 22:4 (May 1934): 377–391.

Meyer, Lorenzo. *The Mexican Revolution and the Anglo-American Powers.* LaJolla: Center for U.S.-Mexican Studies, University of California, San Diego, 1985.

Meyer, Michael C., William Sherman, and Susan Deeds. *The Course of Mexican History.* 7th ed. New York: Oxford University Press, 2003.

Michaels, Walter Benn. *Our America: Nativism, Modernism, and Pluralism.* Durham, NC: Duke University Press, 1995.

Molineu, Harold. *U.S. Policy Toward Latin America: From Regionalism to Globalism.* Boulder, CO: Westview Press, 1990.

Montejano, David. *Anglos and Mexicans in the Making of Texas, 1836–1986.* Austin: University of Texas Press, 1987.

Morner, Magnus. *Race Mixture in the History of Latin America.* Boston: Little, Brown, 1967.

Musolf, Lloyd D. *Federal Examiners and the Conflict of Law and Administration.* Westport, CT: Greenwood Press, 1979.

Neal, Joe W. "The Policy of the United States Toward Immigration from Mexico." MA thesis, University of Texas, Austin, 1941.

Ngai, Mae M. "The Architecture of Race in American Immigration Law: A Reexamination of the Immigration Act of 1924." *Journal of American History*, 86:1 (June 1999): 67–92.

———. *Impossible Subjects: Illegal Aliens and the Making of Modern America.* Princeton: Princeton University Press, 2004.

Noel, Linda. "'The Swinging Door': U.S. National Identity and the Making of the Mexican Guestworker, 1900–1935." PhD diss., University of Maryland, College Park, 2006.

Nonet, Philippe. *Administrative Justice: Advocacy and Change in a Government Agency.* New York: Russell Sage Foundation, 1969.

Nutini, Hugo G. "Class and Ethnicity in Mexico: Somatic and Racial Considerations." *Ethnology* 36:3 (Summer 1997): 227–238.

Pastor, Robert A., and Jorge G. Castañeda. *Limits to Friendship: The United States and Mexico.* New York: Vintage, 1989.

Patterson, James T. *Congressional Conservativism and the New Deal: The Growth of the Conservative Coalition in Congress, 1933–1939.* Lexington: University of Kentucky Press, 1967.

Penrose, Eldon R. *California Nativism: Organized Opposition to the Japanese, 1890–1913.* San Francisco: R and E Research Associates, 1973.

Perales, Alonso S. *En Defensa de mi Raza.* Primero tomo. San Antonio: Artes Gráficas, 1936.

———. *En Defensa de mi Raza.* Segundo tomo. San Antonio: Artes Gráficas, 1937.

Perea, Juan F. "The Black/White Binary Paradigm of Race: The 'Normal Science' of American Racial Thought." *California Law Review* 85:5 (1997): 1213–1258.

Pike, Fredrick B. *FDR's Good Neighbor Policy: Sixty Years of Generally Gentle Chaos.* Austin: University of Texas Press, 1995.

Pops, Gerald M. "Administrative Law as Public Policy: The First Fifty Years." *Journal of Policy History* 2:1 (1990): 98–117.

Raat, W. Dirk. *Mexico and the United States: Ambivalent Vistas.* Athens: University of Georgia Press, 1992.

Reisler, Mark. "Always the Laborer, Never the Citizen: Anglo Perceptions of the Mexican Immigrant During the 1920s." In *Between Two Worlds: Mexican Immigrants in the United States,* ed. David Gutiérrez, 23–43. Wilmington: Scholarly Resources, 1996.

———. *By the Sweat of Their Brow: Mexican Immigrant Labor in the United States, 1900–1940.* Westport, CT: Greenwood Press, 1976.

Robinson, David J., ed. *Studies in Spanish American Population History.* Boulder, CO: Westview Press, 1981.

Rodríguez, Gregory. *Mongrels, Bastards, Orphans, and Vagabonds: Mexican Immigration and the Future of Race in America.* New York: Pantheon, 2007.

Rosales, F. Arturo. *Chicano! The History of the Mexican American Civil Rights Movement.* Houston: Arte Público Press, University of Houston, 1997.

———. *¡Pobre Raza! Violence, Justice and Mobilization Among México Lindo Immigrants, 1900–1936.* Austin: University of Texas Press, 1999.

———. "Shifting Self Perceptions and Ethnic Consciousness Among Mexicans in Houston, 1908–1946." *Aztlan* 16:1–2 (1987): 71–94.

Rosenbloom, David H. *Public Administration and Law: Bench v. Bureau in the United States.* New York: Marcel Dekker, 1983.

———, and Rosemary O'Leary. *Public Administration and Law.* 2nd ed. New York: Marcel Dekker, 1997.

Ruiz, Ramón Eduardo. *Triumphs and Tragedy: A History of the Mexican People.* New York: Norton, 1992.

Salyer, Lucy Elizabeth. "Guarding the 'White Man's Frontier': Courts, Politics, and the Regulation of Immigration, 1891–1924." PhD diss., University of California at Berkeley, 1989.

San Miguel, Guadalupe, Jr. *"Let All of Them Take Heed": Mexican Americans and the Campaign for Educational Equality in Texas, 1910–1981.* Austin: University of Texas Press, 1987.

Sargent, James E. *Roosevelt and the Hundred Days: Struggle for the Early New Deal.* New York: Garland, 1981.

Schoultz, Lars. *Beneath the United States: A History of U.S. Policy Toward Latin America.* Cambridge, MA: Harvard University Press, 1998.

Schwartz, Bernard. *An Introduction to American Administrative Law.* 2nd ed. Dobbs Ferry, NY: Oceana, 1962.

Scisco, Louis. *Political Nativism in New York State.* New York: AMS Press, 1968.

Scott, James Brown. "Nationality." *American Journal of International Law* 24:3 (July 1930): 556–561.

Shapiro, Martin M. "Administrative Discretion: The Next Stage." *Yale Law Journal* 92:8 (July 1983): 1487–1522.

———. "Judicial Activism." In *The Third Century: America as a Post-Industrial Society*, ed. Seymour M. Lipset, 109–131. Stanford, CA: Hoover Institution Press, Stanford University, 1979.

———. "On Predicting the Future of Administrative Law." *Regulation: AEI Journal on Government and Society* 6:3 (May–June 1982): 18–25.

———. *The Supreme Court and Administrative Agencies*. New York: Free Press, 1968.

———. *Who Guards the Guardians? Judicial Control of Administration*. Athens: University of Georgia Press, 1988.

Sheridan, Clare. "A Genealogy of Citizenship: Mexican Americans, Race and National Identity." PhD diss., University of Texas, Austin, 1999.

———. "'Another White Race': Mexican Americans and the Paradox of Whiteness in Jury Selection." *Law and History Review* 21:1 (Spring 2003): 109–144.

Simon, Rita J., ed. *Immigration and American Public Policy*. Beverly Hills: Sage, 1986.

Sitkoff, Harvard, ed. *Fifty Years Later: The New Deal Evaluated*. Philadelphia: Temple University Press, 1985.

Solum, Lawrence B. "Originalism and the Natural Born Citizen Clause." *Michigan Law Review First Impressions* 107:1 (September 2008): 22–31.

Stepan, Nancy L. *"The Hour of Eugenics": Race, Gender, and Nation in Latin America*. Ithaca, NY: Cornell University Press, 1991.

Stephenson, George M. *A History of American Immigration, 1820–1924*. Boston: Ginn and Company, 1926.

Tatalovich, Raymond. *Nativism Reborn? The Official English Language Movement in the American States*. Lexington: University Press of Kentucky, 1995.

Taylor, Paul Schuster. *Mexican Labor in the United States*. vol. I. Berkeley: University of California Press, 1930.

———. *Mexican Labor in the United States*. vol. II. Berkeley: University of California Press, 1931–1932.

———. *Mexican Labor in the United States*. vol. IV. Berkeley: University of California Press, 1933–1934.

Teitelbaum, Michael S. *Latin Migration North: The Problem for U.S. Foreign Policy*. New York: Council on Foreign Relations, 1985.

Thatcher, Mary Anne. *Immigrants and the 1930s: Ethnicity and Alienage in Depression and On-Coming War*. New York: Garland, 1990.

Thurston, Walter C. "Relations with Our Latin American Neighbors." *Annals of the American Academy of Political and Social Science: Elements of an American Foreign Policy* 156 (July 1931): 116–125.

Tichenor, Daniel J. *Dividing Lines: The Politics of Immigration Control in America*. Princeton: Princeton University Press, 2002.

Toggia, Pietro. "The Whiter the Better: United States' Immigration Policies by Racial Design." MA thesis, Arizona State University, 1994.

Tucker, Robert W., Charles B. Keely, and Linda Wrigley, eds. *Immigration and U.S. Foreign Policy*. Boulder, CO: Westview Press, 1990.

University of Texas, Bureau of Research in the Social Sciences. *Texas' Children: The Report of the Texas Child Welfare Survey*. Austin: University of Texas, 1938.

US Attorney General. Committee on Administrative Procedure. *Administrative Procedures in Government Agencies*. Senate Document No. 8, 77th Congress, 1st Session, 1941; reprint, Charlottesville: University of Virginia Press, 1968.

US Congress. *Congressional Record*. 1928–1940.

US Department of Commerce. Bureau of the Census. *Historical Statistics of the United States, Colonial Times to 1970*. Washington, DC: US Department of Commerce, Bureau of the Census, 1975.

———. *Sixteenth Census of the United States: 1940*. Washington, DC: US Department of Commerce, Bureau of the Census, 1943.

US House of Representatives. *Nationality Act of 1940: Conference Report*. 76th Cong., 3rd Sess., October 4, 1940.

———. Committee on Immigration and Naturalization. *To Revise and Codify the Nationality Laws of the U.S. into a Comprehensive Nationality Code*. 76th Cong., 3rd Sess., January 17; February 13, 20, 27, 28; March 5; April 11, 16, 23; May 2, 3, 7, 9, 13; June 5, 1940.

———. Immigration Committee. *Western Hemisphere Immigration*. 71st Cong., 2nd Sess., January 16, 20, 22, 24, 28–31; February 3, 4, 6, 1930.

US Senate. *Revision and Codification of the Nationality Laws of the United States*. 76th Cong., 3rd Sess. September 23, 1940.

Van Vleck, William C. *The Administrative Control of Aliens: A Study in Administrative Law and Procedure*. New York: Commonwealth Fund, 1932.

Wang, Peter H. *Legislating Normalcy: The Immigration Act of 1924*. San Francisco: R and E Research Associates, 1975.

Weiss, Richard. "Ethnicity and Reform: Minorities and the Ambiance of the Depression Years." In *Politics and the Immigrant*, ed. George E. Pozzetta, 398–417. American Ethnicity and Immigration Series. New York: Garland, 1991.

Welles, Benjamin. *Sumner Welles: FDR's Global Strategist*. New York: St. Martin's Press, 1997.

White, G. Edward. "AHR Forum: Constitutional Change and the New Deal: The Internalist/Externalist Debate." *American Historical Review* 110:4 (October 2005): 1094–1115.

Whiteman, Marjorie M. "Green Haywood Hackworth: 1883–1973." (Obit.) *American Journal of International Law* 68:1 (January 1974): 91–94.

Williams, Mary Wilhelmine. *The People and Politics of Latin America*. Boston: Ginn, 1938, 1945.

Wilson, Joan Hoff. *Herbert Hoover: Forgotten Progressive*. Boston: Little, Brown, 1975.

Wilson, Steven H. "Brown over Other White: Mexican Americans' Legal Arguments and Litigation Strategy in School Desegregation Lawsuits." *Law and History Review* 21:1 (Spring 2003): 145–194.

Woll, Peter. *Administrative Law: The Informal Process*. Berkeley: University of California Press, 1963.

Wood, Bryce. *The Making of the Good Neighbor Policy*. New York: Columbia University Press, 1961.

Yans-McLaughlin, Virginia, ed. *Immigration Reconsidered: History, Sociology, and Politics*. New York: Oxford University Press, 1990.

Zolberg, Aristide R. *A Nation by Design: Immigration Policy in the Fashioning of America*. Cambridge: Harvard University Press, 2006.

World Wide Web Resources

Ancestry.com at http://www.ancestry.com

Congressional Biographical Directory at http://bioguide.congress.gov/biosearch/biosearch.asp

Federal Judicial Center at http://www.fjc.gov/history/home.nsf

Handbook of Texas Online at http://www.tshaonline.org

League of United Latin American Citizens (LULAC) at http://lulac.org

McClatchy: The Employee Magazine of the McClatchy Company at http://www.mcclatchy.com/129/

Social Security Administration at http://www.ssa.gov

Index

About the Author

Patrick Lukens is a native of the southwestern United States who received his education at New Mexico State University in Las Cruces (BA, MA) and Arizona State University in Tempe (PhD). Since receiving his doctorate, he has worked as a policy analyst for the Arizona Board of Regents and is currently an independent scholar and instructional faculty in the Arizona community college system.